LUDWIG VON MISES

By the same author:

Hayek: His Contribution to the Economic and Political Thought of our Time (1983)
Milton Friedman: A Guide to His Economic Thought (1985)

Ludwig von Mises

FOUNTAINHEAD OF THE MODERN

MICROECONOMICS REVOLUTION

*

EAMONN BUTLER

Director of the Adam Smith Institute,
London

Gower

Published by

Gower Publishing Company Limited,
Gower House,
Croft Road,
Aldershot,
Hants GU11 3HR,
England

Gower Publishing Company,
Old Post Road,
Brookfield,
Vermont 05036,
USA

ISBN 0 566 05752 2

British Library Cataloguing in Publication Data

Butler, Eamonn
  Ludwig von Mises : fountainhead of the
  modern microeconomics revolution.
  1. Mises, Ludwig von   2. Microeconomics
  — History
  I. Title
  338.5'01   HB172

Printed and bound in Great Britain by
Biddles Ltd., Guildford and King's Lynn

Contents

Preface

Contemporary economists have not convinced us of their power or understanding. They fail to anticipate crises, the economy does not follow their directions, and the side-effects of their policy prescriptions can be bigger headaches than before.

The demise of the giant manufacturing industries has compounded their problems. Today's enterprises are smaller, lighter, more flexible, and more individualistic, giving economic life a new diversity which the old macroeconomic models, either Keynesian or monetarist, are too lumbering to match.

As macroeconomics retires exhausted, more and more people are asking whether the microeconomic approach of the Austrian School of Economics can provide a better understanding of events. Such an enquiry draws them inevitably to the work of Ludwig von Mises, its most thorough and systematic exponent.

However, Mises is a difficult writer, and those new enquirers already trained in conventional economics can find his approach bafflingly unfamiliar, while less experienced students can be quickly overcome by the formidable disquisitions on methodology that permeate his very considerable output.

Hence the need for an orderly exposition of Mises's ideas which explains the unfamiliar, works up gradually to the most difficult material, and offers some occasional criticisms to help place Mises's approach in context.

Sadly, those criticisms, and the inevitable oversimplification required in this task, will undoubtedly draw invective from some of Mises's more ardent disciples. Nevertheless, if more students can be helped to read and understand Mises's books for themselves, that would be a small price to pay.

Meanwhile, special thanks go to John Blundell, Madsen Pirie and Bettina Bien Greaves for their encouragement and constructive criticism.

Dr Eamonn Butler
Adam Smith Institute
July 1987

CHAPTER ONE

Prologue: Mises's Life and Work

> I rather regret that I spent my literary efforts to one
> more refutation of fallacies that had been exploded a
> hundred times before. I regret that I spent too much of
> my limited strength on the fight against pseudo-
> economics.[1]

Ludwig von Mises must be one of the most important and
influential economists of the present century. When he became
a Distinguished Fellow of the American Economic Association
in 1969, he was credited as the author of 19 volumes, many of
them seminal works that were as substantial in size as they were
powerful in argument. Counting revised editions and foreign
translations, the figure reached 46; and since his death in 1973
at the age of 92, dozens more translations, revised editions, and
collections of his essays have appeared. During his long life he
taught an entire generation of economists who went on to
distinction in their own right and who acknowledge Mises as
the modern fountainhead of their approach. Three *Festschriften*
were dedicated to him. Grove City College, New York University, and the University of Freiburg all granted him honorary degrees. A lecture series is named after him in Hillsdale
College. Research institutes are named after him in Auburn
University and in Vienna.

Yet even these honours seem scarcely proportionate to his
extraordinary contributions to economic theory. 'If ever a man
deserved the Nobel Prize in economics,' wrote his fellow economist Dr Henry Hazlitt, 'it is Mises.'[2]

Recusance and rebuff

In the event, Mises did *not* become one of the few Nobel
laureates created in his lifetime; nor did he and his closest
colleagues really suppose that he would. For what he had to say

was not to the liking of those at the top of the economics profession and the other academics who disbursed the top awards. The Nobel prizes and the other most prestigious honours went instead to reward more fashionable economists who sought to apply mathematical and statistical techniques to economic issues – a method that Mises had long argued to be mistaken, hollow, and worthless.

Similarly, while the profession was occupied in teaching its students that these techniques put economics on a genuine scientific basis, little reference was made to Mises's unpopular but uncompromising opinion that they were only a sham. For all his pains, Mises's writings never featured prominently on the reading lists that are distributed to economics students in our colleges and universities. The problem was not just that some of his books are long and may be difficult for the general student to understand clearly; for many less comprehensible mathematical economists are still taught more commonly and accepted more widely. The main reason why Mises remained unpopular with the economics professionals is that he was committed to unpopular views: his recusant writings manifest in every line a revolutionary approach to economics and the study of society that is quite uncongenial to a generation of teachers born in the age of Keynes, schooled in the theory of macroeconomics, and wedded to a fashionable distrust of the market economy.

Rising influence. In consequence of this rebuff from the more modish segments of the profession, it might be quite possible to study economics up to degree level and never hear mention of the name of Ludwig von Mises beyond a few footnotes. Yet it is quite impossible for the modern student, knowingly or other-wise, to escape the influence he has had on the development of economic analysis. At a time when even a patched-up version of the economic orthodoxy that has prevailed for half a century convinces dwindling numbers of people of its power to understand and predict key economic developments, the very principles of the macroeconomic approach are under review. As one inadequate mechanical interpretation of the economy gives way to yet another, more critical minds have looked for a new direction. Some have found it in the work of Mises and his colleagues in the 'Austrian School' of economics, which he consolidated, developed, and systematized into its recognizably modern form. Others have been forced by the logical shortcomings of orthodox teaching into new 'discoveries' that were in fact worked out by Mises long ago. Economics is gradually emerging from its mid-century diversion, and as it does so, the importance of Mises is progressively enhanced.

Mises's key contributions

It is wise for the modern student of economics, then – and to some extent it behoves all those whose lives and fortunes are delimited by the prevailing attitudes of economists – to become more familiar with the thinking of this increasingly important figure whose work has been so methodically overlooked by a fashion-conscious profession. There is no straightforward guide to his work for the general student, as there is *A Guide to Keynes*[3] for example; what discussions exist of his thought are for the most part deep and technical.[4] So a book such as this, which attempts to present and discuss his key contributions in non-technical language, is hopefully of some value in helping that process.

It is almost an impertinence to attempt a short list of the key achievements of a writer so prolific and so varied as Mises, and anyone familiar with his work will inevitably dispute the selection. But six main headings should help to illustrate his unique contribution, and along with other parts of his work, they will be expanded in much more detail in subsequent chapters.

Subjectivism. First, Mises developed and systematized what has become known as the 'subjectivist' view of economics. This view reminds us that human actions, including those of the sort studied by economists, are not mechanical but depend crucially on what the individuals concerned think of events at the time. A rise in the price of sugar, for example, might in one year trigger panic buying among the very same people who in the next see it only as the spur to cut down their sugar

3

consumption and move to a more healthy diet. If such very personal influences on prices, spending, investment, saving, and all the other materials of economics makes life hard for the macroeconomist, who is looking for relationships between one global measure of these phenomena and the next, they make life impossible for the econometrician, who searches vainly to find quantitative statistical linkages between those same aggregates.

Mises was not, of course, the originator of the subjectivist approach. It had already been baptized into economic theory by Carl Menger in his *Principles of Economics*, published in 1871,[5] and it has become perhaps the defining characteristic of the Austrian School of which Menger was the founder and Mises would become the most prominent twentieth-century proponent. A segment of the subjectivist method, in the shape of utility analysis, had been plucked out of its context and clumsily but firmly grafted into the mainstream economics textbooks. The unique feature of Mises's contribution, rather, was to work out with more rigour how the method could and could not be used, and then to apply it systematically across the gamut of economic problems, including those thought previously insoluble, in a way which revealed the serious inadequacy of the orthodox approach.[6]

Monetary theory. A good example of this technique is Mises's substantial reformulation and restatement of monetary theory. It was he who demonstrated that money itself could be subjected to the same kind of utility analysis applicable to other goods, giving us significant insights into its nature and behaviour. At the same time, he distinguished with care and precision the different types of things that are commonly lumped together as 'money', and showed how mainstream economics, overlooking the fact that people react to these things differently, yields mistaken results and ignores some of the most important understandings that could save us from the scourge of inflation and economic dislocation.

The trade cycle. A particular result of these researches, but one which deserves to be mentioned in its own right, is Mises's work on the business cycle. Theoreticians had long sought to explain the rhythmic ups and downs in business activity, prices, and incomes that are discernible from the historical record, but no explanation had been completely satisfactory. Mises, with his insights derived from a more careful understanding of the nature of money, was able to give a comprehensive monetary explanation for these phenomena. He was able to pin down their source as the attempts of governments to manipulate interest rates and the quantity of money in the politically motivated effort to stimulate business, to show why the result was more destructive than most analysts appreciated, and to make prescriptions for a monetary policy that could limit the damage in future.

Capital and interest. The explanation of trade cycles also rests on a view of capital that shows Mises's departure from mainstream thinking. He derived, with careful precision, the phenomenon of interest from individuals' subjective view of the future, whether they thought it worth giving up consumption today to make the fishing nets, the ploughshares, and the machinery that would make production easier tomorrow. And thus he reminds us once again of the crucial importance of time in economic theory – something that is largely eliminated from the 'statics' approach of pure macroeconomics teaching, and largely misunderstood and misapplied in the 'dynamics' approach that is its close relative.

Textbook economics commits other fatal errors in its attempt to simplify the subject for the student, one of which is to treat capital as a homogeneous stock or flow. But Mises, building on the work of his Austrian predecessor, Eugen von Böhm-Bawerk, argued that capital existed only in specific capital goods, each different from the next. A steam hammer, for example, is different in cost, application, flexibility of use, ease of relocation, and in many other different ways from an anvil and a mallet; so precisely what combination of capital goods exist at any time has a crucial bearing on the outcome of our economic activity. Subjective issues are once again in play, but in lumping different goods together under the general heading of 'capital', the macroeconomist will overlook the possibility of investing in the wrong sorts of capital goods, a malinvestment which turns out to be an important stage in the unfolding of the trade cycle.

Calculation under socialism. A fifth key contribution is Mises's undermining of socialist principles on the grounds that economic calculation becomes impossible where markets cease to exist. Where the means of production are owned by the state, and are thus never bought or sold, their price cannot be established. Where the cost of different possible production processes cannot be established, there is no rational way of choosing between them. Waste is inevitable – a waste which the market economy, with its built-in pressure on people to choose the most economical method and so preserve vital resources intact for other production processes, tends everywhere to reduce.

When the debate was raging most fiercely on the European continent in the early part of the twentieth century, Mises's contribution was certainly a telling one, and it remains effective. In response, socialist theoreticians turned to such long-stops as 'market socialism', in which resources are allocated 'as if' markets existed, or else they argued that the problem of deciding between different production possibilities was merely a mathematical one of solving large numbers of simultaneous equations. But time has shown that the first proposal breeds little success, and that only when prices and production processes can be copied from market economics; and Mises himself demonstrated that planning of the second variety, by ignoring that people act differently at different times and in response to the changing circumstances that unfold while the plan is in progress, never has 'simultaneous' data to digest – not that it is theoretically possible to collect and digest such data in any case.

Teaching career. Mises's analysis on these points led him to believe that the only practicable economic system was one where markets, and not governments, allocated resources. Consistently, he applied the same philosophy to other aspects of life, and refreshed the political and economic case for liberalism (which, whenever the word is used by or about Mises 'is to be understood in its classical . . . connotation, not in its present-day American sense'[7]) that the tide of socialism and collectivism was threatening to swamp.

Not just his analytical approach to economics, then, but his thoroughgoing belief in the virtues of free markets and free political institutions, was communicated to the many students who were influenced by him and still remember him as a great teacher. In Vienna before the Nazi occupation, he led a weekly seminar in which gifted young economists such as F.A. Hayek (later a Nobel laureate in economics), Gottfried Haberler (later of Harvard), Fritz Machlup, and Oskar Morgenstern (later of Princeton) could be found. His teaching continued subsequently in Geneva. In America after the Second World War, a new Austrian School grew up around him, including exiles from Austria such as Ludwig Lachmann (the great capital theorist) and American students such as Israel Kirzner (the author of pathbreaking works on entrepreneurship) and Murray Rothbard (well known for his book *Man, Economy, and State*), who as teachers in their own right have now taken the subjectivist approach to economics into its next generation.

MISES'S LIFE

Mises has left us with a biographical sketch of the first sixty years of his long life in the form of his book, *Notes and Recollections*, written when he emigrated to the United States in 1940. It is a sketch which fortunately reveals the intellectual roots of many of his main works as well as the more visible events of his life in Europe.

He was born on 29 September 1881 in the city of Lemberg, about 350 miles east of Vienna. Then part of the Austro-Hungarian empire, the city (renamed L'vov) is now inside the Russian Ukraine. But he grew up principally in Vienna, and entered the University of Vienna in 1900, from which he would receive the degree of Doctor of Jurisprudence in 1906. That time was punctuated by the publication of his first and second monographs, both on economic history, one an account of Galician land tenure arrangements between 1772 and 1848,[8]

7

and the other on Austrian factory legislation;[9] and it was interrupted by his being called up for active duty with the Austro-Hungarian army.

Mises's university years were formative. Like most people of the time, he says, he believed thoroughly in government intervention in the economy, although he found Marxism more distasteful than most.[10] The 'civil service' nature of German-speaking universities had left them populated with dull teachers and those, such as Werner Sombart, who actively advocated the controlling involvement of government in every feature of social life. An exception was the founder of the Austrian school, Carl Menger, and it was Mises's reading of Menger's book, *Grundsätze der Volkwirtschaftslehre* (*Principles of Economics*), that he says first made an economist of him.[11]

Yet Menger was at the end of his teaching career. Mises thought his successor, Friedrich von Wieser, although now remembered as a key personality in the development of the Austrian School, was a poor substitute who did not grasp fully the importance of the subjectivist approach.[12] The university system had effectively kept down other members of the unfashionable and anti-interventionist Austrian school: when Mises graduated with a doctorate in law and economics in 1906, the only prominent advocate and pioneer of Austrian economics was Eugen von Böhm-Bawerk, and even he had left academic life to run the Ministry of Finance in Vienna. Fortunately for Mises, however, Böhm-Bawerk later returned to academe, becoming a professor at Vienna until his early death in 1914. In consequence, Mises was able to benefit not only from Böhm-Bawerk's brilliant seminars, but from his personal discussion about the book Mises was writing, *The Theory of Money and Credit*, which was published in 1912.

Early work in Europe

In 1908, Mises joined the Central Association for Housing Reform, where he analysed the impending proposals to reform property taxation. At about the same time, he began to study in more detail the ideas of nineteenth-century liberalism that he would develop so effectively later on. Soon, Mises's evident talent was spotted by the Austrian Chamber of Commerce (the *Kammer für Handel, Gewerbe, und Industrie*), which he joined in 1909, remaining there until 1934. The chamber was a quasi-official body, which evaluated legislative proposals and advised the government on policy issues. Mises was soon to become its most prominent theoretician.

His status was certainly consolidated by the publication, in 1912, of his thorough and monumental reformulation of monetary theory, *Theorie des Geldes und der Umlaufsmittel* (translated in 1934 as *The Theory of Money and Credit*). Although nominally no more than a senior analyst with the Chamber, he became in reality 'the economist of the country'[13] – although his advice was by no means always taken. He would almost certainly have preferred to work exclusively as an academic teacher, but never really rose very far in that profession, barred, he believed, because of his unfashionable liberal views. He did become a lecturer in economics at the University of Vienna in 1913, but as a *Privatdozent* had to rely on fees rather than a university salary.

Seminars. During the First World War, military service intervened again. After serving as an artillery captain, he was recalled to the office of the general staff in Vienna. In Vienna in 1918–20, he was director of the *Abrechnungs Amt*, an office set up to resolve some of the administrative questions arising from the treaty of St.Germain, a post in which he first met and hired the services of the gifted young economist F.A. Hayek, who came to him on the recommendation of Friedrich von Wieser.[14]

At the end of this period, Mises was setting up the private seminar which clearly gave him the 'greatest sense of satisfaction and accomplishment'[15] and which was undoubtedly instrumental not only in confirming his reputation, but in bringing together a number of fine minds who would go on to develop Austrian economic theory and the liberal approach.

Further publications. Mises's written output continued apace. In 1920 he published an essay on the problem of economic calculation under socialism, which he developed into the towering volume of 1922, *Die Gemeinwirtschaft* (translated as

Socialism in 1936). It began a long debate that peppered books and journals for the next twenty years. Meanwhile, his interest in monetary questions continued, with several long papers, some now collected in *On the Manipulation of Money and Credit*, on money and business cycles. His interest in this was such that in 1927 he founded the *Österreichisches Institut für Konjunkturfors-chung*, a body to promote research into business cycles, in which Hayek joined him.

That same year saw the publication of *Liberalismus* (which came out in English translation in 1962 under the title *The Free and Prosperous Commonwealth* and in 1976 as *Liberalism*), in which he reformulated the principles of the free society. A little afterwards, in 1933, came his iconoclastic work on the theory and method of economic science, *Grundprobleme der Nationalöko-nomie* (the 1960 *Epistemological Problems of Economics*).

Worries at the Chamber. Mises's work on business cycles did nothing to make his prognosis for the Austrian economy any more cheerful. This was, of course, the period of the great hyperinflation in Germany, and Austria was not immune from the same problems. In just a few years, the Austrian currency fell until it took 14,400 paper Crowns to be worth one gold Crown. Mises's agitation for the government to end its deficit and inflationary policies helped prevent the complete collapse that overtook the Germany currency in 1923. But as the theory he developed told him it must, the inflation left severe scars on the Austrian economic system. His research with Hayek made it clear that a banking crisis was on the way, and in 1931, the inevitable happened with the collapse of the major banking institution in Austria. Mises's long battle had won 'nothing more than a mere delay of the catastrophe'.[16]

Geneva and the United States

When Mises was invited to take up the post of Professor of International Economic Relations at the Graduate Institute of International Studies in Geneva, he accepted eagerly. It was not just a sense of relief at being able to escape the shortsighted-ness of Austrian politics: teaching was, after all, his first love.

His second was Margit Sereny-Herzfeld, whom he married in 1938 in Geneva, after a courtship of some thirteen years. She has left a touching testament to him in the form of the book, *My Years With Ludwig von Mises*.[17]

That book describes well the turmoil caused by the rise of the Nazi cause in Europe at the time. Mises's firm and eloquent rejection of totalitarianism in all its forms had made him an exile from Austria and an embarrassment to the Swiss government. In 1940, after a frantic journey across Europe trying to avoid the Nazis at every turn, Mises and his wife finally succeeded in immigrating to the United States, where Mises became a citizen in 1946.

Writing and teaching. Even in America, Mises's liberal views were unfashionable, and he did not succeed in getting an academic appointment straight away. From 1940–44, however, he was a guest of the National Bureau of Economic Research in New York. From 1945–69, he occupied the position of Visiting Professor at the Graduate School of Business Administration at New York University; the appointment was unsalaried but he was supported by the William Volker Fund and earnings from his publications.

The first dozen years after this appointment were very active. Mises attracted students and teachers into his seminars as he had done so effectively in Vienna. Books such as *Bureaucracy*, *Omnipotent Government*, *The Anti-Capitalist Mentality*, and *Theory and History* looked at the deficiencies in non-liberal social policies and their theoretical underpinnings. The very substantial *Human Action*, published in 1949, integrated his economics and methodological views into an impressive whole that is remembered as his *magnum opus*.

In 1962 he published *The Ultimate Foundation of Economic Science*, a systematic account of the subjectivist methodology, by which time the first of his honorary degrees had come. More would follow in his later years.

He died on 10 October, 1973, the undisputed doyen of the Austrian School of economics. His library found a place of honour at Hillsdale College in Michigan, where his name is still remembered in an annual lecture series. Today, the Austrian tradition in economics that he fostered at the University of New York continues there, with growing numbers of students learning about the approach and taking it into new areas of economic debate.

In a eulogy that captures the spirit of the man in but a few words, his wife Margit later wrote of him that:

he never feared to contend against economic error – no matter how popular it was or how powerful were the persons advancing erroneous theories and dangerous policies. He would not give an inch to any argument he thought to be in error. As humble and self-effacing as he was in his personal conduct – and as reasonable and courteous in debate, without personal prejudice to those who failed to understand him – he was absolutely uncompromising on principles he was convinced were true.[18]

It is a tribute to which those who knew Mises readily subscribe.

A BRIEF REVIEW OF MISES'S MAIN WRITINGS

It was not just his uncompromising adherence to beliefs which during his lifetime were unpopular (but which are now fortunately regaining acceptance) that impeded Mises's teaching career. Another factor was that he wrote in German at a time when attention was concentrated on the developments that Fisher, Marshall, Keynes, and others of their mould were unfolding in English. Perhaps because he was seen as slightly detached from the mainstream teaching profession, Mises's works were slow to be translated. Some important items have become available only after his death. Many of his arguments, and much of his power and impact in the continuing debate, were simply unavailable to American and British economists during this delay.

For the student reading Mises in English, all this poses problems. Some translations are better than others, and some of the precision with which Mises chose his words is sometimes lost. Mises's German-language publications retain a preoccupation with the special problems of the German-speaking world. Some, remaining unavailable in translation for many years, deal with issues that are long settled. All of this requires a greater than normal effort of selection from the reader.

Writing in the English language, Mises lacked an easy fluency, and in lectures he had frequent difficulties in finding the right word. Despite his care, his meaning is occasionally obscure and sometimes quite misrepresented by the words he chose.[19]

Additionally, Mises was not only a brilliant analytical economist, but a gifted polemicist who lost no opportunity to criticize the intellectual drift into interventionism and statism. The student of economics will often be astonished and perhaps a little confused to find in his books that the most detailed economic or methodological analysis can be found but a few pages distant from such a blistering attack.

Yet the difficulties these things pose for the casual reader cannot eclipse Mises's contribution or diminish the enjoyment with which his works can be read. His whole approach represents a breathtaking challenge to everything that many students of economics are taught to accept as second nature. And it is partly *because* of his refutations that many once-potent social theories are now untenable and forgotten. His ideas have buried forever an entire family of arguments about the feasibility of economic planning, the uncritical use of traditional scientific methods in the social 'sciences', and the legitimacy of macroeconomic theory and research.

Works in economic theory

The Theory of Money and Credit. Completed in early 1912, *The Theory of Money and Credit* was a brilliant achievement from one so young. Large in scope, innovative in content, and meticulous in detail, it launched the theory of money, credit, and inflation in a completely new direction.

Mainstream Austrian theory employed marginal utility analysis to explain the relative prices of goods, both consumer goods and production goods. Value had always been a problem to the classical school, who thought it a paradox that 'essentials' like water should be cheap while mere 'luxuries' such as diamonds were so costly. The Austrian answer was that

13

it was the usefulness of goods *at the margin* which explained their value. Water might be essential to life, but it is cheap because most individuals can generally get plenty and so have little use for any *more* of it; diamonds might be inessential, but they are expensive because they are scarce and most individuals always cherish *extra* ones. A version of this approach is now familiar to the readers of all economics textbooks, into which it has been lifted.

But this *microeconomic* analysis was hard to reconcile to the theory of money. Money was seen as a mere medium of exchange; it could not be 'consumed' or valued in itself (except perhaps by a miser, though that case would be untypical). Individual values were therefore out, and only the impersonal *macroeconomic* view of money seemed fruitful.

Mises's 'dazzling achievement',[20] which will be examined in more detail in Chapter 12, was to show that money could in fact be subjected to utility analysis. Economics was indeed a 'complete and united whole'.[21] The same supply and demand principles that determine the price of any other economic good, he argued, also determine the 'price' (that is, the purchasing power) of money. In the case of money, the demand is simply the amount people choose to have on hand in their wallets and bank accounts, and it reflects their judgements about the marginal utility of the money unit. The analysis that works for water or diamonds works equally well for money.

Legacy of the theory. It is a sad fact that this persuasive argument was almost entirely overlooked by contemporary American and British economists, being eclipsed by the macroeconomic analysis Irving Fisher had published a year earlier (an approach which Milton Friedman would later revivify).[22] Mises was not in total disagreement with this 'quantity theory' view that an increase in the supply of money would lead to a fall in its 'price' or purchasing power; but he thought it a crude approach. For the link between money and prices is not mechanical; it depends on the value judgements of unique individuals. The same change in supply will therefore have different effects depending on when, where, and how it is made. In each case, different prices will be affected to different degrees, making it wrong to talk of changes in 'the' price level, as the quantity theorists find themselves forced to do.

Mises's work on monetary economics is original, refreshing, wide in scope, and important. It became influential on the continent of Europe, but it represents one of those cases where the lack of an English-language translation for many years meant that others in Britain and America had already taken the subject in new directions before his contribution was published in a form they could understand.

Nevertheless, Mises's views achieved a leverage in other ways. His interwar essays, some collected in *On the Manipulation of Money and Credit*, showed that the irregularity he perceived in the behaviour of prices following government-inspired efforts to stimulate business by artificially depressing the interest rates, caused people to make wrong investment decisions and therefore explained the origins of business cycles. The acceptance of this part of his work outside continental Europe was helped by its English-language development by his student, F.A. Hayek.[23] This monetary explanation of business cycles and the uneven passage of inflation and unemployment through an economy following monetary changes is attracting much more support today, and even diehard quantity theorists are finding themselves obliged to address the point.[24]

There is no doubt that Mises's contributions on monetary theory and the trade cycle are among his most important gifts to the discipline of economics; and indeed, an entire book has been devoted to discussing them alone.[25] However, the intervening three-quarters of a century has not left *The Theory of Money and Credit* in perfect shape as far as the modern reader is concerned. Some parts of the analysis, so original at the time, have now gone into mainstream thinking or address issues long since settled. The segments that are unexpectedly technical and precise (as of course they must be in discussing the difficult issues of money, prices, and value) fit uneasily with the final section, added in 1952, which is more of a polemic scorning the alleged deceitfulness of those who caused the postwar inflations and the stupidity of the public that allowed them so to do. Still, Mises did give his warning, and some irritation is perhaps justified; and in any event, the evident power and penetration of his analysis is not diminished.

Human Action. In his monetary analyses, Mises made some telling criticisms of modern economic theory and showed the fatal weakness of mechanical, macroeconomic approaches that overlook the pervasive importance of individual valuations in the whole of economic life. It was an approach that he would later apply systematically across the entire range of economic problems, and we have been left the result in what is Mises's largest and perhaps most important work, *Human Action*, published in 1949.

Human Action grew out of a German-language forerunner, *Nationalökonomie*, a comprehensive analysis of economic theory bravely written and published in Switzerland in 1940 when Nazism was rampant in Europe. Although *Human Action* could well be described as a textbook, and is today used as such in an increasing number of colleges and universities, it surprises both teachers and students by being very different from any conventional economics textbook. In it, Mises sees economics as merely one part of a more general 'science of human action', much of which can be derived, in his view, from a few self-evident axioms about how human beings can and do act. It leads him to stress the importance of how people as economic agents react to changes, and allows him to examine the importance of time, uncertainty, and speculation in economic actions – things largely or completely overlooked by the 'statics' approach of orthodox textbooks – and to show how the simplifications of textbook 'equilibrium' economics simply assume away everything that we really want to understand. This nonconformist approach, as unveiled so comprehensively in *Human Action*, gives a new understanding of the nature of money, monopoly, competition, inflation, the role of government, and many other crucial issues, which will be considered more fully in Part 2 and Part 3.

The inventiveness and importance of *Human Action* does not make it a perfect book. The attempt to be comprehensive leads Mises to repeat wholesale sections of his earlier books, or to provide overcondensed and less elegant versions of the same arguments. Again, some polemic is mixed in with its purely scientific analysis. But nevertheless, its dazzling insights have inspired a generation of able economists to apply the theory to new problems and in yet greater detail.

Systems of social organization

Nationalism and socialism. For Mises, a proper understanding of the scientific findings of economic analysis yielded important guidance about which systems economic or social organization were practicable and which were not. His great concern for these issues is exemplified in another important early book, which will be reviewed more thoroughly in Chapter 5: *Nation, Staat, und Wirtschaft* (*Nation, State, and Economy*), written in 1919, about the same time as Keynes's *The Economic Consequences of the Peace*. It was, he said, a 'scientific book with a political design'.[26]

It argues that nations (defined, somewhat remarkably, in terms of linguistic groups) are naturally keen to preserve their culture, and so commonly resist immigration by members of other nations; and in the attempt to insulate their own people from foreign developments, erect protectionist economic and migration barriers. The net effect is to trap the population of some nations in poor and overpopulated areas, which sparks a militant nationalist reaction within them and urges them simply to grasp the territory they 'need'. It is the protectionist power of governments that causes national conflicts; only its demise will end them.

This is why, to Mises, socialism is a recipe for international conflict. Socialist economies must insulate themselves; they cannot allow individual migration to upset their careful plans, and they have the centralized power of the authorities to insist on it. Moreover, socialist states are persistently outshone by market economies. To preserve the myth of their superiority, and indeed to survive, they must attempt to socialize all other states, which explains their pervasive imperialism.

Socialism. In *Nation, State, and Economy*, Mises unveils at high speed a number of the arguments that he was to use sub-

17

sequently in his large and important book on *Socialism*, about which more will be said in Chapter 2. It came at a time when the momentum of socialism seemed unstoppable. The promise of the revolution that had occurred in Russia seemed alluring to the splintered nations of the interwar period. Even in Mises's native Vienna, a Bolshevik takeover seemed only a whisper away: everyone was so convinced of it, he wrote, that they were actively intent on securing for themselves a favourable position in the new order.[27]

Mises's critique of socialism was comprehensive and had a profound impact in Europe. It has many poignant comments to make on the inevitable erosion of individual liberty under centralized economic planning, many telling arguments to advance against the Marxian notion of the inevitability of socialism, and many pertinent questions to raise about the meaning of class interest, equality of incomes, and other catchphrases in the socialist lexicon. But it was the unimpeachable demonstration of the impossibility of rational economic calculation under socialism that was the most devastating of its themes.

The non-European world, however, remained largely unaware of this critique. It was not until 1936 that Mises's devastating book was translated for English speakers, and by that time (as Murray Rothbard says), they had been assured that the Polish socialist Oskar Lange had 'refuted' Mises, so spared themselves the bother of reading his arguments.[28] But Mises was correct in his criticism that socialist states cannot calculate economically because their production goods, being 'publicly' owned and thus never bought or sold, lack any market valuation which would tell us whether they are being used efficiently or not. The poor performance of the socialist economies and the fierce protectionism and emigration barriers that seem required everywhere to maintain them, is a practical illustration of the point.

Interventionism. Watering down the spirit of socialism does not make it any more useful, according to Mises: and he argued sternly and at length against the popular (but often feebly thought out) yearning for piecemeal government intervention in the economy. Part of Mises's fight against interventionism found its expression in a series of essays that were eventually published together in German in 1929 as *Kritik des Interventionismus* (the English translation, *A Critique of Interventionism*, did not appear until 1977). His fundamental theme was a straightforward one. Any intervention in the market economy produces unexpected and undesirable side-effects. For example, an attempt to keep down the price of milk raises the demand for milk while making it less profitable for producers to supply it. The inevitable side-effect is a shortage. This needs a further intervention to correct, such as the imposition of production quotas or legal price ceilings on farmers' inputs. The side-effects of this in turn generate demand for more intervention, and so on until the entire economy is under government control. Interventionism, he claims, leads inevitably to full socialism. This idea is given more detailed discussion in Chapter 4.

Various more popular works take up this theme, along with other related subjects. The collection of essays and lectures appearing as *Planning For Freedom* begins with the idea that middle-of-the-road policy leads to socialism and goes on to unveil Mises's determined notion that the only choice, in the long run, is between dictatorship or economic freedom. Likewise, *Economic Policy*, drawn from speeches given in South America and published in 1979, after a clear and succinct description of the true principles of capitalism and the problem of calculation under socialism, goes on to show once again the inevitable instability of the interventionist system.

Later in his career, after his exile to the United States in 1940,[29] Mises made further refinements to his critique of interventionism. His short and readable 1944 monograph, *Bureaucracy*, showed how impossible it was for government agencies to act like efficient businesses. An entrepreneur faces the simple test of profitability; but the (noneconomic) output of a bureau like the FBI is much more intangible and difficult to assess. The businessman must serve his customers; the bureau chief must satisfy not the public but his political masters. Companies are free to innovate and take risks; but there can be no such latitude in government bodies that could put the entire public at risk by their mistakes.

19

The Anti-Capitalistic Mentality, a short popular work that appeared in 1956, looked at some of the reasons why people still yearned for socialism or interventionism, despite its failure: the resentment of those who fail to get to the top, of intellectuals who suppose themselves superior to the rich, and of white-collar workers who sometimes earn less than those in high-demand menial jobs; the constant and sometimes alarming changes in people's careers and working relationships that are needed if they are to succeed in the market economy; and the supposition (completely wrong) that economic growth and the struggle to achieve it eclipses non-material needs.

Deeper critique. At the other end of the scale from his more popular discussions of interventionism is Mises's war book of 1944, *Omnipotent Government*, which took up once again the theme that interventionism was the root of conflicts between nations. It is a strong book, more orderly than many of Mises's writings, which traces the central idea with few digressions. By its deep occupation with historical events in Germany, it perhaps loses some of the impact of F. A. Hayek's contemporaneous volume, *The Road to Serfdom*;[30] but it is grander in scope, almost subsuming Hayek's thesis that socialism leads directly to fascism and then going on to elaborate and refine the details.

Mises's argument starts, once again, from his observation that interventionism produces side-effects that demand more and more interventionism to overcome. The attempts to insulate the domestic economy from the realities of the world market lead to increasing conflicts with trading partners, and allow the rise of nationalism, which engenders strife and war. The effect is reinforced by the fact that the original interventionism lowers productivity and increases the need to acquire more profitable territory, further fuelling the economic nationalism and imperialism that leads to war. In 1944, the message was well taken.

Liberalism. Mises's 1927 *Liberalism*, less negatively, is an elegant, technical, and complete statement of what must be the only alternative once we have recognized that socialism and interventionism are unworkable.

Certainly, economic advancement requires co-operation between individuals, since the specialization of tasks known as the division of labour is plainly more productive than if everyone tried to produce all his or her own needs. But as we have seen, that co-operation cannot be achieved by central planning or the public ownership of resources: only the private ownership of the means of production, and the ability to consume or exchange their fruits freely, will be effective.

To Mises, therefore, the only workable economic system rests on private property and the peace and freedom to enjoy it. From experience (rather than from any higher theory) we have discovered that this peace can be guaranteed only by equal civil and political rights, he reports. The liberal would limit the role of the state to enforcing these rights and preserving peace, recognizing how easy it is for governments to begin eroding private property if allowed any further rein. The liberal system of economic exchange links every trading nation, making conflict more costly and therefore less likely. The greater the individual's freedom to move, work, and invest abroad, says Mises, the greater the likelihood of avoiding war.

Methodological works

Mises's wrote three, densely technical, books on economic theory and method, and a good measure of his work on methodology is found also in *Human Action*. Although separated by three decades, these books interlink. In the 1933 *Epistemological Problems of Economics*, and again in *Human Action*, he sets out that economics is not an experimental science like physics, but a deductive system like mathematics or algebra, in which every theorem can be *deduced* from a few simple axioms. At its base, economics must start from the obvious proposition that people act purposively: and once we have accepted this, we have, he demonstrates, already accepted a great deal about preferences, costs, time, interest, and a number of other things that are the substance of economic theory. Only observation and experience will tell us *what* economic choices people in fact make; but we can derive quite logically a

21

great deal of the essential theorems about *how* they choose, and that is what economics is really about.

Two further books on method round off this cycle. *The Ultimate Foundations of Economic Science*, which appeared in 1962, shows once again why Mises feels the methods of the natural sciences are inappropriate in economics. We act economically because we value things, and from our direct understanding of our own values we can derive the economic concepts of ends, means, success, failure, profit, and loss that are inherent in every action. What more does the economist need? Many people might like to apply to economics the experimental methods of physics, but with society there are no measurable constants and no way of forecasting the behaviour of individuals, whose personal value systems are unknown to outsiders. The mistake that human society is predictable, says Mises, has prompted some to suppose that it is controllable. That mistake not only ignores the human mind: it threatens human freedom.

The 1957 *Theory and History* applies this methodological critique to other disciplines. It is partly a criticism of Marxian theory and method, partly a defence of liberalism. Taking the subjectivist point of view, it argues that the priority of the human mind makes a nonsense of theories that certain historical developments are 'inevitable', as Marx and his followers and other 'historicist' thinkers had supposed. People are inventive and by no means tied to a predetermined fate. And it must be remembered that only *individuals* act: there is no 'group mind' forcing them in certain directions. This is a warning as pertinent to the economists who seek predictable statistical patterns in economic activity today as to those whose dream of the socialist commonwealth has persistently failed to be realized as Marxian theory predicted.

CONCLUSION

Mises himself was pessimistic about the value of his contribution to economics and political theory. During his lifetime, the pull of fashionable socialism and interventionism remained strong in both these disciplines. He had hoped that his writings would have had a more immediate impact on public policy than in fact they did: as in the case of *Socialism*, however, his arguments were often overlooked, or emotional factors proved more powerful than reason. He concluded despondently:

Occasionally, I entertained the hope that my writings would bear practical fruit and show the way for policy. Constantly I have been looking for evidence of a change in ideology. But I have never allowed myself to be deceived.[31]

But in fact, subsequent events have furnished that evidence in great quantity. The fashions which Mises criticized have now revealed their inadequacy in ways that are clear to everyone; in economics as in politics, the interwar and postwar orthodoxy is in decline. The rise of the liberal market economy has helped prevent the spread of the militant nationalism he found so repugnant, and indeed has made allies out of formerly imperialist countries such as Japan and Germany; socialist economies, meanwhile, are failing to keep up economically, as Mises's exposition of the calculation problem warned us they would; monetary factors are receiving new attention in economics now that the disastrous nature of inflation becomes clear; and our transition from large-scale manufacture to a more customized, sub-contracting, small-business, service economy has underscored the importance of the individual and the inability of economists to treat the processes of economic life as they would describe the operations of a machine.[32]

There is, in other words, a marked return to the principles which Mises insisted upon so strongly and argued for so ably; and though the arguments change over the decades, the foundations he laid are proving more durable than he supposed they would. The new intellectual structures that are being built upon them are testimony to an increasing confidence in the value of liberal social and economic institutions for which Mises and his students can take a full measure of credit.

PART ONE: SYSTEMS OF SOCIAL ORGANIZATION

CHAPTER TWO

The Logical Problems of Socialism

Socialism is the abolition of rational economy.[1]

The demise of the mid-century orthodoxy in economics, caused by the very evident inability of those ideas to explain events and save us from inflation and its related disasters that have proved every bit as damaging as the interwar depressions, has generated increasing interest in the economic ideas of the Austrian School. The Austrians' critique of the entire underpinnings of economic theory, and the particular contributions of Mises on such subjects as entrepreneurship, money, interest rates, and the trade cycle are now being reassessed. Were it not for this recent attention on the broader aspects of his work, however, Mises could well have been remembered chiefly (and by some, solely) for his work on socialism, which scored telling points in academic debate long before economists were ready to absorb his other theoretical legacies.

Mises's contribution. The part of this work which is generally considered the most significant is Mises's development of the problem of economic calculation in the socialist commonwealth. However, he has also done us a service in defining the fundamental essence of socialism and separating the various and incompatible philosophies that are often lumped together under its name. In addition, he made it clear how pervasive must be the coercive apparatus required by socialist planners if their programmes are to be fully implemented.

These are the main strands of Mises's thought which will be considered in this chapter. Together with them, and at the deepest level, Mises addressed the theory and philosophy of Marxian socialism, including its supposed inevitability, in technical works such as *Theory and History*; but a review of this critique must wait until the next chapter.

Possible forms of social organization

If it were possible for individuals to exist who were entirely self-sufficient, neither co-operating with others nor wishing to, there would be little matter to interest the social theorist. The most interesting problems come only when people interact and co-operate together to achieve objectives which they could not meet so easily (or at all) as single individuals. They might share tasks, or specialize in particular tasks – what economists call the 'division of labour'. It is then that we have to start thinking more fully about the rules of ownership and exchange, and that relative differences in income and wealth begin to strike our attention. How is the product of the specialist farmer to be divided among non-farmers who need meat and cereals? Who makes the distribution decisions and who owns the resources upon which so many others will depend? How, in short, is a society based on the division of labour to be organized?

Five possibilities. Mises says that 'it is possible to distinguish five different conceivable systems' of organizing the co-operation of individuals in such a society:[2]

1. the system of private ownership of the productive goods themselves, which, in its developed form, is called capitalism;
2. the system where the means of production are still privately owned, but there is a periodic redistribution of personal wealth;
3. syndicalism, where ownership of the productive equipment is vested in the workers themselves;
4. the system of public ownership of the means of production, known as socialism or communism; and
5. interventionism, where the means of production are nominally in private hands, but official directions are issued to control their use.

It was under the system of private ownership, observes Mises, that humankind first started to develop and prosper. Although its opponents are fond of pointing out that private property did not exist in the village communities of human prehistory, this is no argument that it could be abolished without damage to the advanced civilizations of today. The second principle, periodic distribution of property among others, is persuasive in many simple agricultural communities, and is thus sometimes called 'agrarian socialism', though it is nothing like true socialism as Mises would define it. Where more refined and complicated farming and manufacturing processes arise, however, this principle is unthinkable; it is senseless and pointless to break up a successful farm or a rolling mill so that everyone can get a little bit of it, for only together are those pieces most useful. Syndicalism, once a popular attempt to adapt the ideal of equal distribution to large-scale modern industry, failed because some industries proved more prosperous than others, in which case the worker co-owners of different industries would become very *un*equal. Interventionism has its own problems, which will be considered at length in Chapter 4. That leaves 'socialism or communism' as the object of the present enquiry.

Definition of socialism. Some readers today might be alarmed at this glib union of socialism and communism. Socialism, very frequently, is seen as something much less strong, a philosophy which tries to combine the best elements of private enterprise with the general principles of central planning. There are other overtones as well: communism tends to be thought of as the actual practices, including the political institutions, of a number of (often totalitarian) states, while socialism carries the connotation of being a more democratically achieved economic structure in which political freedoms still exist.

As Mises uses the words, however, there is no such distinction. He is interested in distilling the essence of socialism which can be subjected to analysis by scientific economists. The subtle additional connotations which inhere in the words as they are used in careless everyday language must be set aside if a proper understanding of the principle itself is to be gained. To him, accordingly, socialism boils down to being 'a policy which aims at constructing a society in which the means of production are socialized'.[3] More bluntly, he says:

29

The essence of socialism is this: all the means of production are in the exclusive control of the organized community. This and this alone is socialism. All other definitions are misleading.[4]

Mises's uncluttered definition of the concept, therefore, makes socialism a basic ingredient that might be found in many different social philosophies, including both those which refer to themselves as a particular brand of socialism, and others which today are called by quite different names. It is, however, this basic ingredient which must be the focus of analytical attention; and according to Mises, his own definition commands agreement among the scientific students of the subject, and allows the claims of socialism as a system of economic organization to be investigated single-mindedly.

Socialist theories and their origin

Nevertheless, it is also interesting to look at the wide variety of different systems of social organization that do contain this basic ingredient of having the means of production controlled by some central apparatus. The history of socialism has seen so many different variants emerge, that critics must be careful to distinguish each one clearly when reviewing their particular nature.

Early socialism. It is doubtful whether this defining principle was clear to the early or *village socialists*, comments Mises. When villages were isolated communities, the question of centralized production planning probably did not arise, only that of how to share out the results of production. The nineteenth-century growth of international trade, however, made the socialists raise their sights and expand their ideas into a national or even world socialism. But it was a utopian vision, not a practical programme, and the socialist philosophy was quietly buried. It took Marx to resurrect it.

Other varieties. Once revived, the idea was joined by many variants, which Mises traces in Part 3 of *Socialism*. For example, there is *military socialism*, found in states that rely on conquest for their continued wealth. Naturally enough, this booty has to be deposited in a central treasury for subsequent distribution, and then the same principle of distribution begins to seem appropriate for home production as well, and mechanisms are devised to impose it. Then, there is *war socialism*, an idea common in the First World War, that collective action was necessary for wartime production.[5] Actually, declares Mises, the opposite is true: socialism has not proved able to increase production, and when imports are difficult because of wartime threats to shipping, price controls and other government measures merely compound the shortages. Nevertheless, his point that people believe in the efficacy of collective action during wartime was underscored when the electors of the United Kingdom dismissed Winston Churchill in favour of a socialist government that advertised itself as intending to use the same collective methods to achieve peacetime prosperity.

Next come the various brands of *state socialism*, where the attempt was made to introduce nationalization, economic planning, and the distribution of wealth, not on the grand scale of the utopian socialist visionaries, but more practicably and only within the boundaries of a particular country.[6] Where any variety of state socialism was tried, however, it soon failed, and some blamed this on the replacement of entrepreneurs by bureaucrats when industries were nationalized. Thus came the compromise of the *planned economy*, where businessmen were left to own enterprises, with the state taking an interest here and there. But whoever is nominally the owner, the resources in such a system have to be controlled, ultimately, by some agency of the collective; and it is not surprising that we find this 'mixed' system to be unstable, with government agencies quickly usurping all the important functions.[7]

Quasi-socialist ideas. Both the mixed economy and *profit sharing* have become widespread ideas. Of the latter, Mises notes that it is not really a socialist principle according to his definition, because like agrarian socialism, the means of production are actually controlled privately, despite the fact that the wealth, income, or profits derived from them are subsequently confiscated and distributed according to some predetermined prin-

31

ciple. But this mechanism, as well as being not a true brand of socialism, is inherently unsatisfactory to the socialist: if enterprises share profits only with their own workers, it creates differences in income 'which fulfil no economic function, appear to be utterly unjustified, and which all must feel unjust'.[8] The alternative method, of imposing high taxes on businesses and distributing from a central exchequer the revenue raised, simply takes away the rewards of success and therefore discourages entrepreneurship and reduces productivity.

The idea of *syndicalism* is much less common today. The word has two meanings, according to Mises: one indicates Georges Sorel's idea that unions should take 'direct action' to smash capitalism; in the other, syndicalism is seen as a programme of social organization in which the means of production are taken out of the hands of private owners and made over to the workers themselves. But as we have seen, this system of management by worker-shareholders cannot bring about equality, because enterprises are not uniformly productive or profitable, and so it does not achieve one of the background purposes of the socialist movement. Also, the principle completely ignores the impact and importance of change. Shifts in consumer tastes may make the distribution of profits, and therefore incomes, even wider still. And how do we allocate shares between workers, given the emergence of new productive processes and the failure of old ones, and the frequent movement of workers between different productive units?[9]

Although 'one cannot take the syndicalist programme seriously, and nobody ever has', Mises detects its outriders in numerous 'pro-worker' policies: enforced profit-sharing, the obligation to appoint worker-directors, and the restriction of workplaces to union members. What might be beneficial to the workers in any particular firm, however, is by no means so when spread over the entire economic system.[10]

Socialism after Marx

Marx, of course, completely changed the course of socialist theory and provided an analysis which is fundamental to most socialist discourse today. He is often credited with making the subject 'scientific'. But as we will see, Mises insists that his true effect was actually to preserve the vague and utopian features of the early socialism and insulate it from genuine scientific analysis. The utopianism came from his doctrine that the world was moving inexorably towards socialism; and Marx's rejection of any criticism of this doctrine on the grounds that critics were using a false, 'bourgeois', logic provided the necessary insulation against any further scientific discussion.

Mises's exposition of the many errors that underpin Marx's approach are reviewed in more detail in the following chapter. For the moment, we need to understand only that Marx's success rested on his ability to capture the human yearning for a better world and to make that dream immune from criticism:

The incomparable success of Marxism is due to the prospect it offers of fulfilling those dream-aspirations and dreams of vengeance which have been so deeply embedded in the human soul from time immemorial. It promises a paradise on earth . . . Logic and reasoning, which might show the absurdity of such dreams of bliss and revenge, are to be thrust aside.[11]

Many people were inspired by this comfortable, quasi-religious vision of a better world in which all inequalities would be ended. But the socialist vision of Marx and others was so carefully cocooned against critical argument, protests Mises, that it was able

to win more and more ground without anyone being moved to make a fundamental investigation of how it would work. Thus, when one day Marxian socialism assumed the reins of power, and sought to put its complete programme into practice, it had to recognize that it had no distinct idea of what, for decades, it had been trying to achieve.[12]

The arguments surrounding Marx's philosophy of history and the scientific (or unscientific) nature of his beliefs can appear deep and technical, particularly to untutored members of the public. But the effect of any brand of political principles on the economic interests of ordinary individuals is usually clear enough, and was so with socialism. The most severe problems for the socialists, therefore, began not so much in academic discussions but when they tried to put their programmes into practical effect and came up against the grim logic of economics. And on this point, Mises has left us with a powerful discussion of why those problems were inevitable.

THE PROBLEM OF CALCULATION UNDER SOCIALISM

We need to understand the true nature of ownership and the different types of goods that can be owned, states Mises, before we can begin to appreciate the full severity of the problem of economic calculation in the socialist commonwealth.

Ownership of production and consumption goods

In economics, we are told in the opening chapter of *Socialism*, ownership means simply the power to dispose of a good. It is absurd to describe someone as the owner of a house, a machine, or a book if he or she has no power to decide how it is used and whether it can be transferred to others by gift or sale. The socialist ideal of equal *ownership*, therefore, really means equal *control* or equal *use*. This is a valuable point which is often forgotten in the debates about 'public' ownership today.

Consumption goods. Can we achieve this ideal and divide up the control and use of goods equally between individuals? Not always, answers Mises. Consumption goods pose an immediate problem, because many of them lose their quality as goods when they are used. A can of hair spray is no use to anyone when it has been fully discharged, for example, and a cigar that has been completely smoked by one person thereby becomes useless to everyone else. It is, of course, true that things of this kind are sometimes said to be owned jointly, like a bar of chocolate given to two children; but any such good must be divided before it can be enjoyed, whereupon the joint ownership ceases. The real economic ownership – the use – of a non-durable consumption good must always be exclusive.

The same is true even with durable consumption goods. There is a slight difference, in that one person's enjoyment of the good does not exclude its enjoyment by others later on: a coat can be worn by one person and then sold to another. Ownership, in other words, *can* be divided in a certain way, and commonly is. But the socialist's notion of joint ownership is still invalid, because simultaneous use of such goods will disturb the enjoyment of others. Two people cannot wear the same coat at once.

When the problem is carefully examined, it becomes clear that the ownership of consumption goods is not fertile a promising starting point for socialist reformers:

it would be quite absurd to think of removing or even of reforming ownership in consumption goods . . . consumption goods cannot be the joint property of several or the common property of all.[13]

Mises's point is that it is simply impossible to build, or even conceive of, a society in which all goods, including consumption goods such as coats, cars, shopping bags, food, pets, or wristwatches can be owned in any meaningful joint fashion. Indeed, in support of his argument, the fact that real-world socialist communities rely on market structures to deliver these goods to consumers and that even in such communities they can be bought and sold for exclusive personal use clearly reminds us of their non-collective nature.

Production goods. Proposals to embark on equal ownership, therefore, have concentrated on *production* goods. They serve enjoyment only indirectly, being employed to produce consumption goods. Many people can benefit from their services without the need to divide them up, like a bar of chocolate, before consumption takes place. They *can* be shared.

At first sight, this straightforward observation makes the socialist ideal of the shared ownership of the means of production a plausible goal. It certainly does make sense to describe a factory, a large farm, or a service company as having more than one owner. Those who invest in a company quoted on the stock exchange are, in a very real sense, co-owners of the company;

and their collective decision at a shareholders' meeting is necessary before its assets and personnel are put to work on major new projects. Partners often jointly control smaller companies such as accountants and firms of lawyers. And many other forms of shared ownership actually exist already under modern capitalism. So is it not simply a question of extending this joint ownership more widely?

Socialist theoreticians, reports Mises, went to some lengths to show that joint ownership in the widest sense was actually far from uncommon. They believed they could demonstrate that shared ownership of land, an important production good, has long been a common principle, and that in historical terms, private ownership is a recent institution. Even though economic history can easily defeat this contention, however, we should remember that a long pedigree is not enough for the common ownership principle to work. The advanced civilization we enjoy today is very distant from that of the primitive hunter-gatherer groups who shared an area of hunting and grazing land, and probably many other productive resources as well. The problems of social organization where the major productive investments are steel plants, rolling mills, engine factories, and car production lines, are quite different in character. These things are not just large, but integrated; we have to decide which processes to opt for, and having done so we face a constant stream of future choices about the degree to which they will be maintained, renewed, and replaced – a process that requires a much more sophisticated way of making decisions regarding them than that needed by the primitive village group. In Mises's words:

The experiences of a remote and bygone period of simple production do not provide any sort of argument for establishing the possibility of an economic system without monetary calculation.[14]

Even if the widespread existence of joint ownership of land and other resources in historical periods were an accurate interpretation of events, Mises concludes, the advocates of common ownership would still have no safe haven. Common ownership of consumption goods is obvious nonsense. And the proposed principle of common ownership of production goods contains an inherent flaw which makes it impossible to operate in practice: it leaves us with no means to make rational economic calculations and decisions about what to produce, in what quantities, and by what methods. It is this point that Mises next goes on to explore.

The problem of calculation

The discovery of this problem of economic calculation under socialism as it has been described thus far is not, in fact, completely original to Mises. However, his own particular version of it is a particularly careful, comprehensive, pertinent, and powerful one. Before going on to look at the next steps in his argument, it is perhaps worth a brief look at how the debate stood when the publication of *Socialism* took it into a completely new phase.

Prehistory of the problem. The problem of how to choose rationally between different possible production processes in the absence of market prices was in fact glimpsed very early in the development of modern socialist ideas. Even Marx's collaborator, Friedrich Engels, seems to have been aware of it,[15] although neither his work nor that of Marx addresses and answers the point squarely.

The true magnitude of the problem became more clear in 1854, when H.H. Gossen (whose early subjectivist treatment of human values and utility analysis secures his claim to be a solid precursor of the modern Austrian School economists), pointed out that only a system of private ownership could provide a yardstick to decide how much of different goods should be produced, given the existing resources – a problem that was also considered by the great Vilfredo Pareto[16], though without a clear conclusion. Early Austrians such as Wieser and Böhm-Bawerk pointed out that the socialist society would still need ways to settle important features of production such as rents, interest, and profit ratios, and that copying those found in market societies was likely to be the only, if inefficient, method.

On a related point, P. H. Wicksteed raised the question of

how people were to be remunerated under socialism if money wages were to be abolished.[17] The Dutch economist N.G. Pierson (later to become a co-author, with Mises, of *Collectivist Economic Planning*) took up the same challenge in 1902, rejecting the pious socialist hopes that people could be rewarded according to their 'contribution to society' because, in the absence of a labour market, it becomes quite impossible to determine the specific contribution that clerks, managers, and manual workers make to the end result of a very complicated production process.[18]

For the socialists, Enrico Barone argued in 1908 that the decision of what and how much to produce was simply a matter of solving a large number of simultaneous equations describing supply and demand conditions, and by 1919, others such as Otto Neurath and Otto Bauer (with whom Mises undoubtedly debated the issue at length in Vienna) had added their own support to the belief that socialism could in fact work without money prices.[19]

Mises's statement of the problem. It was against this background that Mises's contribution to the debate was made. With brave originality it started from the question of how goods are valued and how choices are made between them, and then went on to show that the problem of calculation under socialism applied not only to production goods but to semi-manufactured goods going through their respective production processes. The calculation problem, he concluded, not only concerned choices that were deeply personal and impossible for socialist administrators to decide objectively, but was much more complex than socialists had understood because those allocation decisions had to be made about a much wider range of goods than they had supposed.

Valuation and calculation. As Chapter 7 will explain and explore more fully, human values are very individual, and people disagree about what things they want and how strongly they want each one. Without any way of choosing between these conflicting views, it is impossible to make any rational choice on the matter of which ones should be satisfied. This is the root of the socialist calculation problem, and it is worth beginning here, as Mises does.

Every human action, says Mises, springs from a decision about which things the individual concerned values most. People act because they are not satisfied with the present state of things. They seek to replace their present condition with a preferred one, to gain new things they value or to exchange some of what they have now for other things that they value more. It is not an altogether straightforward process: there may be many possible improvements that could be imagined and grasped, many different gains that might be achieved through different expenditures of time and effort, and many potential exchanges of new things for old on offer. Everything human beings do, therefore, requires a personal review of how they value the assortment of things they already enjoy and assess each of the new possibilities unfolding before them.

The decision is even more complicated than this, of course, because as well as having to make choices between what we want to achieve, we also have to make choices about the various ways of achieving them. A change in our condition cannot be conjured up just by wishing: resources are limited and men are not omnipotent, so it will take the application of time, effort, and materials to produce the improvements we seek. But in what combination? There will almost certainly be many possible production methods that would achieve the desired results, each of them using different combinations of resources – that is, using up different amounts of things which we also value. Naturally, we want to achieve the most valued improvements, but we do not want to use up too many highly valued resources in the process. We have to make a series of comparisons between all the things we gain and lose from each process, before we can begin to act rationally.

Immediately we begin to do anything at all, therefore, we must make a number of value judgements. Making decisions about which consumption goods we prefer might be relatively easy, but if long and complicated production processes are required in order to make those consumption goods, the choice might be very hard indeed. We might readily appreciate the benefits of electricity, but should we produce it by mining more coal or building a new hydraulic dam? Whichever process we alight on, it will mean giving up other things, including time, labour, land, and other materials that we might well be able to use elsewhere to satisfy our other desires.

The problem is compounded still further because a large number of different people will be involved in any complicated production process, and its benefits will be spread to a large number of others. Those individuals involved may value the gains and losses quite differently. Environmentalists, for example, may value an undisturbed waterfall far more than the electric power derived from the new dam. People's values may not be concurrent, and indeed, they may clash significantly.

The need for a unit of calculation. For the socialist planner, deciding whether or not to embark on a new production process is therefore a very problematic business. The divergent values of everyone involved must somehow be weighed so that resources are used effectively to produce the optimum results. But the more sophisticated the production processes used, the wider the choice of different processes and different potential results that presents itself, and the greater the number of people who will be affected by the outcome, the more difficult that problem becomes.

To make sure that resources are used rationally, then, we need to make comparisons between them, and also between the different products that emerge from their use. Particularly where the choices we face are very large or complicated, we need some sort of common unit in which we can make careful computations to decide whether an undertaking is sound or unsound.

Unfortunately for the planner, we have no units which could measure individuals' own valuations of different commodities. Judgements of value are very personal, and even changeable. Outside observers have no direct access to them, and no unit by which they could be measured. One person's values cannot be balanced against another – just as we cannot measure the balance one person's grief against another's happiness or a third's physical pain.

Calculation by money. However, in the free economy, there is a straightforward way in which we can gain an indirect access to the process of personal valuation, and that is by examining the actual choices which people do make between one thing and another. We can measure quite objectively the proportions in which people are in fact prepared to exchange different things. This 'objective exchange value', as Mises calls it,[19] the going rate of exchange (that is, the price) of one good against another in the market. Moreover, it takes account of the preferences of everyone engaged in trade, applies to production goods as well as consumption goods, and allows us to reduce the different choices people make to a common unit. That unit is money.

Of course, calculation in terms of money has its limits. It does not help us to make decisions between non-economic goods such as health, honour, or beauty. It does not measure value, which is inherently personal and unmeasurable in any case. But it does at least give us an indicator of the proportions in which people are in fact willing to exchange marketable commodities. It offers us a guide through the bewildering throng of economic possibilities by providing a common unit of account for every consumption good and every production process.

Calculation under socialism. The socialist economy denies itself this happy prospect, but cannot escape the need to make choices between different courses of action, and for some principle on which those choices can be based. One popular belief is that calculations in kind can be substituted for calculations in money. But that, says Mises, leaves no common basis of measurement by which production decisions can be made. A socialist society could certainly see that 1000 litres of wine would be better than 800 litres. But is it better than 500 litres of oil? We still need some single measure to compare different things. Without a common unit to help compare them, only the will of some person – a politician or an official – would decide. In the socialist commonwealth, the objective measure of market price, based as it is on the choices of the whole community of trading individuals, must be replaced by the subjective judgement of a single individual or group.

41

When production processes get really complicated, we see the full absurdity of all attempts to do without the common accounting unit of money. Take the maze of decisions involved in the construction of a new railway line, suggests Mises. Should it be built at all? Which of the possible routes should it cover? Would the reduction in transport costs it produces be worth the expense of building it? What mix of skilled and unskilled labour is best, and can the coal, iron, and machinery be more productively used elsewhere? At every stage of the decision process, the socialist planner would be trying to balance things that are as different as oil and wine. Denied a unit of calculation, rational choice is impossible:

All economic change . . . would involve operations the value of which could neither be predicted beforehand nor ascertained after they had taken place. Everything would be a leap in the dark. Socialism is the renunciation of rational economy.[20]

Rational economic action, then, the rational exchange of one state of affairs for another, is impossible without the very unit of account that is done away with in the socialist philosophy.

Production goods and goods in production. A telling objection to Mises's complete denial of the practicability of socialism is that socialist economies do not in fact abandon the use of money completely, so his picture is merely a caricature. As a practical measure, people in socialist communities are paid in money and consumption goods are bought and sold with it. So a unit of account does exist, and can be used to make decisions between different economic choices.

Nevertheless, Mises quite rightly reminds us that because of the very nature of socialism as he has defined it, this accounting mechanism cannot possibly be extended to production goods. For under socialism, production goods are held in common ownership: they are never traded, never bought and sold, but continue as the joint property of the commonwealth. But if things are never exchanged, they never get the chance to manifest an objective exchange value. In other words, there is no way in which such goods can ever acquire prices. They are never exchanged and so never fall within the scope of the universal accounting unit provided by money. The problem remains, even when money is not abolished completely.

Another point which Mises added to this discussion, and which was to prove important in the subsequent debate, is that this calculation problem extends not only to production goods, but washes over to all goods in the process of production. At any time in the socialist community, there will be thousands of different production processes going on. Only a few will produce finished consumption goods: most will produce capital goods and semi-manufactures, which again are not subject to market exchange. (To borrow an example from Mises's Austrian School predecessor, Carl Menger, every loaf of bread requires also the production of flour, grain, ploughshares, and iron ore.) At every stage in the life of each of these millions of intermediate products, managers must decide whether more work on them is justified and, if so, what is the best process. But without knowing the expenditure incurred in their production so far, or the cost of future possible stages, no such calculation can be made. To extend the example from Menger: should more effort be put into growing better strains of wheat or developing stronger steel for the ploughshares, and what strategy would work best in each case? Is the benefit of a greater yield worth the extra effort to make the ploughshares sharper and sturdier? What effect will more investment in mining equipment have on steel production and the efficiency of agricultural production, and does the outcome justify that expenditure? Is more bread needed enough to make us put more work into threshing, or is some waste at that stage acceptable? And in a similar way, the problems continue right through the economic process. In the socialist commonwealth, therefore, not just production goods but most of the commodities in the economy can never be rationally compared. The whole economy is affected by the impossibility of economic calculation that arises when certain goods are specifically excluded from exchange.[21]

Socialist production and planning

Socialism has always claimed as a major strength its supposed ability to replace the 'anarchy' of production under capitalism by a 'rational' system of overall economic planning. When we are aware of the severe problem of calculation that exists in the socialist commonwealth, however, we see that production under socialism must be anything *but* rational, because there are simply too many possibilities to weigh against one another, each of them using up different resources. As Mises says,

No single man can ever master all the possibilities of production, innumerable as they are, as to be in a position to make straightway evident judgements of value without the aid of some system of computation.[22]

The aims of capitalist and socialist communities alike is to achieve a 'profit' – that is, to satisfy more urgent needs over others. Capitalism does this at every stage because it has a unit of calculation, based on people's actual choices in the market-place, upon which careful computations can be made. In the socialist economy, the process is far from automatic. Someone has to decide what people's needs are, which are most urgent, and how production is best steered to that result. It is a problem that no amount of technology can solve: technology can tell us what we *can* achieve, but not what we *should* aim to achieve.[23] What the market decides routinely, therefore, the planned economy finds a major obstacle. Without a unit of account,

The human mind cannot orientate itself properly among the bewildering mass of products and potentialities of production . . . It would simply stand perplexed before the problems of management . . . [24]

The burden cannot even be rationally shared out between a larger number of individuals on a committee or planning board, because the problem of calculating in the absence of market prices still exists, no matter how many people apply their minds to it.

The socialist response

A possible objection to Mises's analysis is that the socialist commonwealth might adopt an objective unit of account other than money. But, he retorts, the possibilities would be somewhat limited in an economy where neither money nor exchange were present. We have already rejected the possibility that things can be calculated in kind: wine, oil, railways, and electric power are completely different and cannot be added or subtracted against each other. Similarly, any idea of a measure of personal value, a 'quantity' of 'utility' is out: our values are not mathematically precise, and certainly cannot be measured against those of others. So what options are left?

The labour theory of value. Only labour, Mises concludes, would seem to be a credible candidate as an accounting unit of value that could be applied to all commodities in the socialist commonwealth.[25] And this, in fact, is the idea that Marx adopted and upon which his entire economic theory rests: that the objective value of any good is simply the amount of labour put into its production.

However, Mises detects two crucial weaknesses in this approach. First, it is quite possible for two goods to need precisely the same amount of labour to produce, while one takes a larger input of materials. We must give up different quantities of our valuable resources to produce them, and yet they still rank equally in terms of socialist calculations. Obviously this is unsatisfactory. Facing such a choice, we can of course select the process which uses up the smallest volume of the necessary inputs: but what if the resources used in each process are quite different? Again, we might rate some resources much more important than others, even though the labour put into acquiring them might be the same. The quantity of labour expended patently does not provide an adequate basis for such a decision. And second, labour is a poor unit of account because it is not in fact uniform, as a unit of account must be. The different skills and different types or qualities of work put into a product are crucial in determining how we judge the value of the outcome.

Simultaneous equations. Some socialists, notably Enrico Barone, argued that making decisions in the socialist economy was simply a case of having enough computing power. We do not need money prices to calculate how we can use our resources to the best advantage: all we have to do is to solve a long series of equations that describe economic relationships (simultaneous equations, in fact, because the use of any one commodity will to some extent determine how we can best use others).

The trouble with this idea, says Mises, is that economic relationships are far from static. People act with the intention of producing *change*, and when they do, they stimulate further actions by others that produce yet more changes in a sort of 'chain reaction' process. The course of this chain reaction is unpredictable; the 'data' that we would need for our simultaneous equations are uncertain and in constant flux.[26]

This is a point on which Mises's student, F.A. Hayek, has contributed some very valuable insights. Not only are the economic possibilities so infinite and intertwined that no computer could ever solve them, he argues, but it would be impossible even to collect the necessary information in the first place. Markets are active: by the time information about local conditions is gathered, collated, despatched to the central decision makers, and processed, it would be already out of date. And by the time the decision has been made, orders have been given, and implementation begins, conditions could be completely different and the new policy completely inappropriate.[27]

Hayek developed an even more subtle point, made also by Mises and Wieser, which was largely overlooked in the debate at the time but is nevertheless a crucial one. The socialist decision maker, trying in the absence of prices to weigh up the costs of one production process against another, faces the insuperable problem that costs are not in fact objective entities. They are what an individual has to give up to achieve some end – and individuals can put very different valuations on the same thing. An expenditure of a given amount of time in pursuit of some goal may be seen as a horrendous cost to bear for one who values leisure, a trifle to a workaholic. There is an infinite number of projects for which that time, or any other scarce and valued resource, could be used, but each individual may well rank them quite differently. The socialist planner has no objective way to decide between such ranking. The only question is: whose judgements are to prevail, those of the planners or those of individuals?[28]

Other methods. To all but the most intransigent socialists who dismissed Mises's arguments as mere propaganda and unworthy of discussion, it became clear during the course of the interwar debate that, whether they were determined by planners or by consumers, prices of some sort were still needed. The search for a non-monetary way of deciding the proportions in which different commodities should exchange in the planned economy led socialist theoreticians into many and diverse proposals. H.D. Dickinson, for example, suggested that these prices could be set in the absence of market exchange, by the technique of estimating the demand curve for each commodity. But in his 1939 book, *The Economics of Socialism,*[29] he acknowledged the crudeness of this device and abandoned it.

Others, however, continued the search to find some principle that would maximize consumer satisfaction if, as they believed, capitalism was unfitted for the task. Thus, thinkers such as Oskar Lange and Abba Lerner developed the principle of 'market socialism', in which an 'ideal' market would be constructed, with prices set by the administrators. Lerner suggested simple rules to instruct managers – for example, that they should aim for the level of production at which the prices of the goods sold equal their marginal costs of production.[30] If prices represent the value of goods sold and costs represent the value of goods used in the process, then such a formula would, Lerner maintained, ensure that nothing was used up in any process that could not generate greater value elsewhere.

Good classical textbook economics that might have been, but it ignored Hayek's point that costs are in fact a matter of judgement for each manager, rather than an objective measure. And Mises was pleased to reply in *Human Action* that perfection and balance could never be found in the real-world economic process, which involved the continual motion of complex, diverse, and inter-related events, and could certainly never be summarized or directed by simple rules.

In *Human Action*, Mises also replied to the argument of Oskar Lange that under market socialism, the administered prices would be adjusted in response to any surpluses and shortages that arose, and again that managers would be given straightforward instructions to produce at the minimum average cost. This 'final refutation' of Mises, however, still ignored Hayek's insights that costs are not objective and that centralized collection and processing of market information is not so easy. For his part, Mises observes that it must be a very poor mechanism for dealing with the constant movement of complex variables that we find in the real market economy. Crucial features of economic life lie outside the mere management of corporate concerns. Entrepreneurs are incessantly hiring and firing managers, opening and closing down complete production units to meet changes in consumer needs and their own judgements about how best to satisfy them. Market socialism can never mirror market exchange rates just by trying to avoid surpluses and shortages in the commodities traded today, because that ignores the role of innovation for tomorrow. Rejecting private capital ownership (like all forms of socialism), it overlooks the value of capital: it cannot mimic entrepreneurs' judgements about what capital goods are worth and how they should be used in the face of an infinite number of production possibilities.

Socialism in practice

The logical conclusion of all these arguments seems to be that:

Every attempt at socialism, however brought about, must founder on the impracticability of setting up a purely socialistic economy. For that reason, and not because of deficiencies in the moral character of mankind, socialism must fail.[31]

In practice, however, socialist states have persisted for some time, as Mises accepts. However, he says, this is only because they have reduced their calculation problem somewhat by referring to the price relationships that do in fact occur in capitalist countries. Prices in the rest of the world can thus be used as a basis for calculation in the socialist commonwealth. But, Mises cautions, this practice has its limits – particularly in view of the socialist objective to bring socialism to the whole world:

> Without the basis for calculation which capitalism places at the disposal of socialism, in the shape of market prices, socialist enterprises would never be carried on, even within single branches of production or individual countries.[32]

In other words, the dream of spreading socialism throughout the globe would be self-defeating, because it would kill off the last vestige of any basis for economic calculation.

THE EROSION OF FREEDOM

In Part 4 of *Socialism*, Mises spends some time reviewing the battery of arguments that allegedly demonstrate the moral superiority of the socialist ideal. One of the most important of these is the slogan of 'economic democracy', the transfer of decisions about economic life from a few owners of productive property to the general mass of the people. But in Mises's view, the ideal and the reality are inevitably different. The removal of the means of production from private hands raises a wide variety of problems about how to manage them, problems which draw us quickly into the establishment of institutions that turn out to be dictatorial and the antithesis of the free and equal society that socialism advertises.

The socialist state

We have already noted Mises's definition of socialism:

> socialism means the transfer of the means of production out of the private ownership of individuals into the ownership of society. That alone and nothing else is socialism.[33]

But the obvious question is how 'society' manages these resources once it has taken them over. The answer, he maintains, is quite straightforward; it manages them through the coercive apparatus of the state.

This is, of course, a very embarrassing answer to the socialists who have built their careers on prophesying the 'withering away' of the state and who regard any idea of an authority above the community as utterly distasteful. But how are decisions to be made and executed where resources are held by a union comprising all people? Marxists talk glibly about the 'unitary will of society' without revealing how 'society' can express this 'will'; but plainly it requires some organ of control.

Competing ideals. When we move from the world of utopianism, and actually begin to look at the practicalities of how economic life is to be organized in the socialist commonwealth, it becomes clearly apparent that the individuals who make up society, even those who are committed socialists, are far from unified in their views about what things ought to be done. Accordingly, there are bound to be heated disputes about the question; and so much is at stake – the organization of an entire community – that the divisions are likely to be severe. Let us not suppose that socialism automatically produces perfect harmony:

> Many popular fallacies concerning socialism are due to the mistaken belief that all friends of socialism advocate the same system . . . If a man says socialism, or planning, he always has in view his own brand of socialism, his own plan. Thus planning does not in fact mean preparedness to co-operate peacefully. It means conflict.[34]

So there will be inevitable disputes about what the 'will' of 'society' really is; and however it is arrived at, there is no guarantee that those who are strongly opposed to the decision will accept it meekly. Both they, and others who might have no strong ideological commitments but who will willingly flout the agreement in order to further their own ends, must be brought firmly into line. In other words, there must be some office vested with supreme authority to prevent any deviation from the common purpose and to give the orders necessary to ensure that it prevails.[35] Because it is responsible for every element of production, the coercive might of the socialist state must be, and is, considerably greater than any other.

This coercive power does not cease to exist simply because the word 'state' is denied a place in socialist theory. We must beware of the doctrine of Marxian socialists

that state compulsion would be superfluous in a society not based on private property in the means of production. They argue that in the socialist community 'obedience to the simple fundamental rules governing any form of social life will very soon become of necessity a habit' but this is backed up by a hint that 'evasion of regulation and control enforced by the whole people will undoubtedly be enormously difficult' and will incur 'swift and severe punishment' since 'the armed workers would not . . . let themselves be mocked'. All this is merely playing with words. Control, arms, punishment, are not these 'a special repressive authority' and thus according to Engels's own words, a 'state'?[36]

Concentrated power. Other Marxist phrases betray the iron fist concealed in the velvet glove of words. The 'army' of the workers strongly suggests a single purpose, for example; but what of those of us who are conscripts and conscientious objectors?

To Mises, it hardly matters how the supreme authority in the socialist world is set up. The important point is that it must have complete control. There is no room for conscientious objectors: the minority 'will have to bow to the will of the majority'.[37] And the fact that power over all aspects of life is concentrated makes it easy to deal with the minority:

Within a socialist community there is no room left for freedom. There can be no freedom of the press where the government owns every printing office. There can be no free choice of profession or trade where the government is the only employer and assigns everyone the task he must fulfil. There can be no freedom to settle where one chooses when the government has the power to fix one's place of work.[38]

With all this being implied in the very nature of the socialist state, it is hardly surprising that dictatorship has in reality been the very obvious characteristic of most countries that have aimed to establish socialism. It was obvious from the very start

51

of the Russian revolution and found its most pithy expression in the view of Trotsky that the successful dictator has to be the most ruthless one.[39] There was no 'withering away of the state' in that particular community.

Looked at carefully, therefore, the socialist society is no equal society. It has to delegate complete power to some ruling body if it is to make and execute any decisions at all. Thus:

The socialist community is a great authoritarian association in which orders are issued and obeyed. This is what is implied by the words 'planned economy' and the 'abolition of the anarchy of production'.[40]

CONCLUSION

When we reflect on Mises's contribution to the debate on socialism, we have to agree with him that his arguments were sadly overlooked in Britain and the United States in particular. In those countries, it was thought that Mises had done no more than concentrate the minds of socialist theoreticians on the practical problems of calculation that had, in principle, been solved anyway by Barone many years before. Lange's reply, it was understood, had met Mises's view head on and had triumphed, leaving the intellectual field clear for a practical test of market socialism. In fact, Mises and Hayek had denied the ability of planners even to acquire the kind of information that Barone's strategy of simultaneous equations would need in order to work, and Lange's reply completely failed to meet Mises's analysis of the complexity of price adjustments in a world of change and innovation.[41] Today, many countries are suffering the practical effects of these early theoretical oversights.

There is no denying the penetration of Mises's argument. His point that the absence of a market in production goods leaves us with no yardstick to make production decisions is telling. His extension of that argument to cover semi-manufactures and intermediate capital goods reminds us that the calculation problem absorbs the whole economy, not just an isolated and manageable part of it. His observation that the valuation, and therefore the use, of such commodities depends upon the judgement of individual entrepreneurs at the time and is thus impossible to recreate by planning, reinforces his argument that markets are always in flux and simply cannot be commanded into a textbook equilibrium. It is absurd to suggest that 'ideal' markets can be created along the lines of 'perfect competition', as did Lange, because the notion of perfect competition is an abstraction that filters out, for the sake of simplicity, all the complicated processes by which markets actually work. In Part 2, the analytical background to these points will be examined more fully.

Definition and practice of socialism. It may be objected that Mises's arguments on socialism are generally theoretical, and do not take sufficient account of the practical successes that socialist states would claim. Also, socialism as he defines it would seem to be quite rare in the thoughts and actions of practical politicians: something less than complete common ownership of the means of production is a much more prevalent argument.

While Mises is correct that most analysts of his time accepted a definition of socialism much like his own, there were exceptions even then. What he was really attacking was Marxian socialism, which by the opening of the twentieth century had smothered the other, less radical, varieties in which limited common ownership and some reliance on market principles were retained. To help clarify this point, one recent writer has distinguished four varieties of projected socialism:

1. Marxian communism, in which money and prices are abolished and production and distribution is directed centrally;
2. communist production, but with a market existing for consumer goods only;
3. systems which suppress the operation of the market and so produce some of the features of the first two kinds; and
4. 'market socialism' in which both consumer and producer goods are exchanged.[42]

Although it might appear at first glance that Mises's arguments apply only to the first system, his incorporation of capital goods industries and semi-manufactures into the analysis also shows how the next two are also fatally tainted throughout with the lack of direction caused by the absence of exchange and therefore prices in their production processes. His criticism of market socialism is perhaps a little different: first, the administrators cannot collect the information they need to operate it, and second, it seems to aim only at reproducing by decree everything that the unfettered market does spontaneously, which seems to make it but a pale and inefficient version of everything that true socialists have been attacking for decades.

Of course, it was the theoretical essence of the socialist argument that Mises set out to attack; and having neutralized its pure form, he has indirectly weakened its less pure versions. In the meantime, actual events seem to be bearing out his concerns. Where socialism has been tried with most conviction, in Cambodia or under Chairman Mao, the repression of dissenters has been at its most barbarous. And where, such as modern China, it is being relaxed (whether its name is retained or not), prosperity and human freedom seem to be on the rise again.

CHAPTER THREE

The Theoretical Basis of Marxism

> It is useless to argue with mystics and seers. They base
> their assertions on intuition and are not prepared to
> submit them to rational examination. The Marxians
> pretend that what their inner voice proclaims is his-
> tory's self-revelation. If other people do not hear this
> voice, it is only a proof that they are not chosen.[1]

There is one particular brand of socialist theory that has
maintained a powerful influence within the minds of intellectuals for more than a century. It still retains the basic socialist
principle of communal ownership of the means of production,
but adds a persuasive philosophy of history which appears to
show that socialism is not only desirable, but inevitable. Furthermore, the theory suggests that those who argue for other
systems of social organization suffer either from a clouded
vision of the world or are deliberately mischievous. With all this
to recommend it, there should be no surprise that so many
intelligent thinkers have embraced the body of thought that we
call Marxism.

Marx's difficult task

According to Mises, the classical economists of the eighteenth
century had already worked out much of the theory that
explained why a system based on private ownership, incor-
porating the liberal institutions that guarantee peace and
stability, was likely to produce the most rapid increase in
human prosperity. Their arguments made an intellectual
mockery of what proved to be a practical impossibility in the
machine age: the attempt to impose the tenets of a village
socialism appropriate to the agricultural community onto
industrialized societies. It might seem reasonable to divide the
available land between farmers, but to share out the bricks and

pistons of a steam-mill to the workers was plainly ridiculous. As international trade grew, the primitive and utopian socialists of the time raised their sights wider and wider, and yet seemed less and less able to devise a practical programme for such a burgeoning new world.

It took a writer of Marx's skill to resurrect the utopian brand of socialism that had been entombed by the stony logic of economic theory and left for dead by practical men and women. Yet he was able to do so, comments Mises, only by insulating it securely and systematically from scientific criticism. In the first place, Marx argued that history was moving inexorably from the feudal era that preceded capitalism to the socialist paradise of the future: since socialism was inevitable, there was not much point in anyone trying to show it would not work. Furthermore, he maintained that different rules of economics apply in each of the stages of history: so present-day economics is the wrong tool to criticize the socialist future in any case. This analytical moat allowed Marx the additional safety of being deliberately vague about how the socialist commonwealth would in fact be arranged. Lastly, Marx said that the way people think was crucially dependent on their class allegiance and outlook, making him able to repulse any attack on the grounds that it rested on a 'bourgeois logic' that was necessarily inferior to the superior understanding of the socialists themselves.[2]

Many were inspired by this comfortable, quasi-religious vision of a better world in which all inequalities would be ended. But Marx's vision was so carefully fortified against critical argument, protests Mises, that it was able to win more and more ground on its emotional appeal alone, without anyone being moved to make a solid investigation of how it would work.[3] This oversight led to evident problems when Marxian socialism assumed the reins of power.

What, then, comprises this body of theory that has proved so durable and convincing to the intellectuals? Mises devotes the whole of Part 3 of *Socialism* to a consideration of the argument that socialism is inevitable and that capitalism is bound to end in monopoly, poverty, and oppression. His later work, *Theory and History*, reviews even more closely the philosophical roots of this idea, the notion that history is moving through a series of identifiable stages, with one form of society giving way to the next until, inevitably, the ultimate stage in the shape of world socialism is reached; and before we consider the other defences that Marxism has raised on the surface, it seems appropriate to examine this substructure first, and to look at Mises's biting critique of it.

THE STAGES OF HISTORY

The origins of dialectical materialism

The roots of Marx's thinking are in the German philosopher Hegel, who sought to explain historical change as a clash of opposing ideas out of which emerge the new ideas which go into the next round. This is the logic of the *dialectic* method, in which it is held that a *thesis* meets an *antithesis* (that is, the negation of the thesis), and thereby generates a *synthesis* that is the negation of the negation.

This explanation of how thought develops has a revolutionary appeal to it – ideas do not evolve slowly but emerge from the conflict of existing systems – that made it attractive to Marx and his collaborator, Frederick Engels. But as the basis of their own social studies they wanted a doctrine that was less woolly, more in tune with the materialism and the experimental approach that had proved so effective in the natural sciences, such as physics. And thus was born the notion of *dialectical materialism*.

Absurdity of the doctrine. Marx and Engels did not realize, complains Mises, that it was nonsensical to uproot dialectics from its home in the world of ideas and attempt to apply it to the physical events observable in the universe. Doing so led Engels to silly interpretations: butterflies 'come into existence from the egg through negation of the egg . . . they are negated again as they die' and so on. Mises wastes no sympathy on this nonsense:

It did not occur to Engels that he was merely playing with words . . . if one is committed to such inappropriate and logically vicious metaphorical language, it is not less sensible to call the butterfly the affirmation of the egg than to call it its negation. Is not the emergence of the butterfly the self-assertion of the egg, the . . . fulfillment of all its potentialities?[4]

This 'dialectical materialism', then, proves precisely nothing about how the world actually works. We can use it to interpret the world in any way we choose – and indeed, it is possible to construct interpretations that are completely contradictory.

The importance of this point as made by Mises is plain enough. Marxism deploys the dialectical analogy in the attempt to show that certain forms of human society, certain stages of history, must inevitably give way to specified others. But in fact, the substance of any such prediction would hinge on the particular analogy we adopted. A different interpretation of events is quite possible, and could lead us to predict an entirely different outcome.

The forces of production

Undeterred, Marx and Engels went on to apply this language to economic matters, an approach which automatically implied that capitalism was the 'negation' of what had preceded it and would be replaced by a further 'negation' (which turns out to be the socialist commonwealth). To do so, however, they had to rarify the theory yet further.

The 'materialist' view of the world on which Marx and Engels wanted to impose their revolution-inspiring dialectic method is really a *technological* view, argues Mises. In it, the 'material productive forces of society', the modes of production of material things, are said to condition the social, political, and intellectual aspects of human life. Eventually, the argument runs, these material forces will come into contradiction with the social relations they produce. In the case of capitalism, for example, industrial conurbations bring together vast numbers of downtrodden workers who then see their common interest in overthrowing the system, and social revolution will ensue.

In other words, the very shape of human society, how people see their social relationships and how they desire their world to be, is rooted in the techniques of production. The primitive economy based on agriculture generates one set of relationships (feudal relationships, according to Marx), while industrial capitalism generates yet another. And the values which determine human relationships in these various social stages are simply different: we cannot judge the standards of an earlier or later stage by those of our own. (A point, says Mises, which helps Marx insulate his vision of world communism from the criticism of those living in the present.)

Mises's criticism. Do the techniques of production ultimately determine what society and ideas come into existence? Most writers agree that technological inventions produce changes and liberate people for artistic and intellectual achievements. Many people would agree with Marx that the social relationships found in a society based on steam mills are likely to be very different from the way of life prevailing when only hand power is available. But Marx is attempting to do more than this. He wants to argue that a change in the ownership of productive goods would by itself change our ideas, values, and relationships very much for the better. To argue this, he has to maintain that *only* tools and machines are important and that all else is a necessary superstructure on top of them. There are, Mises suggests, three objections to this.

First, technological inventions are themselves the product of mental processes. We have to have an idea of what we want to achieve, and theories about how to achieve it, before we can set about the task of constructing the tools for the job. The means of production do not determine ideas, rather it is the other way around. Second, social relationships such as a respect for property and personal security are necessary if people are to accumulate the capital required to construct new productive processes: once again, the social rules precede the tools and processes they make possible. Third, the use of productive machinery rests on co-operation through the division of labour: the decision to co-operate, and the belief that co-operation is practicable, must obviously come first. In all these ways, then, it becomes clear that a society cannot be explained by reference to its tools and machinery because those things in turn can be the result only of prior social bonds.[5]

Marx's determinism. Being unable to detect these shortcomings, Marx thus propounded the view that mankind was moving steadily through various preliminary stages up to the final paradise of socialism. Each stage rests on a particular state of technology; human will and reason are powerless to stop the process because society, will, ideas, and reason are themselves a mere corollary of the prevailing technology. We might fool ourselves that we are free to choose, but in fact it is only providence acting through our thoughts.

As Mises correctly points out, this is an entirely mystical doctrine. The only proof offered for it is the equally mystical dialectical reasoning that capitalist private property is the first negation of individual private property, which then begets the common ownership of the means of production with the same inevitability as the other applications of the dialectical method that we have seen.[6]

The death-knell of capitalism?

The notion that disembodied material 'forces' explain historical change is plain nonsense, according to Mises.[7] It is impossible to describe historical development without reference to human minds, choices, values, and beliefs. Nor is it clear why the alleged supremacy of the material forces of production should lead to a progression of historical stages. Something more is needed if the promised transition is to occur – something human.

In the case of capitalism, Marx saw the proletarian workforce as the engine of change, just as the acquisitive bourgeois merchants of the middle ages had formed the vanguard in the overthrow of feudalism. The capitalists, having the ultimate control over the material productive processes, would bid down the wages of their workforce to subsistence levels in their dog-eat-dog competition to serve the idle rich. With no prospect of improvement under the prevailing system, and with a new consciousness of their interests brought about by close proximity in the factory towns, the proletariat would hold the key to the future. To survive in the cutthroat world of industrial capitalism, businesses would have to grow larger and larger in the struggle to achieve the economies of large-scale production and so underbid and supplant their competitors. But as the dialectic predicts, this same growth and concentration undermines the very system that produces it. The days of big business would be numbered.

The trouble with this analysis, says Mises, is that Marx completely forgot that big business exists to serve the masses, not the rich minority. Small groups can be served by specialist producers and shops, and millionaires in any event consume a tiny fraction of a nation's product. But the whole rationale of large businesses is to supply the demands of the millions of ordinary people. Far from grinding the masses into poverty, capitalism has always brought them material improvements.[8] The owners of capital would never profit by trying to suppress or contradict the wishes of the majority, but (a point to be covered more extensively in Chapter 10) must follow the commands which the general public express in their role as sovereign consumers. Marx's failure to grasp this harmony of objectives is just one aspect of his classist analysis of society that is, in Mises's eyes, every bit as vicious as the racism which modern Marxians decry today.[9]

CLASSES, IDEOLOGY, AND TRAITORS

To Marx, the capitalist era in which different social classes struggled to assert their contradictory interests, was just one tableau in the inevitable pageant of history. He took it that there could be no doubt about the existence of these classes, nor about the solidity of their respective purposes. Under capitalism, it was just a plain fact that the class interests of workers and capitalists were different and could not be reconciled.

Ideological basis of thought

The introduction of classes was a vain attempt by Marx to bring some human element into his mystical theory of the stages of history; but it was more. By insisting that people

61

thought and saw the world in terms of their own particular class perspective, Marx was able to deflect all criticisms of his socialist dream merely by exposing the critics themselves as members of a hostile class whose minds were glued up with a false logic.

In a class society, argued Marx, individuals are unable to see the world objectively. Their thoughts and theories are tainted and distorted by their class interests: their views can never be the truth, but are really an aspect of *ideologies* determined by their class position. Thus he was able to maintain that the economists of his day were merely apologists for the bourgeoisie. Without realizing it, they promoted economic doctrines that were not valid for every society, but were merely justifications for the capitalist system. The teachings of these 'vulgar economists' of the capitalist era are so impregnated with a class ideology, in other words, that present economic theory cannot even begin to discuss the principles of the socialist order to come.

Mises's criticism. Mises rejects this line of argument for many reasons. First, Marx and his followers only assert that there *is* a difference in the logic systems of the bourgeois class and themselves, but never explain precisely what it is. Such a gap is hardly likely to win rational converts to the new thinking, or to allow any judgement of its merits. Second, Mises argues that even if economic theories *were* constructed solely for furthering the power and position of the authors, that goal could still be achieved far better by breaking away from ideology and seeking out theories that were correct rather than ideologically tainted. By definition, a correct theory is better and more useful (for whatever purposes) than one which is made false by bigoted thinking.[10] Third, 'bourgeois' economics might well have been devised at the outset as a mere rationalization to counter feudal beliefs, and might still be used to bolster the claims of the capitalists; but that does not make it incorrect. It might have been devised originally in order to promote the interests of a particular group, and yet still be valid.[11]

Nevertheless, says Mises, it is not sensible to declare that ideas are a product of class or personal interests. Ideas and reasoning tell people what their interests are, and as circum-stances change, people adapt and change their ideas about what courses of action would best serve their interests.[12] There is nothing immutable about our thinking: our group membership and class allegiances do not tell us automatically what to believe and do.

Marxism, however, must go even further away from this commonsense point. For Marxism, the 'interests' concerned are but an aspect of the unfolding design of the superhuman material forces of production, not something originated in the minds of mortal men. The proletarian class which leads the revolution is a mere tool in the historical process. Given this view, it is not surprising that the Marxian theories do not admit the possibility of the proletariat deviating in the slightest from the ideas that are preordained for their class.[13] This leads on to a second batch of cricitisms from Mises.

Definitional shortcomings. It is quite legitimate to divide people into classes of any kind that helps analysis – men and women, dark and fair, able-bodied and handicapped, for example. It is not legitimate then to argue that these classes, which are merely how analysts divide the world arbitrarily, have any mind of their own. Thoughts and decisions are inherently personal, and cannot be ascribed to arbitrarily drawn groupings. But this, says Mises, is precisely what Marxian theory does. It forgets that any classes selected on one criterion might differ in other ways. For example, the class of capitalists would undoubtedly benefit from free trade and the absence of protectionism; but those in each sector of the capitalist economy would still welcome protectionism in their own sphere. What is beneficial to certain members of a class can harm the rest.[14]

Marxism, however, imagines that there should be a unity of thought and interests among the whole membership of each class, and admits no deviation. Its problems become rather obvious when such deviation *does* occur, however.

If the interests of a particular class are obvious, what are we to make of those members of the class who deviate? They can only be class traitors – bought out by the capitalists to espouse bourgeois arguments. The fact that a class's interests are plain should mean that members of the class have no choice in how they act; deviation would be irrational. And yet it exists: even Marx and Engels in the *Communist Manifesto* complained about competition *within* the proletarian class, indicating that there was less than complete agreement on the matter.[15] But, counters Mises, if complete agreement does not exist within any class, and its interests are not obvious to everyone, who is to decide what its interests are? As he puts it:

What reply can Marxian socialism make to those who, precisely on behalf of the proletarians, demand private ownership of the means of production, and not their socialization? If they are proletarians, this demand alone is sufficient to brand them as traitors to their class, or, if they are not proletarians, as class enemies.[16]

And who does the branding if there is disagreement? Who is the arbiter of what opinions are sound proletarian ideas and which are not? In fact, we discover, the only authority is the Marxian authority himself. The argument is completely circular: the Marxian justifies his or her vision of future socialism with an argument about how class unity and the conflict between different classes produces inevitable historical changes. Anyone criticizing this argument, whatever his or her origin, can be dismissed as misguided because they cannot see the inevitable unfolding plan.

Socialism is not a proletarian doctrine. Sadly, of course, Marx and Engels were not of proletarian origins themselves, says Mises gleefully in a slightly undignified but nevertheless effective piece of polemic. One was the son of a well-off lawyer who married into the German nobility and lived surrounded by the luxuries of middle-class comfort (including a housemaid), while the other was the son of a wealthy businessman. It is difficult to see, therefore, how they escaped 'bourgeois' thinking themselves while others apparently remain incapable of it.

Indeed, asserts Mises, socialism never has been a proletarian doctrine: those who devised it and fought for it were intellectuals with impeccable bourgeois backgrounds. For their part, the workers always wanted improvements *now* rather than the promises of some socialist paradise to come; they formed unions and negotiated for improvements in wages and conditions, instead of campaigning for the abolition of the wages structure completely as Marx had hoped and expected. Sadly, it came to appear to the disappointed Marx of later years that a sizeable fraction (if not most) of the working class was taken in by capitalist bribery: they were no more than 'petty bourgeois'.[17]

Any conclusion justified. In summary, then, Mises's view is that the Marxian refusal to meet rational argument directly, by dismissing all opposing ideas as stemming only from self-interest, means that *any* conclusion can be justified. If Marx had proposed some other development than socialism on the basis of dialectical materialism, the simple expedient of branding all objectors as myopic (or treacherous) fools would serve the same end of preserving it from attack. But on close inspection, this expedient can be shown to rest on a completely mistaken view of how human ideas are formed.

Marxism and the classical school

Mises was always mindful that economic and social life is a series of changing and complex relationships between individuals, not something that is static or mechanical like the textbook models of orthodox economics. It is therefore in character that he should trace some of the Marxians' errors in approach back to the work of the classical economists – even though the classical writers are often presumed to be in favour of free trade and unrestricted markets, and so quite unlike socialists of any description.

The Marxian contention that capitalist enterprises inevitably become larger and larger until the whole system is dominated by a few, all-powerful monopolies, is an example that illustrates Mises's point of view. Orthodox economics starts out with the 'perfect competition' assumptions that all suppliers are identical and that the products traded on each market are indistinguishable. When these oversimplifications are compounded with the commonsense observation that products manufactured on a larger scale can usually be produced and supplied more cheaply, it is only a short step to the conclusion that businesses will continue to grow and that larger suppliers will remorselessly squeeze out their competitors in every area of trade. But this view, argues Mises, is completely wrong. As the Austrian approach reminds us, neither suppliers nor consumers, nor the products they exchange, are ever identical: there are infinite gradations of quality of price, and the preferences of consumers are individual and divergent. There is no single and homogeneous market that can be captured simply by cheaper manufacture. Small specialist suppliers can be (and always have been) persistently successful, and innovators can whittle away the custom of even the largest and most well-established firm by producing something that is not necessarily cheaper, but better or more popular.

Through arguments of this sort, therefore, Mises can offer a critique of Marxism that is often difficult or impossible for orthodox economists, simply because many of the mistakes of Marxism are rooted in the classical analysis that still exerts a profound influence on how the mainstream practitioners of the subject think today. Mises's approach gives us a powerful vehicle for analysis where non-Austrians are often seen to flounder.

Misunderstanding of science. Another and deeper mistake of the neoclassical thinkers that also helped to reinforce Marxian errors, says Mises, was their yearning to make their subject into a 'science', bringing it the esteem enjoyed by the natural sciences and promising it an equally rapid progress. Thus, great emphasis was put on anonymous 'forces' similar to those which could be found in physics, and little mention was made of individual motives and values. The method of the natural sciences was thought to be wholly transferable to the study of human society, including economics. It was assumed that the same principles by which physical or chemical processes could be studied, measured, and predicted, were equally applicable to social phenomena:

The very idea that a discipline dealing with 'practical' problems like prices and wages could have an epistemological character different from that of other disciplines dealing with practical matters, was beyond the comprehension of the age.[18]

This mistaken methodology, soon to be countered by the subjectivist approach of the Austrian School of which Mises was a representative, was a strong undercurrent in the work of Marx and his contemporaries, whatever their political colour. Even in the field of personal morality, John Stuart Mill and Jeremy Bentham were looking for 'objective' standards. Auguste Comte similarly sought for 'laws' of sociology. And in the same vein, Marx himself came to devise a theory of history in which the material productive forces, quite independently of the will of individuals, were seen as producing social relationships that would bring about socialism with the inexorability of a law of nature.[19] This entirely mystical doctrine, in other words, was presented to the public under the guise of being a 'science'.

The truth of the matter, however, is that there are no objective 'forces' ruling history. Only *individuals* think and act. It is true that individuals might be members of particular groups which colour their thinking; but each individual is a member of many different groups, tempered by a different variety of experiences and forming a different set of opinions about the world. Individuals, and their thoughts, cannot be predicted merely by reference to their group allegiance.

Furthermore, it is the thoughts and actions of particular individuals, alone and in groups, which shape history, not some superhuman force. The development of events is not willed by a group mind, but by the practical actions of individuals and how those actions interact together.[20] Because individuals in themselves are hard or impossible to predict with any degree of certainty, Mises argues, it is simply mistaken to believe that economic and social events could ever be predicted in the way Marx tries to predict them:

Nobody is in a position to predict with the same assurance with which the natural sciences make predictions how he himself and other people will act in the future. There is no method that would enable us to learn about human personality all that would be needed to make such prognostications with the degree of certainty technology attains in its predictions.[21]

CONCLUSION

According to Mises, then, Marx's alleged 'scientific' predictions of the future course of history amount to a mere sham. They are based on a 'historicist' view that events are moving inexorably from one definite stage to the next; but when we look closely, we find that those supposed stages are no more than a particular way of interpreting events. Marx drew attention to the means of production and the economic relationships as the defining characteristics of each stage. Other thinkers might propose completely different things that would categorize past events in quite contrary ways. Marx predicted the demise of capitalism on the grounds that it would oppress and impoverish the workers; in fact, capitalism exists to serve the mass of the population, who form the core of its market. Marx imagined a trend towards uniformity and monopoly when in fact the course of capitalism has presented consumers with increasing variety and choice.

Mises does not stress this point overmuch, but events in the real world have certainly disposed of Marx's predictions. The revolutions he urged and forecasted, for example, have generally occurred in agricultural economies, not in advanced industrial countries. So glaring was the gap between the theory and the real outcome that Lenin chose to revise Marxism very substantially, introducing the new factor of socialist party organization to explain why revolutions occurred when and where they did. And capitalism has not been extinguished, but persists in the developed countries, where millions of ordinary people live and work together in crowded cities without any thought that they are oppressed; indeed, Mises is correct that it is those ordinary people who have derived the biggest benefits from capitalism, being brought the luxuries of everyday life by the mass markets that industrialization makes it possible to serve.

In the face of this hostile evidence, Marxians have been grateful for the logical insulation that other parts of Marx's theories have provided them. Mises's early criticisms did little to dent that barrier in the first half of the century, particularly in the English-speaking countries where socialism became so popular. More recently, however, his arguments have been echoed more and more widely, and the academic debate has certainly swung. It is, of course, a moot point whether that change has been due to the strength of the intellectual case, or whether the deficiencies of practical Marxism – the impracticability of socialism which Mises analysed – have sunk with them the Marxist philosophy.

If such extreme forms of socialism fall because of the problem of economic calculation and the mistaken foundations and predictions of their theory, what are the prospects for its milder representations? Characteristically, Mises is not short of an answer; and this can be found by going on to examine his critique of other anti-capitalist ideas.

CHAPTER FOUR

Anti-capitalism, Interventionism, and Bureaucracy

The idea that there is a *third* system – between socialism and capitalism, as its supporters say – a system as far away from socialism as it is from capitalism but retains the advantages and avoids the disadvantages of each – is pure nonsense.[1]

If socialism is based on such false rationale and unveils the dismal vision of despotism, why does there persist so much evident hostility to capitalism? Partly, Mises suspects, because capitalism is no respecter of vested interests and therefore tends to arouse resentment among large numbers of people who think they ought to be better off; also because of the success of socialist propaganda that capitalism is in a crisis; and partly because of the widespread belief that there exists a middle way between the supposed extremes of socialism and capitalism.

Mises has bequeathed us some interesting and effective work on these points, much of it written for a general public and therefore not as technical as some of his other works, but nonetheless rigorous and innovative. His book, *The Anti-Capitalist Mentality*, examines the source of some of the common complaints against the unfettered economy, and having been written in 1956, draws upon observations of the intellectual world of the United States, in which – despite the devotion to economic independence and personal freedom normally associated with that country – Mises was surprised to find a widespread acceptance of a weak form of socialism.

This weak socialism, based on the suppositions that the free market must be nudged in the right directions if consumer satisfaction is to be maximized, that this control should be limited, and that such a policy was a practicable alternative to full socialism, had already drawn Mises's fire. In the 1920s and

1930s he had been criticizing just this philosophy, although his work had not become available in English before *Human Action*. Some of his other essays had to wait until the publication of *A Critique of Interventionism* in 1977.

Meanwhile, in 1944, Mises took up a specific aspect of the argument in his short book, *Bureaucracy*, which gained enough attention to go through several editions. In it, he looks at the patterns of control that must dominate enterprises owned by the government or constrained by political objectives. It is a neat explanation of what many politicians have only now, after years of running state businesses and using regulations in the attempt to control private ones, begun to accept – that organizations aiming at political targets instead of financial targets are inherently difficult (perhaps impossible) to manage efficiently.

THE ANTI-CAPITALIST MENTALITY

There has always been resentment about the operations of the market economy – precisely because the market rewards people dispassionately for the goods and services they produce for others, and thus frequently gives many groups less than they feel they 'deserve' (an idea that goes right back to the ancient aristocratic writers, including Aristotle and Cicero).

Groups opposed to capitalism

Insecurity and resentment. Many groups display more than their fair share of resentment against capitalism and have the ability to make it vocal. White-collar workers, for example, often find that manual workers in routine or dirty jobs are paid better than they. On market principles, this might be quite justified, since people do not like menial or unpleasant jobs and have to be paid well to do them; but the office worker sees only the fact that someone who is far less accomplished is actually receiving a much greater reward. In addition, white-collar workers are always in contact with more successful people – their bosses or those they serve – fuelling their resentment yet again.

Furthermore, the market economy brings constant change. The demands of consumers change, new production technology comes into operation, and workers in old industries and experts on old equipment can find themselves having to accept lower wages and might even be put out of a job. The working out of this market process is bound to make people feel less than fully secure, even though the power of the market to absorb change is actually its greatest strength. So insecurity remains a prominent cause of anti-capitalism, even though a static economy would quickly reduce us all to poverty.[2]

Intellectuals, teachers, and literati. Teaching is another source of opposition to capitalism. Teachers in tax-supported institutions depend upon the government sector for their livelihood and are hardly likely to oppose it too vigorously.[3]

Many university teachers are former government bureaucrats and so take easily to authoritarian views and habits.[4] Historians talk of industry being 'imposed' on the population instead of mentioning the benefits it brought to all, while economists simply assume the wisdom of interventionist doctrines. Old ideas, born when theoretical socialism was at its zenith, have proved slow to change. It takes a long time for people, including teachers, to admit that they were wrong.[5] In the meantime, generations of students have been influenced by their outmoded views.

Writers, actors, and artists are also peculiarly disposed to attack capitalism. It may be that the romantic tends to rebel against reason, or that the benefits of capitalism are diffused and hard to portray, while its deficiencies, as Dickens found, are easy to dramatize.[6] But the 'social novels' of middle-class authors such as Emile Zola entertain us with homilies, not facts. Capitalism *reduces* poverty and provides opportunities for personal improvement that simply did not exist in the static agrarian economy that preceded it.

Pressure groups. Such is the nature of representative politics that pressure groups can have a great influence on politicians. Government today is characterized as having a duty to help deserving groups, and there are plenty of groups and coalitions being formed to insist that their own cases are particularly deserving. Only the general public is unrepresented by the professional lobbyists, says Mises. Much effective opposition to the free economy, therefore, comes from people who are simply trying to achieve a privileged position within it.[7]

Mises has no doubt that all modern party ideologies originated as 'special group interests fighting for a privileged status',[8] warning that a parliament comprising only special interests is doomed to disappoint everyone in the long run. And this is a principle of growing importance, which serves as the point of departure for a complete modern school of economics in its own right, the Public Choice School.[9] Under this approach, the mathematical principles of game theory are employed to illustrate the general possibility that by defending their own special interests, political groups can generate a result that is actually in the interests neither of themselves nor of others. If Mises can be credited with helping to initiate this new approach (and by and large its authors do sympathize with him and the other Austrian thinkers), it is an extremely important by-product of his work.

The 'failure' of capitalism

Another source of opposition to capitalism is that the market economy is often misunderstood. Those who play a part in it, such as the trade union official and the entrepreneur, often feel qualified by their office alone to decide questions of political economy. The tendency for economic analysis to be reduced down to easily understood models and principles serves only to reinforce their impression that economics is simple and that economic relationships are straightforward and manageable. In reality, however, the market process is subtle and involved, and many of those working within it get a distorted view of its operation. Those who work for large industrial companies, and especially their trade union leaders, might imagine they have a practical knowledge of how the economy functions, for instance, but in reality they are very far from its cutting edge and may completely overlook the importance of entrepreneurship and innovation in the development of their own industry and therefore of others. Mises cautions:

On no account must a disposition to avoid sharp words be permitted to lead to a compromise. It is time these amateurs were unmasked.[10]

Confusion of science and values. It is not just amateurs who have misrepresented capitalism, however. Professional economists and historians must bear much of the blame. The Swedish economist Gunnar Myrdal, who went on to share the Nobel Prize with Mises's follower, F.A. Hayek, argued that demands for higher wages and shorter working hours, together with the strikes that sometimes support them, are in reality a striving for power and justice by a social class that simply feels oppressed. Mises retorts that such arguments are hopelessly confused. The principles of economics remain unaffected: however much resentment any group may feel, their wages cannot remain above the market level for very long in any economy – or at least, not without generating the worse evil of unemployment.[11] We may sympathize with certain groups, but our values do not change the irrefragable logic of economic science.

Industry and poverty. Capitalism is also accused of generating poverty. Mises finds this a bewildering view, since the truth is precisely the opposite. The *laissez-faire* capitalism of the nineteenth century actually converted the landless poor into wage earners, he notes; that is, it *abolished* poverty rather than caused it. From our comfortable world today, we may not care much for the conditions of the urban poor at the time, but life for them was certainly better than the poverty and early mortality that was guaranteed on the land. Capitalism gave them a crucial first step on the ladder; as it grew, so did wealth, personal saving, insurance, and the productive capital that continues to make work less laborious and more fruitful.

Is Mises correct? Critics of capitalism nevertheless abounded in the nineteenth century, and if we are to form a sound judgement about whether Mises's panegyric is justified, it is worth asking what was the source of their objections. It might be mentioned that the enormous changes inherent in the industrial revolution would tend to make any economist gloomy, much as modern economists are dismayed about the short-term consequences of the information revolution, whatever its longer-term benefits to human society, for we all tend to see events in terms of our rather immediate and localized concerns. Some modern economists, on the other hand, have argued that the increasing concentration of the workforce in industrial towns conspired with a lack of sanitation to produce increases in infectious and sometimes fatal diseases. In nineteenth-century Britain, where the capitalist boom was at its most pronounced, it is certainly true that life expectancy did not rise much; the population grew, but only because more and more youngsters survived into adulthood. But this in itself must be considered a benefit, and one concentrated on the poor. For where the rich had luxuries before, including those of relatively good sanitation and adequate food, the poor were able to afford them only on increased wages available in the industrial towns, to which they (for the most part) freely migrated. Boots replaced clogs, hats replaced shawls, and items such as clocks and handkerchiefs began to enter the scheme of expenditure, tea and sugar fell in price, and newspapers and schools prospered, giving evidence that the poorest people were, for the first time, raised well above the level of mere subsistence that was all their predecessors could hope for on the land.[12]

Mises's own conclusion from the evidence is that it may take time to abolish poverty, but capitalism is the surest way to do it. We should remember that the pre-capitalist economy supported only a twentieth of the population that the industrial revolution made possible. To scrap capitalism would certainly consign the vast bulk of the population to oblivion.[13]

A crisis of government. There is no doubt, agrees Mises, that our age is beset with considerable economic problems. But we must be clear about their source. The only way to increase our standard of living is to build up the capital resources, the tools and equipment, that make human effort more productive. Capitalism has a profound tendency to do this, of course, and so it raises wages and living standards into the bargain. However, that tendency can be stifled by taxes that eat into capital or make its accumulation less worthwhile, and by regulations

75

which inhibit its use. This is precisely the effect of most government economic policy of today. We are told that the world economy is in crisis. However,

this is not a crisis of capitalism. It is a crisis of interventionism, of policies designed to improve capitalism . . . [14]

but which plainly fail to do so. (Later sections of this chapter will explain exactly how interventionism, in Mises's judgement, erodes the efficient functioning of the market economy and so produces all of the problems it is supposed to cure.)

Visions of a new society

Anti-capitalist writings are long on slogans and short on workable economic systems, Mises tell us. Among other things, they call for 'economic democracy', 'an end to social injustice', and the 'equal distribution' of property. These slogans are powerful, but the reality which adheres to them is undesirable.[15]

Economic democracy. The idea that 'the people' should take over the administration of the economy sounds attractive, but is a hollow concept. As we have seen, such administration can be achieved only through some coercive organ (that is, the state, whatever name is in fact given to it) with powers to regulate all economic life – something very far from the idea suggested by the original slogan. Furthermore, the purpose of political democracy is to keep the peace by giving everyone a say in political decisions. But in economics, no special institutions are required to give everyone a say in economic life. Competition alone is quite sufficient, because producers in a competitive world are effectively governed by the wishes of consumers; unless they satisfy the most urgent needs of the general mass of consumers, expressed through their demand in the market-place, they will not stay in business. In the free economy, in other words, production is directed by the mass of consumers already. Why attempt to replace this rule of consumers by the rule of producers?[16]

76

Still, the idea of 'economic democracy' has proved strong, and one of the principal vehicles for it has been heavy taxation on businesses. It is imagined by some 'social democrats' that taking away large proportions of the profits earned by ordinary producers, and distributing them more generally throughout the population, can increase the degree to which we all benefit from the good fortune of successful businesses. Unfortunately, this principle takes the rewards away from those successful enterprises without sharing any of the risk that is involved in running every commercial firm – for no tax system ever helps enterprises in trouble with the same efficiency and generality that it taxes those which prosper. That is an imbalance which can only depress people's efforts to succeed by serving consumers:

Today the state shares in the profits of enterprises without being obliged to co-operate at all in the management of the production process and without being exposed to harm in any way by possible losses of the enterprise.[17]

Social injustice. 'Justice' is another slogan that Mises feels is often misused. There is a pervasive idea that nature has provided our wealth and resources without favour, so we have a duty to share them equally. Again, careful scrutiny shows this to be completely false. Nature does not create wealth. If we do nothing with the resources of nature, we will have poverty for sure. Only *people* create wealth, by the efficient use of labour, by specialization, and by the steady accumulation of capital that has been possible in free societies. Capital makes our labour more productive, so increasing our standard of living; but it is not one of nature's bounties. However, it has to be accumulated – saved for by forgoing current consumption – and can be wasted easily. If we remove the incentives for people to save and thus to accumulate and preserve capital, we will not bring about justice, only poverty.

Property. The more equal distribution of private property is, of course, at the heart of most socialist criticisms of the market economy. Some argue that property derives solely from violence and conquest in the past, others that it is less efficient than common ownership. In reply to the first, Mises is blunt:

That all rights derive from violence, all ownership from appropriation or robbery, we may freely admit . . . But this offers not the slightest proof that the abolition of ownership is necessary, advisable, or morally justified.[18]

Even then, it should be remembered that we have come a long way from the property disputes of early communities. Ownership today takes nothing from others: one of the benefits of modern capitalism, suggests Mises, is that an individual can start from the very bottom and by working and saving, build up completely new property that never existed before.

Indeed, it is the fact that property *is* distributed according to these rules that makes production and the standard of living as high as they are. If property is not used and maintained, the income it helps us generate must fall. Private owners are likely to use and maintain their property more carefully than others, so its distribution across the whole population, including those who were much less careful, would bring only a loss. The social income in fact *depends* on how private property is held.

Let us remember finally that property also provides a necessary bastion for the individual against the erosion of freedom by strong governments: a 'sphere of independence' that is not available where all property is controlled by the state.[19] Mises takes up this argument in detail in *Liberalism*, and his views on this principle will be discussed more fully in the next chapter.

INTERVENTIONISM

Even those who were once the strongest supporters of socialism, claims Mises, have now generally wilted under the logical attack on it in which he played a part. Somewhat optimistically, perhaps, he announced in his 1929 volume that only the names, and not the substance, of the various brands of socialism and communism had survived. Their place, however, had been taken by a new form of political belief that appeared milder but is, upon examination, just as impracticable and undesirable. This is the principle of interventionism. Thus,

> the socialist ideal itself has ceased to exert a political effect. Its followers, even those who were willing to shed blood to bring it about a few years ago, have now postponed it or given up entirely. But interventionism . . . now dominates the climate of opinion.[20]

The search for the middle way

The phenomenon of interventionism, Mises alleges, arises partly from the clear failures of socialism and partly from the misunderstandings and doubts about capitalism already described. Some adopt it as a Trojan horse within which full socialism can be smuggled into an unsuspecting society. For others, it is an end in itself, representing a middle way between socialism and capitalism, a system in which the market economy can be 'regulated', or transformed into a 'mixed' economy that combines the best features of each system. Whatever their motives, both groups agree that interventionism is the best policy.

Marx himself, and the older Marxists, poured scorn on this moderate approach, dismissing it in 'frank language as reformist nonsense, capitalist fraud, and petty-bourgeois idiocy'.[21] They were not searching merely for a system of private property that is hampered, regulated, and directed through government intervention: they sought completely new institutions that would outlaw private property and make it impossible to buy and sell labour or any other productive resource. Merely tampering with the market economy completely misses their point.

Types of socialism. The reason why we find so many modern Marxians lurking inside the Trojan horse of interventionism, maintains Mises, is that it *does* in fact bring about the triumph of socialism. He explains that there are two different patterns for the realization of socialism, and that the 'hampered market economy' resulting from interventionist policies differs from one of these brands only in degree.

The first kind of socialism is that on the 'Marxian or Russian' pattern, where all the means of production are owned and operated by the government. Every farm, shop, or plant is a mere department of the state, and those who work in them are bureaucrats carrying out the orders of a central administration. The hampered market economy is not much like this. But it is very much like socialism on the German *Zwangswirtschaft* pattern, where farms, shops, and plants are *nominally* in private ownership but are directed by the government how and what to produce, and whom to trade with at what prices. The trappings of capitalism – ownership, markets, prices, interest rates, and wages – are maintained, but they are a sham. So-called entrepreneurs still buy and sell, pay the workers, contract debts and pay interest, but they are not genuine entrepreneurs. In Nazi Germany they were called shop managers of *Betriebsführer*. In reality, they are told what to produce, for whom, and at what price, by the government. It is a *socialist* system because the government authority directs all production, but it is socialism with the outward appearance of capitalism.

In passing, it might be said that Mises has made a very interesting point here, which can help explain and avoid some mistaken impressions about the Nazi era which still persist today. The fierce anti-communism of the Nazis leads many people to suppose that their economic organization, and that of the Italian fascists, rested on a complete *laissez-faire* principle, in which large industrial capitalists were allowed a free rein – and perhaps contributed in some measure to the oppression and bellicosity of the age. In fact, Mises is reminding us, the economic principles of the Nazis were socialist principles: although it might have appeared to possess all the features of unbridled capitalism, in reality the German economy had never been so tightly controlled before. Fascism and a free economy are two very different things indeed.

Anyway, the main point is that interventionism and socialism are often confused. The difference, declares Mises, is that the hampered market economy is still a market economy. The purpose of interventionism is merely to influence it, to make production and consumption develop along the lines chosen by the authorities rather than those which emerge from the free interplay of buyers and sellers. But the doctrine is definitely seen as the middle way: the interventions that are proposed and put into effect are isolated and designed to regulate only particular markets, and are not intended to become instruments of more widespread and general economic control.

The main thrust of Mises's critique of interventionism is that, unfortunately for the interventionists, their limited objective cannot be realized. Markets are very complicated, and an interference with them at one place produces unwelcome side-effects in another. For example, the government might decide to boost employment by spending public money on labour-intensive projects. But that money has to come from somewhere: if it comes from taxes, he says, it abolishes on the one hand as many jobs as it creates on the other (more, we would say today, because of the inevitable churning of the labour market in response to fickle tax policies); if the spending is financed by borrowing, it means credit expansion and inflation. And other interventions have yet other kinds of adverse effects. There is consequently a great pressure on the regulators to attempt to contain the problems caused by their initial policy. They are pushed to intervene more and more until, eventually, the system has degenerated into complete German-pattern socialism, an economy that is capitalist in its outward appearance, but which in reality has become completely controlled by the authorities. As Mises puts it:

The middle-of-the-road policy is not an economic system that can last. It is a method for the realization of socialism by instalments.[22]

And it is so whether we recognize the fact and embark on the policy deliberately, or whether we unwittingly fall into it because we do not understand the nature of interventionism and that it cannot be sustained.

The nature of interventionism

To see why Mises thinks this is so, we must examine his concept of interventionism more closely. Intervention, he explains, is a limited order by a social authority forcing entrepreneurs and the owners of the means of production to deploy their resources in a manner different from that in which they otherwise would.[23]

Content of the definition. This definition is quite restrictive, and we should be mindful of the economic policies that Mises has deliberately left out. A measure designed to preserve property and to allow the market to function – the institution, say, of a police force and a punishment system for those involved in theft or fraud – is obviously not an intervention in Mises's opinion. On the contrary, the preservation of a functioning framework for economic activity is an essential duty of government. With this we can readily assent; such policies are not designed to steer production and consumption in particular ways, but simply to generate an atmosphere of peace and stability in which economic life can proceed with certainty and without coercion. But other exclusions from Mises's definition of interventionism are not so fully in line with the customary meaning of the word, and in discussing his views, we need to be careful that we have a clear understanding of what his definition rejects. This is not always easy, because Mises's own view appears to have changed between his early essays in the 1920s and his more comprehensive analysis in *Human Action.*

In this context, it might come as a surprise that according to Mises's early views on the subject, at least, the government using market principles to promote particular ends is not an intervention. An example would be the government buying milk on the market in order to give it to destitute mothers, or the subsidization of private schools.[24] But in *Human Action*, he later came to absorb this type of policy into his definition.

Similarly, a partial socialization of the means of production, such as the nationalization of a railroad, or the ownership and operation of other means of production by the government or the municipalities, would not constitute intervention.[25] First, the aim of interventionism is to direct private property, not to own and control it. Second, all these enterprises exist against a background of private ownership, and they must fit into the mechanism of the market economy. If their losses are covered from taxation, it might well shift the pattern of production and consumption – but that will happen according to the process of the market, and not according to the wishes of the authorities. That is, at least, the view expressed in Mises's earlier writings. In *Human Action* he seems to accept that, even though this result is unintended, it is rather similar to the unintended consequences of other interventions.

Main thrust of interventionism. In summary, then, Mises stuck to the definition that:

Intervention is a limited order by a social authority forcing the owners of the means of production and entrepreneurs to employ their means in a different manner than they otherwise would.[26]

Although in later years Mises broadened the range of policies covered by this definition, it did not change his original opinion that the interventionist arsenal is furnished with two main weapons: price controls, including controls on wages (the price of labour) and interest rates (the price of borrowing); and controls over production and trade, including import controls. It is around these two weapons that Mises's argument against interventionism revolves.

Intervention in theory and practice

Price controls. Wage and price controls have a long history, as long as forty centuries.[27] But even when they were sanctioned by the death penalty, as in the reign of the emperor Diocletian and the French Revolution, they failed to achieve the desired results. Why should that be?

Mises explains it through the example of a typical price control set by a government in order to keep down the price of some necessity like milk.[28] Having declared a maximum price for the sale of milk, the government might pride itself on easing the burden for those who need milk and can least afford it. Unfortunately, the lower price encourages people to buy more milk, while it makes milk production less attractive. Some producers may even start to make losses at the new lower price, and will sell their herds for slaughter. With demand high and supply shrinking, there simply will not be enough milk to go round. The government will be disappointed. It wanted people to get more of the milk they needed by making it cheaper for them to buy. But now, there is *less* on sale and people are getting less than before. To meet this problem, it might try rationing, so that the available supply goes mainly to deserving people, such as young children. Whatever it does, however, it does not get round the fact that there is still a smaller quantity of milk available for consumption than before.

Another strategy might be to help producers by fixing lower prices for fodder, with the intention of restoring their profitability and thus tempting them to replenish milk supplies. Then, of course, exactly the same happens: fodder production drops and the government must move on to control *its* production costs, and so on. The government originally wanted to control only one price, but now it finds itself obliged to control more and more if it is to contain the undesirable consequences. And, concludes Mises,

as the government goes farther and farther, it will finally arrive at a point where all prices, all wage rates, all interest rates, in short everything in the whole economic system, is determined by the government. And this, clearly, is *socialism*.[29]

Rent controls are another classic case.[30] They may be introduced in an effort to help needy families to get somewhere to live, but they make it unprofitable for people to rent out houses. The inevitable result is that there is a serious housing shortage wherever there is rent control, making life *harder* for people who want to rent.

Wage controls. In the case of wages, governments generally want to demonstrate their help for the working poor by fixing *minimum* rates of pay.[31] Higher statutory wage rates, however, increase the production costs of business enterprises. They might try to pass these increased costs on to the public in terms of higher prices: that will reduce the demand for their products (particularly the demand from poorer people, who are forced to economize), and force cutbacks and unemployment; or they might reduce their labour bill directly by laying off workers.

The larger the coverage of wage controls, the more pronounced will this unemployment be. Yet further intervention will be suggested as a cure, such as new rules to force businesses not to dismiss workers, or higher taxes on business in order to compensate the unemployed. The only option then left by which businesses can absorb the increased costs is to run down their productive equipment. That is a waste of capital which will generate more unemployment later.

On this subject, Mises stresses his distinctly 'Austrian' view of the problem.[32] If only some industries are affected by the wage maxima, as is quite probable under the piecemeal programme of interventionism, they will be affected worse than others. Or again, capital-intensive industries may weather the storm better than labour-intensive ones. Wage controls, therefore, have a marked tendency to change and distort the entire pattern of production. Before the intervention, resources were deployed for the best possible satisfaction of the most urgent needs of consumers; now, they are employed differently, implying that satisfaction has been unintentionally reduced.[33] And if the pattern of production has changed, the workers laid off in the shrinking industries may be unqualified for new jobs, or will have to be retrained, making the unemployment effect even more pronounced.

Import restrictions. Similar problems arise with import controls, which Mises cites as an example of regulations over production and trade, rather than wages and prices. Tariff barriers are often invoked as a way of protecting home industries against less expensive goods coming from foreign competitors. Their effect, however, is to force and encourage production to be made domestically even though this is more expensive. More expensive production processes mean that fewer resources are available to be diverted into the payment of wages. While a tariff might seem to help a particular industry, therefore, its net effect is to lower living standards generally.[34]

Conclusion. These examples show that interventionism, as defined by Mises, cannot persist for long. If the government, faced with the undesirable side-effects of its first intervention,

is not prepared to undo its interference with the market and to return to a free economy, it must add to its first measure more and more regulations and restrictions. Proceeding step by step in this way it finally reaches a point in which all economic freedom of individuals has disappeared. Then socialism of the German pattern, the *Zwangswirtschaft* of the Nazis, emerges.[35]

Mises suggests that the acceptance of this state of affairs by the public might not take long. The very failure of the hampered market economy, its tendency to deliver the opposite of what was promised, reinforces the layman's conviction that private property must be controlled more rigidly, if necessary by the coercive instruments of socialism.[36]

Is Mises correct?

The question of whether Mises is correct in this analysis is a pressing one today, since there is a good deal of allegiance to the principle of interventionism and the philosophy of the 'mixed economy' (that form of organization excluded from Mises's definition of interventionism, where the government or the municipalities actually own and control a modest number of enterprises within an economy where private ownership is prevalent and resources are guided by the market, rather than by the authorities). Indeed, comparatively few commentators in the West today would urge the 'extremes' of complete socialism or unhampered capitalism, most believing that it is right for the government authorities to give some measure of direction to producers and consumers in the interests of 'social' policy. Since this concept is so common, it becomes a matter of the utmost concern whether it is also durable.

Some economists, including even modern representatives of the Austrian School, have found it hard to be completely convinced by Mises's analysis. Their doubts have hinged on whether the examples he uses are genuinely sufficient to undermine the whole principle of interventionism, and whether his definition is so restrictive that it automatically produces the answer he wants and (unfortunately for us) excludes the very types of interference in the marketplace that are most common and important today.

Controls. Mises's main argument against price controls is repeated over and over again throughout his work, and he cites his demonstration of the self-defeating nature of interventionism as one of his principal contributions to economics.[37] But it is hard to agree that his treatment finishes the job.

It is certainly true that price controls generate shortages, which were no part of the original intention. That does not necessarily imply a steady drift into socialism until the policy is reversed. People might in fact be happy to accept a limited rationing system, considering it to be fairer than a market which gives better choice, or access to essentials, only to the rich. Or the controls might be introduced with the deliberate intent to engineer a shortage and drive people elsewhere, such as using rent controls to kill the private rented property sector and drive people into owner-occupied or state-provided housing. Without some further argument and evidence, however, it is not clear that the effects of this rationing or direction really will spread more and more widely into other markets and bring us closer to comprehensive government control.

It might be that intervention is somehow self-limiting, and as such can be endured without full socialism emerging. By Mises's own admission, the economy is enormously complex and difficult to predict and control. Perhaps, then, it has the power to absorb the shock of intervention without being fatally overcome, just as the human body (another very complex system) can accommodate extremes of heat and cold by sweating or shivering, and does not die immediately the air temperature changes by ten degrees. It could be that the undesirable results of interventionist policies spread themselves so thinly across the population that no strong political pressure exists for further intervention to alleviate them, for example, or that people just accept the consequences as an acceptable price to pay.

As we have seen, wage and price controls have been around for some thousands of years. They have often been modified or abandoned, but have led comparatively rarely to complete socialism developing. The most robust socialism found in the globe today is usually, on the contrary, the result of armed revolution, not a gradual drift. Rent controls, to take Mises's example, are found in many countries and have operated for many years; but not everywhere is there a pressure on politicians to alleviate the shortages they cause by building more houses in the public sector. People can foresee the harmful effects of such a move just as clearly as they can see the present problem.

Similar arguments can be set against Mises's discussion of *production* controls. In addition, it has other features that leave critics less than convinced. In places, for example,[38] it becomes mixed in with wage controls and import tariffs, both of which might be regarded as just another form of price control (one designed to raise prices rather than reduce them), and therefore insufficient to prove the point. He does of course refer to genuine production controls, such as restrictions on working hours or the use of child labour, making the case that these reduce production and so result in a general fall in consumption. But once again, as Mises recognizes, people might be prepared to pay this price for the 'social gains' of the new law. That is,

the recourse to restriction is justified from the point of view of their value judgements. They incur costs and pay a price in order to get something that they value more than what they had to expend or forgo.[39]

Perhaps a measure of intervention, then, could be accepted and remain quite sustainable in the long term. Mises's belief, that wage, price, and production controls cannot last without calls for further intervention that must lead inevitably to socialism unless the initial interventions are repealed, seems hollow. Economic systems containing just these kinds of intervention have been around since the dawn of time. Interventionism seems the most common economic system: does the 'middle way' not in fact exist?

88

Subsidies and nationalization. Another question, raised recently by the Austrian School economist Donald Lavoie,[40] is why Mises originally excluded subsidies, interference with the market through taxation policy, and control of macroeconomic variables such as the quantity of money from his original definition of 'intervention'. A subsidy to schools, designed to induce more people to become teachers and more students to enrol, plainly distorts production much as he fears price controls do. And since subsidies are paid out of taxation, Mises is hoist by his own belief that taxes are never neutral but always cause distortions in production and consumption. Likewise, the whole Austrian School approach reminds us that government manipulation of macroeconomic factors such as the quantity of money and credit must produce harmful effects on the operation of the market, and push entrepreneurs into acting in ways they would not have considered beforehand. It must therefore be regarded as an intervention, as Mises went on to accept in *Human Action.*

Lastly, Mises's exclusion of scattered nationalization from his definition of interventionism is troubling. It is not interventionism nor socialism, he says, if only parts of the means of production are socialized. But again, if these concerns are financed through taxation, it will affect consumer spending, and so the market is distorted. And even if they are profitable, their buying and selling will still affect producers and consumers. A nationalized oil industry in pursuit both of economic and 'social' objectives, for example, would affect almost every other industrial sector.

The importance of this issue is made more urgent because price controls, around which Mises's argument hinges, are no longer seen as the mainstay of the 'middle way' economy, whereas scattered nationalization and the mixed economy is. Moreover, some socialists see the nationalization of the dispersed but 'commanding' heights of the economy as a means of establishing effective control over all productive resources without the legal transfer of ownership to the state. Unfortunately, Mises's discussion of interventionism threatens to leave us almost unclad against this chill wind.

Some of Mises's successors have therefore gone further than

89

he, warning that *any* government economic interference, whether through price controls, production quotas, licences, taxation, subsidies, or piecemeal nationalization, invariably divorce people from their property or some part of its use, and thus always jolt the delicate mechanism of the market out of synchronization.[41] Despite the sweeping nature of this conclusion, it must be admitted on Mises's own principles that they have a point.

BUREAUCRACY

However, Mises offers some comfort against the threat of nationalization in his discussion of bureaucracy. He is not clear on the point, but seems to suggest that nationalization of specific enterprises can occur without it leading to socialism, as a rigorously pursued policy of intervention would do. But even if its spread is not inevitable, he argues that it still has severe drawbacks, being inherently less efficient because the aims of the nationalized industry – partly to cover costs and partly to meet an indistinct array of 'social' objectives – are confused and imprecise.

Public enterprises and bureaucracy

In the market economy, prices and consumer preferences dictate how production proceeds. Entrepreneurs direct resources to where they think consumers' needs are most urgent. If they are right, they will be rewarded by profitability. The public enterprise, however, does not exist principally to produce a profit. It is set up with non-profit objectives in mind – objectives such as providing cheap transport or other services that the government believes are essential.[42]

Monitoring and management. Immediately this happens, problems arise. What services should be supported in this way? Which are useful, and which not? Since profitability is not the hallmark of success, simply providing the services that most consumers want and are willing to pay for (as the private enterprise would do) is not enough. For the commercial business, life is easy: it aims to make a profit, and in the process satisfies the needs of consumers. The aims of the public enterprise, however, are much more vague. It has to override consumer behaviour and decide which services are 'socially' necessary. It is not instructed to make a profit, and may be expected to make a loss, but it is expected to maintain 'essential' or 'desirable' services.

Even if it is straightforward inefficiency that produces the public enterprise's losses, these can be explained away by the necessity for it to provide unprofitable lines. The vagueness of its objectives means it is hard to check its performance. Is a particular bureau necessary? Is it overstaffed? If its output is hard to measure (like the output of a police department or the FBI, for example), can we be sure we are getting value for money? The human tendency of the manager, faced with vague goals, is to fight for a larger staff, better equipment, and service improvements, letting his or her superiors worry about the cost to the taxpayer. After all, who would dare to put a price on essential services?

Bureaucratic rules. To keep managers and their budgets under control, therefore, it is necessary to impose an overlay of rules and regulations on the public enterprise, so that there is a set procedure determining where resources should be committed and to what degree. But the manager thus becomes a mere bureaucrat who has to ask a higher authority if he can step outside the normal framework. This process of bureaucratization, Mises conjectures, is not a problem of the size of any enterprise: it is the result of not aiming at the single and clear objective of profitability.[43]

Bureaucratization of private enterprises

Exactly the same problems can beset a commercial enterprise that is hampered by interventionist policies, avers Mises. Once again, the general public's view is that commercial firms become bureaucratic when they become large, but this is not so: whatever the size of a firm, its owner has to control it carefully if it is not to be supplanted by a more efficient one. An enterprise is not necessarily bureaucratic when it is large, only when complicated rules and regulations have to be introduced within it in order to keep it operating when clear direction is lacking.

It is the swamping of the simple directive to act profitably by the imposition of confused political objectives that makes the private firm become bureaucratized. Government approval or disapproval of different hiring practices, rules requiring firms to distribute instead of retain profits, price controls, taxes on 'windfall' gains – all these tend to make enterprises no longer interested in generating and increasing profits.[44] The precision of cost accounting gives way to imprecise efforts to meet changing and conflicting political aims, and

private enterprise begins increasingly to adopt the mode of management of public enterprises, with their elaborate apparatus of formally prescribed rules and regulations. In a word, it becomes bureaucratized.[45]

The results of bureaucratization

The first obvious result of this process is that the structure and operating systems of all enterprises that are hampered by political objectives become rigid. This is inevitable, because bureaucratic management relies on formal rules and practices rather than on personal initiative and flexibility. In a changing world, however, rigidity amounts to petrification and death, so it is hardly surprising that

the public realizes that whenever enterprises are nationalized and municipalized or government otherwise interferes with economic life, financial failure and serious disruption of production . . . follow instead of the desired consequences.[46]

In the market, a single individual can pioneer a completely new way of doing things, such as a new production technique. The manager in a bureaucracy, Mises points out, has to seek higher authority to institute reforms. It is a deadening process when a board or committee has to be convinced: committees are rarely inclined to introduce bold innovations. And again, the owner of private capital is free to take risks and make mistakes. A bureaucracy will be much more cautious, particularly if public money is at stake, and managers will not be given much leeway to manage.

Patronage. Consumers are merciless: they are happy to go to another firm if they get better or cheaper products. So private employers must hire the most able workers, not just those they like. In a bureaucracy, however, the career of a worker depends on the personal judgement of superiors, not the quality of his or her work. Furthermore, when the government puts appointees on the boards of bureaucracies in order to 'represent the public interest' or some such goal, it provides plenty of scope for patronage. Pro-government employees and executives come to be preferred over those who might in fact be better at their job.

Bureaucratization of the mind. Mises conjectures that the mental effects of bureaucratization can be sweeping. Bureaucrats regard themselves as holders of a public trust; as administrators of the law, guardians of the statutory principles under which the enterprise delivers its important services to the public, they regard themselves as a little above it. No matter how detrimental those laws might be, the bureaucrat can take pride in executing them faithfully. Their exalted position reinforces this complacency: the private hotel porter might perform an essential service, but it is the ambassador who is regarded as the 'pillar of society'. The architect may be a superlative expert on planning and construction, but only the government official has the power to dictate to the public which houses will or will not be built.

The rising generation. Young people probably suffer most from the spread of bureaucratization, postulates Mises, because they thrive on the challenge to remodel society. Where bureaucracy prevails, they face instead the dull prospect of climbing slowly through the ranks.

This part of Mises's analysis was undoubtedly tempered by his own experiences in Austria. He complained, for example, that the universities in the German-speaking world were regarded as a part of the civil service, and that bureaucratic attitudes prevailed within them, stifling all change and innovation and keeping out talented youngsters. This is perhaps more questionable in other countries where a premium is put on individualism. Nevertheless, the point is well taken that the spread of bureaucratization, due in large part to government interventions that confuse the objectives of all enterprises, takes its heaviest toll on the young.

Is there a remedy?

There is no solution to this problem. It stems from the vague objectives that are imposed on government enterprises and on hampered private enterprises alike. Where there is no simple guide such as profitability, and no obvious way of measuring success precisely, rules have to be imposed from outside. Rules and their bureaucratic application are indispensable to public administration.

It is no use insisting that the government bureaucrat should act commercially, proclaims Mises:

A government enterprise can never be 'commercialized' no matter how many external features of private enterprise are superimposed on it.[47]

The objectives of the commercial firm and the bureaucracy are simply different, and it is this very difference that explains their divergent methods and success. The bureaucracy, being directed to non-monetary objectives, cannot use the cost-accounting techniques used by the business to achieve a profit, so the 'commercial' approach cannot be grafted on to it.

Not even the introduction of entrepreneurs into government concerns can save them. Their commercial attitude arises only from their position in the competitive economic process and is lost outside it, where the objectives are very different. Thus, an entrepreneur transplanted into a public agency

ceases to be a merchant and becomes as much a bureaucrat as any other placeman in the public employ.[48]

CONCLUSION

From all this we see that the bureaucratic system, which has enough problems running the Post Office, is simply inadequate as a model for administering the wider economic process. It arises because of the same calculation problem that disables all socialism – where targets are multifarious and perhaps even confused or contradictory, there is no way of making an objective judgement of whether they have been achieved as well as possible. The role of bureaucratization is more to keep an enterprise on some predetermined path, rather than to let its personnel come up with new ways of doing things that may not fit in with the established scheme. Just as the socialist rulers must override individual judgements of value if their plan is to be pursued, so must the bureaucratic manager be brought into line. The growth of such a system into a Russian-style bureaucratic organization in which all enterprises are just bureaux of government, would be a depressing prospect.

On the other hand, Mises fears the degeneration of interventionist controls over prices and production into a German-style socialism in which the name of private ownership persists but the reality does not, resulting in an equally grim prospect. Each intervention throws up side-effects that are not only unforeseen but which demand yet more intervention, so that there is a constant pressure for more and more control to be exercised over every aspect of economic life. As Mises was obliged to admit in his later writings on the subject, government action of almost any kind will distort the smooth operation of the market, and so the pressure is likely to be powerful. On the other hand, it is a fact of life that this policy of the middle way has seemingly endured for many decades, if not centuries, so the power of Mises's theory might be debated.

It is nonetheless true that the world is drifting away from the fashionable anti-capitalism against which Mises railed so passionately on discovering it to be so widespread in the United States. There is today a greater confidence that the free market can provide, and provide more adequately, when it is liberated from governmental interference. Government itself is no longer seen as the disinterested and staunch defender of what is right, but as the end result of a process in which vested interests all have their say, but in which the public is unrepresented. And decades of government attempts to run large and important enterprises have raised serious doubts about whether such efforts will ever succeed. The privatization movement that is spreading across the globe, sweeping up with it not only the developed nations but third-world and even communist powers,[49] is ample testimony to the fact that politicians are no longer sure that they can control the public sector: they are forced to admit that the better answer is to turn it over wholesale to private individuals.

To Mises, the practical evidence was plain, but the theoretical arguments led to a conclusion that was even more clear and less open to optimistic interpretations. The only stable economic system that will not consign us eventually to poverty is the market system. And he goes on to contend that the only social system that will save us from the irreconcilable conflicts that are a sure path to disruption and destitution is the liberal framework from which that market order springs.

CHAPTER FIVE

Nationalism versus Liberalism

> . . . the science of economics proves with cold, irrefut-
> able logic that the ideals of those who condemn making
> a living on the market are quite vain, that the socialist
> organization of society is quite unrealizable, that the
> interventionist order is nonsensical and contrary to the
> ends at which it aims, and that therefore the market
> economy is the only feasible system of social co-
> operation.[1]

Mises lived through two world wars, each of which had shattering consequences for his native Austria. The books he wrote at
the time, *Nation, State, and Economy*, and *Omnipotent Government*,
give his explanation of the roots of militant nationalism and
how it might best be avoided in future. A third, *Liberalism*,
outlines the social and economic system that he thinks is the
only candidate suitable for the task.

Mises's work on liberalism was an important contribution,
revising the old liberal ideas and restating them in modern
language, a task continued with energy and with success by F.
A. Hayek in particular. Indeed, Mises's work on this subject
served as a rallying starting point for a number of his younger
contemporaries who might otherwise have been swamped by
the socialism that was fashionable at the time. Before considering it in detail, however, it is interesting to pause briefly to look
at the militant nationalism that twice threatened to extinguish
it entirely.

NATIONALISM AND ITS ROOTS

The idea of a nation

Mises proposes a very simple definition of the term 'nation'. To
him, a nation is simply a speech community. It does not rest on

race, nor necessarily on geography. The place where a person was born does not define his or her nationality, except in the sterile legal sense. The idea of a nation rests on what language and what dialect people speak.

This is perhaps a startling conclusion, but Mises points out that language is crucial to shaping an individual's ideas, and so it does unite communities and divide them from others:

> In learning a language, the child absorbs a way of thinking and expressing his thoughts that is pre-determined by the language, and so he receives a stamp that he can scarcely remove from his life . . . Community of language binds and difference of language separates persons and peoples.[2]

Those who are fluent in two languages, Mises continues, see the world from both points of view and so can be said to be members of two nations; a deaf mute can be a member of none.

A correct theory? It might be hard for the modern reader to accept this hypothesis without qualm. Mises suggests, for example, that the United States and the United Kingdom are two different states, but still one nation; although today's transatlantic travellers will discover considerable but unstated differences that might deny this view. Similarly, Mises attributes the hostilities in Ireland to religious and political, rather than national differences; yet again, some observers would argue that two different nations with very different attitudes and traditions are involved, even though they both happen to use the English language.

Language and dissent. But be that as it may, what Mises wants to demonstrate, and demonstrates with success, is how crucial language can be in generating conflicts between different people in the same geographical area.

Take the problem of a country in which there are two language groups. The administration of government would obviously be hard to achieve if all officials had to be fluent in both languages. A single administrative or 'official' language will certainly arise. But what now of the educational system? Is

98

schooling in the official language to be compulsory even to those in the minority group? The judicial system, too, can be unfair to linguistic minorities if they cannot represent themselves ably in the official language. And the parliament would be split irrevocably, with the major grouping tending to think and act together to the exclusion of the minority.

We can continue from Mises own argument to say that the same kind of problems are likely to arise whether language or some other characteristic is the thing which separates the residents of a piece of territory. Racial or religious differences, even in those speaking the same language, often engender fierce arguments about the placement of officials, the allocation of housing, social services, and schools to each group, and many other policy matters.

Whatever sources of dispute one should include, Mises does have a point when he says that in such territories, even a democratic constitution is insufficient to ease the conflicts:

Majority rule signifies something quite different here than in nationally uniform territories; here, for a part of the people, it is not popular rule but foreign rule.[3]

The machinery of the state, in other words, carries the potential for violent disputes. The more embracing the state, the greater the likelihood of conflict.

Protectionism as a source of nationalism

In the international sphere too, interventionism breeds conflict. As we have seen, interventionism requires import and migration barriers to protect it: for instance, it is useless to set high minimum wages if cheap labour floods in from abroad. Similarly, people will not tolerate the shortages caused by price controls if they can buy imported substitutes. Where there is free trade, foreign competition would quickly frustrate the aims of domestic business regulation.[4]

The threat from foreign labour is particularly menacing. Naturally, people in poor parts of the world are ready and willing to move to places where wages are higher. But that would produce plummeting wages in the rich countries as cheap labour flooded onto the market, and would threaten the linguistic unit of the rich nations. It is no small problem:

If there were no migration barriers today, probably twenty million people would try to reach the United States every year, in order to get higher wages.[5]

For those who live in countries such as the United States, this potential influx of 'cheap labour' from the poorer countries of the world is a very unhappy prospect. American workers, after all, do not wish to see their wages undercut by anyone, and the sudden influx of new racial, religious, or language groups can cause unrest and tension. Accordingly, the calls for immigration controls usually meet success.

The origin of imperialism. Noting that this protectionist zeal is strongest in the common people, Mises suggests that we should look there for the origin and power of imperialism. Modern imperialism does not stem from the expansionist designs of kings and princes, but the mass of people who look on it as the best way to preserve their threatened national independence.[6] Where different nations live side by side, the threat is persistent and severe: the only permanent solution is seen to be the extinction of the others. Thus arises the attempt to build as strong a national state as possible, one that can extend its control over all threatening territories. Such a state might expand its empire far across the globe in the effort to find safe havens in which the identity of its nationals can be preserved.

It is hard to believe that this kind of attitude must be the *inevitable* result of different language groups being forced to live in a delimited area – Switzerland, with no expansionist designs, may be a case in point, though it is true that the different language communities there are in fact rather separate geographically. Presumably Mises would not want to present this thesis as an unbreakable rule of nature. But the important point is this: where imperialist expansion is observed, it is not a capitalist phenomenon, as Marx originally suggested and Marxians now repeat as if there were no room for doubt on the matter. It is not businessmen who seek to acquire foreign territories: if trade were free, they could buy their raw materials on the market, and would not actually need to own the mines and plantations themselves. There is no '*economic* necessity' there.[7] Only '*political* necessity' would explain it: the fact that the interventionist or socialist state can offer more to its citizens, and protect its nationals from the threat of other nations more thoroughly, when its territory is expanded.

This aggressive nationalism, then, is no product of capitalism, and would be evident even if a Marxian commonwealth covered the globe. For in its attempt to promote global equality, such a commonwealth would undoubtedly feel the need to move large populations from poor and unproductive areas where they are presently trapped by immigration controls, into the richer territories whose governments now exclude them. Wars between national communities would be the inevitable result. Sharing their incomes equally with the impoverished millions on the other side of the world is not what most socialists in wealthy countries have in mind when they propose international socialism.

The total state and total war

The rise of powerful governments that can constrain the working of the economic system, Mises informs us, has made conflict a much more serious business than in times past. Modern war, he surmises, is not a war simply of royal armies, but a war of peoples, a *total* war in which complete economic systems and national identities are at stake. It cannot arise from capitalism, where the state is assigned a very minor role: only interventionist or socialist policies, where the individual is subordinated unconditionally to the state, can produce it.

This over-vaunting faith in state institutions, backed up by concentrated power, that Mises says is found in socialism and interventionism alike, he calls *etatism*. He explains that it is a comparatively recent idea, but has grown to major proportions:

The most important event in the history of the last hundred years is the displacement of liberalism by etatism. Etatism appears in two forms: socialism and interventionism. Both have in common the goal of subordinating the individual unconditionally to the state, the social apparatus of compulsion and coercion.[8]

Mises sees this phenomenon, this view that the state is the pivot of human organization, as the cause of the total wars of today. It sees the economic process as something which should be ordered and protected by the state authorities, but by attempting to control the economic process and insulate it from the policy objectives of other countries, a state makes necessary the institution of protectionist barriers against others. In raising barriers, it generates the hostility of outsiders. The hostility of outsiders makes its people feel under threat and prompts the political leaders to expand its territorial control in an effort to guarantee its own preservation.

Capitalism as the only escape from war

This process is an economic cause of war. But it is not a capitalist one. On the contrary, liberal capitalism gives a much reduced role to the state and so avoids the strains that lead to war. It promotes the interests of its practitioners not through conflict but through co-operation. It requires that trade between people in different parts of the world is carried on freely, without tariffs or controls, that people are free to invest where they choose. It rests on such a powerful interdependence between people that war would be folly:

In an age in which nations are mutually dependent on products of foreign provenance, war can no longer be waged.[9]

The free movement of capital and labour leaves no cause for imperialistic campaigns because it makes no difference whether a nation's sovereignty stretches over a larger or smaller territory.[10] Durable peace, therefore, is possible only under such a system of thoroughgoing liberal capitalism.

A naive view? It is easy to see Mises's point. The large government institutions that are necessary to administer a socialist or interventionist system are also best equipped for warfare; a system which lets individuals run their own lives has no such coercive strength.

Nevertheless, it is harder to believe that his vision could ever be implemented. One of the pillars of the individualism Mises advocates is the right of every person to live wherever he or she wants – in other words, the removal of immigration barriers.[11] In a world where national identities and jealousies still exist, however, is this not inviting serious conflict of the sort for which Mises castigated the notion of world socialism? And the question of how one might gradually move to open immigration, with the major shifts in global population and strains that it implies, is still unsettled.

For his part, Marx believed that capitalism would lead to war. Mises, however, has given us a valuable counterargument by showing that, in its pure form, capitalism need bring no such result. But what passes for 'capitalism' around the world today is really something quite different: it is a series of interventionist orders based on the concentrated power of state institutions. We do raise barriers to protect (private) industries, and invade countries to protect their supplies. Mises acknowledges that a 'radical change in ideologies and economic policies' would be needed in order to head off this incessant tension,[12] and every idealist who agrees with his analysis would support that view. But some states remain deeply anti-capitalist and it seems likely that the threat of war would still persist, no matter how widely liberalism spread throughout the remainder of the globe.

Whatever the practical difficulty of changing attitudes quickly throughout the entire world so that the economic pressures for war are eliminated, some successes can be scored in the more immediate term. The liberal order Mises envisages has benefits other than that of preventing wars between nations, and liberalism may be easier to apply on the more modest scale. Its important features of liberalism are therefore worth our enquiry.

THE LIBERAL ALTERNATIVE

Mises does not base his liberalism on any uncontestable theory of 'natural' rights to freedom or equality of treatment, as the founding fathers of the American constitution based theirs. Liberalism, he says, is to be preferred as a social order because it *works*. It limits conflicts and makes possible a beneficial and productive co-operation between people, and does so without the need for them to be forced to co-operate.

Development of liberal ideas

Though perhaps not the most pristine experiment, the period from Napoleon to the First World War, where freedom of domestic and international trade prevailed, was also a period of the greatest rise in human welfare, Mises reminds us in the preface to the 1962 edition of *Liberalism*. The freedom for individuals to co-operate economically without the overbearing direction of central governments brought gains to everyone, particularly those formerly condemned to poverty on the land.

Origins of liberalism. The eighteenth-century liberals who first formulated the liberal philosophy made possible this incorporation (albeit a limited one) of liberal principles into public policy during the nineteenth century. Without the political ideas of John Locke and the demonstration of liberal economic theory by Adam Smith, the experiment would probably never have occurred. By no means all of the demands of the eighteenth-century liberals were met; but the experiment was still sufficient to achieve major improvements in wealth and population growth. Moreover, the prosperity engendered by the liberal age was not concentrated on a minority, but spread widely throughout society.

It was not just free trade between nations that typified the liberal era. Domestic regulations also became less rigid. In the eighteenth century, there were all kinds of restrictions on common workers. The rural population was expanding, but townspeople raised protectionist barriers against them, rules and regulations on trade well itemized and described in Adam Smith's 1776 treatise on economics, *The Wealth of Nations*. In response to this protectionism, some started to organize shops and industries outside the towns, catering for the needs of the growing population. It was the start of the mass production idea.[13] The prosperity of the liberal age was not concentrated on a minority, but was spread widely throughout the population. The very success of liberalism generated its future growth. The new industries based on the division of labour prospered, and could sustain greater numbers of people.

A fatal flaw. But while those working inside the liberal order enjoyed its benefits, Mises contends, they did not understand its structure. The eighteenth-century founders of liberalism thought that everyone would see the clear benefits of co-operation, and so would accept readily, and would work to maintain, the free economic institutions that made it possible. Their theory showed conclusively that the best interests of all individuals lay in the general absence of protectionism and restrictions. But unfortunately, they had an overoptimistic view of human beings' understanding of their own 'rightly understood' or long-term best interests. As it turned out, everyone could see the apparent and immediate gains of intervention, such as tariffs on competitive foreign goods; but it took a considerable degree of enlightenment to see the real and general benefits that arise over longer periods when the shroud of interventionism is cast off. Those lucky individuals who were able to win concessions for themselves had little time for this more abstract point of view. It was perhaps inevitable that the liberal era would end in quotas, tariffs, and interventionism.

Thus, concludes Mises, it must be one of the key differences between classical liberalism and its twentieth-century revival that liberal theoreticians can no longer assume this natural tendency of individuals to aim for long-term general gains instead of short-term personal ones.

Revolutionary nature of liberalism. The classical liberals were perhaps naive about the rationality of the ordinary public. But they predicted correctly that the ordinary public would gain most from liberalism. For liberalism is a *revolutionary* doctrine. As a political creed, it is unusual, because it does not seek to bring benefits to particular groups and does not derive from any vested interests of its adherents. It is not a dogma that is intended to secure the privileges of the rich, the intellectuals, or anyone else. On the contrary, it challenges privilege and restrictions on personal freedom, contending that a liberal order leaves more scope for co-operation and thus better advances human welfare as a whole. Accordingly, those most likely to be helped by liberalism are those who were previously impoverished and oppressed by the rules and regulations of the ruling elites.

Of course, liberals believe that government functions should be performed by those best able to govern, says Mises. But liberals believe that such individuals are more likely to come into government if they have to convince their fellows of their ability, rather than if they are able to seize power by force. Democratic institutions, therefore, with each individual enjoying equal political rights and an equal say in the choice of leaders, are part of the liberal approach.

At least some of the classical liberals claimed to deduce the idea of equal political rights from an alleged 'natural' equality. Mises holds that this idea is wrong, unnecessary, and impossible to prove. It is another view which distinguishes classical liberalism from its modern successors. His own assertion of the necessity of freedom and equality is much more utilitarian; he supports them because they do in fact bring about social co-operation.

Liberalism, co-operation, and progress

The most remarkable thing about the liberal society, thinks Mises, is this ability it has to make possible a high degree of co-operation between people, despite their differences. And in a very real sense, liberalism achieves this highly desirable result *because of* their differences. The reason is that people will enter into a voluntary exchange only if their valuations of the goods traded are different.

A simple example might illustrate Mises's point. If one individual gives up an hour's labour in return for a sack of flour, for example, it indicates that he or she values the flour more than the hour's labour that is given up for it. But for that exchange to be made, there must be another person who ranks those two things in the opposite order, and values the person's

106

labour more than the sack of flour given up. For a voluntary exchange to take place, in other words, each individual must value what is received more than what is forgone. Because their views are different, they both count themselves as gainers from the exchange, and each one's satisfaction is increased. And the wider the disparity in their respective valuations, the more they will be satisfied and the more eagerly are they likely to enter into the exchange. The liberal principle of voluntary exchange therefore has a remarkable power to bring into harmony the different and often conflicting views and values of individuals.

Although each individual enters into exchange for purely personal gain, therefore, it actually benefits the other party as well. The more widely the exchange principle spreads, the more general and widespread is the gain. In the free-exchange society, people unwittingly help their fellows even as they pursue their own particular objectives, and it is this that Adam Smith meant when he talked of the 'invisible hand' that guides human affairs, not any idea of a supernatural providence:

In the market economy, everyone serves his fellow citizens by serving himself. This is what the liberal authors of the eighteenth century had in mind when they spoke of the harmony of the rightly understood interests of all groups and of all individuals of the population.[14]

Marxist objections. It was this doctrine of the harmony of individual interests that the socialists naturally had to oppose if they were to forge a new society. They alleged instead that only conflict could be found in the market economy, a conflict between rich and poor, buyers and sellers, workers and owners – in short, between *classes*.

Mises finds this notion quite absurd. The revolutionary doctrine of liberalism, he says, has the effect of *reducing* tensions because it replaces birth and privilege with mobility and equality. Nobody is stuck in a downtrodden class with no hope of escape except violence. Under liberalism, professions are open to everyone, whatever their origin; and anyone can become rich simply by serving other people well. Liberalism does not promote conflict – it preserves peaceful co-operation.

Of course, it may not be able to achieve this result perfectly.

As Mises himself has noted, capitalism has features that form its own source of resentment and hostility – the resentment of those who feel they should have higher status, the insecurity of people faced with technological change, the ambitions of those who want to impose their own opinions on the whole market structure, and all the other aspects of the anti-capitalist mentality. And this, Mises acknowledges, is a persistent problem. So it seems that he is not claiming that liberal capitalism ends every conflict, just that the tensions it generates are milder and more likely to be defused peacefully.

Freedom versus design. Liberalism, as we have said, is quite unlike most political doctrines. It does not seek to design a society as one would design a machine, with each individual, each component, serving a particular role in its operation towards some purpose. Liberal principles merely establish a *framework* of peace, stability, and equality before the law – a framework within which people are free to co-operate in any way they see fit. The liberal or market order is just an *arrangement* of individuals; no advance decision settles what things should be produced in what quantities, or what the distribution of wealth and income should be. These things are merely the *outcome* of the complex interplay of individuals co-operating freely, so cannot be predicted.

To Mises, 'society' is not something with a life and will independent of the people who make it up;[15] only *individuals* live, breathe, think, and act, while *society* is merely the pattern in which they do it, not something that exists in addition. Forgetting this produces absurd collectivist errors in which individuals are told they must be subordinate to the directives of a (mystical) 'group mind'. Society is not a machine of which individuals are mere cogs, not an organism in which we are only cells.

Unfortunately, it is all too easy to slip into inappropriate metaphors when discussing this subject; Mises himself drifts into the 'organic' fallacy at one point by complaining that socialist proposals to re-create society are as absurd as trying to re-create a flower. And having said that it is not consciously designed for a purpose, he goes on to call it a machine that needs a will to operate. So care is needed when thinking about this point.

If analogies are helpful, a good one might be that devised by Carl Menger and elaborated more recently by F.A. Hayek: the analogy of language. The rules of grammar constrain how we use language, but within those rules an infinite vocabulary can be used and an infinite variety of meanings can be communicated. Acceptance of the rules of grammar in no way dictates what we will in fact communicate at any time; the form of our expression may be constrained, but not its actual content. In the liberal order, likewise, the framework of rules makes possible an enormous variety of interpersonal action that could not conceivably be imagined before it occurs. Liberalism allows people freedom of thought, movement, and action, but it nevertheless generates a smoothly functioning social order and not chaos; just as the rules of grammar generate language, not gibberish. The rules of grammar generate sentences that are structured, but do not specify in advance what people can say. The rules of the liberal society produce a social order, but it is a *spontaneous* order born out of people's actual interaction, not an order designed in advance by some political authority.[16]

To Mises, the liberal framework not only allows individuals to co-operate freely, but in so doing produces a social order that is a very efficient one. It uses our different abilities to their best advantage; it allows people to specialize in the extraction of natural resources that will always be unequally distributed; and it allows us to share the burden in undertakings that are beyond the abilities of a single individual.

The foundations of the liberal order

In Mises's judgement, the foundations of liberalism are peace, freedom, and property.[17] These are the requirements that are necessary before people can co-operate effectively and efficiently together and so generate prosperity.

Liberalism, as we have seen, helps to generate peace, but it can prosper only against a background of *stability*. Rational economic action requires us to take decisions based on our assessment of their future outcomes, but no outcome is certain in a state of war; international hostilities make trade and its benefits impossible; civil war destroys the opportunities for co-operation by the division of labour. To take a simple example that illustrates Mises's point: a farmer must have reasonable confidence that the land he seeds and the crops he grows will not be torn away from him by hostile foreign powers, nor by enemies living in the same country. Only with the assurance that a return will follow his effort will he bother to make that original investment. Similarly, the large and complex industrial processes that we rely on today require an everyday co-operation between workers with different skills; where civil strife divides a community, that co-operation is likely to be replaced by suspicion, and some workers may refuse to join the enterprise entirely, so that it may not be possible to acquire the very best mix of skills and productivity must decline as a result.

Freedom is another precondition. The classical liberals had the abolition of serfdom as a priority, even though some slaves themselves objected (slavery at least guarantees a secure living, which is more than the market does). Technological developments in the nineteenth century would probably have made slavery outmoded anyway; but in Mises's judgement, the argument of the liberals was, and remains, the utilitarian one that 'free labour is incomparably more productive than slave labour'.[18]

The third condition is the existence of *property*. Again, the reason is utilitarian: specialization, the division of labour, is much more productive than everyone trying to be self-sufficient, but it does presume that what each individual creates can be exchanged voluntarily against the products of others. In other words, there must be personal property that can be traded. Also, to make our labour as productive as possible requires the acquisition of productive machinery and equipment: it requires the right tools for each person to work with if specialization is to bring its full rewards. And as we have seen already, only when those means of production are owned privately can they be put to work with any sense of direction. The ownership of property is an essential part of the economy based on specialization and exchange.

The role of the state. For the system of voluntary co-operation to work, the liberal framework of peace, stability, freedom, and property must be preserved. The state, which is no more than an apparatus of compulsion,[19] should not be used to force people to act in particular ways, only to preserve this framework against the ravages of human nature so that the sphere of voluntary, rather than compulsory, action can be maximized:

This is the function that the liberal doctrine assigns the state: the protection of property, liberty, and peace.[20]

The benefits of liberalism

The liberal capitalist system, particularly with the heavy reliance on personal property that Mises emphasizes, is sometimes caricatured as just another doctrine that is intended to benefit a particular class. The beneficiaries of liberalism, it is supposed, are those with property: the rich.

As we have seen, Mises utterly rejects this charge, because to him, liberalism is a framework of rules which make human society possible and efficient, not a political strategy aimed at helping any special group. Nevertheless, his dogged insistence that property is a crucial part of the liberal order can have the unfortunate effect of making him sound, on occasions, like an apologist for those with property and wealth. Subsequent liberal writers have tended to stress the importance of justice and equality under the law as the hallmarks of liberalism,[21] although all these things are inseparable. However, when we place Mises's commitment to the principle of private ownership in the context of his views that only when the means of production are owned privately are they likely to be deployed efficiently, the reasons for his insistence can be seen. And it should be noted that while property ownership makes possible the material prosperity generated by a liberal society, there is no compulsion for individuals to pursue material wealth under the system. Liberalism leaves people free to set and achieve their own targets, to reduce the barriers of privilege and the threat of coercion for everyone. It does not aim at helping those with property more than any others. His conclusion is that:

111

Liberalism champions private property in the means of production because it expects a higher standard of living from such an economic organization, not because it wishes to help the owners.[22]

Serving the masses. On the contrary, the poor are likely to benefit most. Under liberalism, even those without any property at all benefit from the rising standard of living.[23] As successful businesses grow, they offer higher wages to attract new and better workers; as workers migrate from other work (such as agriculture or domestic service, for example), they raise the demand for labour, and the amount which must be paid to attract it, in those employments too. The wealth generated spreads right through the community.

We must remember also that the main interest of capitalists is in serving the masses, not minorities. The age of capitalism has been the age of shops and industries designed for the many, the age of mass production. An entrepreneur cannot force members of the public to take his goods; they will buy only if it improves their satisfaction. Any other form of economic organization makes ruling elites supreme, but capitalism makes the consumer sovereign:

The profit motive is the means of making the public supreme. The better a man succeeds in supplying the consumer, the greater become his earnings. It is to everybody's advantage that the entrepreneur who produces shoes at the cheapest cost becomes rich; most people would suffer if a law were to limit his right to get richer.[24]

In practice, capitalism has brought not just shoes, but other basics, within the grasp of the bulk of the population; and it has done so at unprecedented speed. Once, it was the ownership of shoes, food, and shelter that distinguished rich from poor. Things have changed, and now the distinction is confined to luxuries:

In the United States today the difference between a rich man and a poor man means very often only the difference between a Cadillac and a Chevrolet.[25]

The lifestyle that is possible for even the poorest section of the population in those rare parts of the world where capitalism has been allowed to proceed with minimal political interference is in very pointed contrast to the Marxian prediction that the conditions of the workers would get steadily worse until they fell to subsistence levels.

In fact, the living standards of the nineteenth-century industrial workers were far higher and more secure than they could ever have expected on the land (although the point is often forgotten).[26] Once the basics were provided, it was natural that growth should be rapid. Mises stresses that the accumulation of capital goods raises prosperity because the use of tools and equipment simply makes work more productive. Individuals who rise above subsistence, as the poor were able to do under early capitalism, are able to save and to build up a capital fund that can be used for precisely such improvement. The benefits of capitalism are explosive.

The poor abroad. It is not just the domestic poor who are helped by liberalism. One of the principles of liberalism is that people should be able to trade freely in any market, anywhere in the world. Accordingly, the capital funds built up by people in one country can be invested in capital goods in another – and those capital goods, by making labour in the recipient country more efficient, help generate additional prosperity. The free movement of capital spreads prosperity far and wide.

Why are some countries poor? It is not just a function of their natural resources, since some countries without resources are rich while others with great resources are poor. Nor would any national characteristics explain it, since those who migrate from poor countries often become rich and show an entrepreneurial flair to match anyone's.

The difference, explains Mises, is the supply of capital: some countries have not had sufficient time to build up their capital structure, others have resisted foreign investment. But capital is vital if the productivity of labour is to be raised, and the role of foreign investment has been crucial in lifting many countries out of poverty. In fact, says Mises, England is the only country to have provided its own capital base. It helped with the capital necessary to build railways in Europe and in North and South America, to provide gas for lighting and heating in Paris and other capitals, and much more.

Foreign investment is therefore the very opposite of the 'exploitation' it is billed to be by Marxians: in general it is a crucial catalyst of economic development. But to attract it, foreign investors must know that they will not be expropriated. Arbitrary taxation or nationalization on the part of the recipient countries is guaranteed to keep foreign capital out, and so keep their own residents in poverty.[27]

Planning versus control. Another advantage of the liberal system is that it allows planning to be done by those who do it best – individuals – rather than by submitting all production to the will of a supreme dictatorship. Some people suppose that 'planning' has to mean planning by a central authority, but this is not so. We all plan. The choice is not between planning and no planning, but *whose* plan should prevail.[28] If we allow the judgement of some planning authority to prevail, we consign ourselves to its rulings and to the coercion of the state apparatus that sustains it. But it is obvious nonsense to suggest that any such body, however expert, has a better idea of our true needs, or how to achieve them, than we. Only each individual can know his or her own values, and without that information, planning is pointless.

This is a point on which there have been considerable strides by modern proponents of the Austrian School. In particular, the application of contemporary information theory has shown that the centrally planned economy is less able to deal with the vast complex of changing, incomplete, and dispersed data that the market economy, through the price system, processes routinely.[29]

For Mises, however, central planning is inadequate for the simple reason that only *individuals* can know their own needs, values, and choices (and even then, they may not be able to say how they would choose until the situation actually arises). So the central planner does not face a scientific or mathematical task, but the impossible job of anticipating other people's judgements about what they want.

The process of the market

From this, we begin to see why liberalism works and why it is very much more effective at satisfying human needs than central planning. The market is a *process* by which different people adjust their actions to the actions of others. There is no compulsion about it, so each person can gain only by co-operating with others. High prices indicate that a demand is inadequately satisfied, and prompt entrepreneurs to adjust production to meet it; low prices indicate that productive activity is more wisely deployed elsewhere. Without the need for any conscious direction of the economic system, the price mechanism tells entrepreneurs what to produce and how much to produce in order to satisfy consumers' demands. It is, in fact, a superlative guide for private planning.[30]

Consumer sovereignty. Such a system means that it is consumers, not capitalists, who ultimately decide the structure of production. In the market, consumers are constantly making choices, selecting which goods they will buy and which they will leave on the shelf. No capital is secure from the ravages of this selection process. Entrepreneurs *must* obey the demands of these sovereign consumers, always searching out cheaper and better products, if they are to remain entrepreneurs. It is not producers who decide what and how much will be produced, but consumers. And consumers ultimately determine even prices, for no good will remain on sale for long at a price which misjudges the strength of their demand for it. But these points must wait until Chapter 9 and Chapter 10 for a more detailed exposition.

Some critics object that consumers are not really sovereign at all, but are taken in by advertising – a 'wasteful' activity which would therefore be banned in the socialist commonwealth. But Mises asks how this could be, for even in the socialist state there would be a need to tell people what new goods and services were available – precisely the main function of advertising. Like the bulk of the goods produced in the market economy, advertising is aimed at the masses, and so might seem tasteless to intellectuals: but it *conveys information*, which is a precious commodity in a world of change. It allows people to compare quality, availability, and price, and introduces new products. But no advertiser can *force* members of the public to take goods they do not want.[31]

Competition and change. This market *process* as described by Mises obviously puts entrepreneurs under a strong pressure to seek out cheaper production processes and come up with new ideas which – they hope – will prove attractive to consumers. It is therefore quite unlike the 'perfect competition' model of the market that is found in most economics textbooks, where an infinite number of identical producers supply a homogeneous product to an infinite number of identical consumers. For Mises, competition works because there *is* differentiation and change. The mainspring of progress is not the unchanging uniformity we find in the textbook model, but the constant competitive pressure to develop new products and more efficient processes that we find in the real world.

Entrepreneurship. An important feature of this market process, then, is the entrepreneur. Yet the entrepreneurial function is one which many textbooks ignore and most misinterpret. In Mises's view, the entrepreneur's crucial role is in pushing out the boundaries of progress. The entrepreneur is not merely a technician who organizes production and gets a 'wage' for doing so, but someone who forms a judgement about how consumers might be served better and takes the risk of trying it out in practice. Profits are not a return on capital, something that comes naturally to those rich enough to invest. People have to *decide* how to invest capital, and profits come solely from making investments based on a good decision about how consumers can in fact be served. Mises's contribution on this point, developed in detail by his follower, Israel Kirzner, is an important advance on the classical textbook treatment of the subject, and something that we shall explore in more detail in Chapter 9.

A materialist view? From all this discussion of economic matters, it might be imagined that the market system concentrates only on material things; but Mises rejects this criticism entirely. The striving for higher things presupposes that people's material welfare is already satisfied, he asserts, and the market system is the only arrangement guaranteed to achieve this condition. By liberating us from our material needs, the market makes us more able to attend to non-material values. And the liberal order in fact assists that spiritual development by ensuring that the state has no power to control our expression of religion, art, literature, or thought.[32]

CONCLUSION

It is an interesting and effective counter to the traditional Marxian argument for Mises to contend that imperialism is not in fact the outcome of capitalist structures, whereby businessmen are seen as pursuing aggressive expansion plans in order to secure their supplies and their markets abroad, but that it is the result of socialism and too great a reliance on the power of the state to solve economic problems. It is certainly true that governments and their panoply of state are usually in a better position to pursue wars against others than unarmed and unorganized businessmen.

For this thesis to hold, however, we have to understand that Mises is discussing the theoretical concept of a rather pure form of capitalism. He would not so define the economic structures that exist today, even in the West. To him, those economies would be interventionist by nature, and so just as reliant on the power of the state, just as likely to come into conflict with other states, as if they were socialist.

Only where liberal principles have a free rein can these threats of war be avoided, concludes Mises, because the liberal order places its emphasis on individuals, not on states. The free movement of people (or at least capital) around the world makes it unnecessary for particular groups to expand aggressively to maintain their economic interests. Why take over a foreign mine by force when you can buy shares in it?

Prospects for liberalism. Mises recognizes that while the general absence of coercion and regulation implicit in liberalism would be to our advantage, the chances of us recognizing it are slim; human beings tend to sacrifice their intangible and long-term interests for their evident and immediate ones. The prospect of liberalism sweeping the globe was an ideal for which Mises held out less and less hope as he gained more and more experience of human nature.

117

Today, however, things look brighter. In many countries, the old rules, regulations, and privileges that dominated economic life are being slowly but surely relaxed. As national markets become integrated into single world markets through the use of quicker and cheaper communications, the barriers that were once seen as protecting national interests are now seen only as a clutter that prevents the smooth flow of people and resources across the new international marketplaces. In addition to this rising chorus favouring more liberal trading structures, the complexity of some new markets and the speed with which they have developed and can direct information and resources is making it hard or impossible for state authorities to effect any control over them in any case.

It appears, then, that the free exchange system is bursting out of the cage designed for it by interventionists. But its new importance raises more urgently the question of whether it can, in fact, promote human welfare more efficiently than any other system. It is to this aspect of the system that attention must now be turned.

CHAPTER SIX

Welfare, Taxation, and the Market

> State interference in economic life, which calls itself
> 'economic policy' has done nothing but destroy eco-
> nomic life.[1]

The conclusion which Mises forms as a result of his theoretical
analysis of socialism and interventionism is that almost any
form of government interference in economic matters, by its
very nature, is bound to lead to a reduction in human welfare.
The idea that government action is the best way to promote
prosperity and eliminate poverty is entirely wrong: the unhampered market, he avers, is a far more promising vehicle.

POVERTY, INEQUALITY, AND INSECURITY

Mises wastes no time in discussing grey areas. He sees a plain
antithesis between the market principle and those policies
which are commonly but mistakenly described as advancing
the 'welfare' principle.[2] Of course, nobody is opposed to
improvements in human welfare; the trouble is that the word
itself has been captured by propagandists who apply it to a
definite interventionist programme, says Mises. In consequence, they imply that anyone who does not support this
programme is selfish and ill-intentioned. And whatever benefits the profit motive has brought, they add, the market does not
distribute wealth equally and has not wiped out poverty.
Profits should therefore be substituted by the 'welfare' principle.

Poverty and the market

The charge that the market economy breeds poverty is one of
the most ridiculous, according to Mises. In those few areas of

119

the globe where the market has been allowed to prevail in a reasonably unhampered fashion, there is a marked absence of the sort of poverty that prevails in noncapitalist societies. There may be relative differences, but even those at the bottom of the capitalist economy are far ahead of those in other systems:

In the eyes of the Asiatics, the American automobile worker is an 'aristocrat'. He is a man who belongs to the 2 per cent of the earth's population whose income is the highest.[3]

As mentioned already,[4] Mises believes that it is the poor who in theory should, and in practice do, benefit most from capitalism. In the precapitalist society where the division of labour is scarcely developed and self-sufficiency is the norm, the independent farmer has a hard enough time digging out the necessities of life, he argues. Those without land are in a much worse state, having no useful position within the society. In the capitalist world, however, any able-bodied person can find a niche within the production structure, a niche which is useful to others and therefore brings its rewards in the form of wages or profits.

The natural inclination of the capitalist is to seek out the widest market, which means producing for the masses rather than minorities. It is to supply the basic necessities of life to the general population which is the first benefit of capitalism, raising people quickly out of their deep precapitalist poverty. When these basic needs have been satisfied, less urgent needs and more specialist and minority tastes can be catered for, but the poor are always the first to benefit.

As Mises expresses this argument, it appears to be something of a blend of economic analysis and politics. He excelled at both, but it is sometimes difficult to know where the boundary of one finishes and the other begins. Precapitalist societies, for example, cannot be characterized as universally poor or hard: Europeans quite understandably regarded the simple hunter-gatherer communities of Tahiti and the Hawaiian Islands as paradise itself. Furthermore, under Mises's own principles, the market order does not automatically eliminate unemployment and poverty. Mismatches between the demand for particular skills and those offered at any time and in any place on the labour market, gaps in the spread of knowledge about market opportunities, and simple mistakes by entrepreneurs in anticipating demand or in acquiring the appropriate kind of capital goods can all produce hardship. It might not last for ever nor be general, but it can be severe as far as any individual is concerned: and Mises himself warns us against forgetting the individual when we survey the general economic landscape.

Unemployables. When we speak of 'poverty' in the context of capitalist economies, argues Mises, it is not in terms of the grinding destitution that pervades noncapitalist societies, but in terms of the relative hardship of those who cannot find a role and reward in the structure of production because they are not 'able-bodied'. Is the traditional *laissez-faire* answer, that those in this group who are not taken care of by their families should rely on private charity, really a sufficient answer in a society that is really concerned to promote human welfare?

Mises thinks that it is, and considers the two main objections to his belief that charity can and should provide.[5] The first is that the resources available within the charitable sector are inadequate to the task. But, he objects, the faster that capitalism progresses, the more becomes available and the fewer individuals there are in need. As people grow more wealthy, they can spare more for charitable giving, and even those with moderate incomes protect themselves against incapacity or bereavement with insurance policies. It is interventionist governments, with their encouragement of credit expansion and fondness for inflating the quantity of money that eat up capital, thereby making businesses less able to generate steady employment, workers less able to provide for themselves out of their savings, and charitable institutions less able to meet this burgeoning call on their services because they too are expropriated. Naturally enough, this increases the calls for more public spending on welfare; but it is such demands for government expenditure that prompt credit expansion and inflationary policies in the first place.

Turning to the second objection, that charity relies on personal compassion only and gives the indigent no legal right

121

to help, Mises concedes the point. But would such a legally enforceable 'right to support' be expedient? Mises believes that there is ample evidence that it has the undesirable effect of making people less concerned to provide against misfortune and less quick to climb out of their hardship when it strikes. And it remains an open question whether the discretion of bureaucrats who administer these welfare systems is better for the recipients than the charitable compassion of independent donors.

Inequality

Even if we are to concede that the unhampered market economy would be well equipped to eliminate poverty, it remains true that inequalities of wealth and income are one of its inherent features. Does this imply, once again, that the market order is deficient from a welfare point of view?

Mises gives a firm negative response. In the first place, the role of income inequality in the market society is quite different from that in the precapitalist world. In the market society, wealth and income is freely voted to entrepreneurs and workers by consumers, as a reward for the benefits they bring to others in the process of economic co-operation. Yet we must remember that this inequality rests not on privilege but on the voluntary actions of other people. It lasts only as long as those others derive a benefit from the entrepreneur's activities, and so it needs constant vigilance to maintain. It is perfectly possible (and not uncommon) for a wealthy businessman, through negligence or miscalculation, to lose everything because the trust and patronage of the consumers is transferred elsewhere.

The inequality of wealth and income that exists under the liberal order, therefore, is not a pernicious one. In the first place, the existence and lure of profits and higher wages has the effect of urging individual suppliers always to adjust their action to bring the greatest benefit to their customers (as judged by those customers themselves) and to seek out new ways of providing more and better services cheaper. That benefit is by definition a welfare gain.

Second, the inequality found under capitalism is not a lasting one. There might always seem to be rich and poor, but the individuals who populate those categories change constantly. The relative wealth of an entrepreneur is not set for all time, but persists only as long as he or she is producing benefits for others; it can disappear as quickly as it can be gained. By contrast, in the feudal society and other noncapitalist orders, inequalities are a fact of life; they are decided by birth or by the arbitrary gift of those in authority, not by the mass of the population. Far from spurring people to progress, they imprison individuals in predetermined niches.

Natural inequality. The liberal philosophy that gave rise to the market economy was from the first opposed to all the traditional caste and privilege structures that prevailed prior to its development. Whatever the language it came in, this revolutionary view did not rest on the 'natural law' principle that all men are biologically equal ('manifestly contrary to fact', says Mises[6]) and therefore entitled to an equal share in everything. It rested instead on the understanding that equal treatment, meaning the absence of privileges – equality before the law – was necessary to preserve the framework of peace in which people can co-operate most efficiently.

Let us not forget the point made already, that co-operation based on the division of labour and the exchange system is possible only *because* people are not the same. It takes two people to disagree on the value of commodities before they will trade them. Indeed, the greater the difference between their judgements, the more they gain from the exchange. The astonishing power of the market economy is that it can integrate the actions of people with completely different, even opposing, views.

The liberal doctrine of equality under the law, therefore, is not aimed at removing the natural differences which make people what they are and which foster trade and progress. It aims instead at the utilitarian targets of making it possible for people to occupy any niche in which they feel comfortable serving others, without the hindrances of caste or privilege, and of allowing consumers, rather than the authorities, to decide who should direct production.

Modern ideas of equality. In the precapitalist economies it was hard to amass large amounts of wealth, and to do so was to risk the suspicion and retaliation of the authorities, who considered their privileged position threatened as a result. Consequently, capital was not accumulated very extensively, and the productivity of labour remained low. A similar abhorrence of large fortunes, says Mises, pervades the minds of welfare propagandists today. The only difference is that it is confiscation through taxation rather than through official discretion that is seen as the appropriate response.

It is easy to caricature those who make large fortunes as essentially selfish, and undoubtedly it *is* personal motives that cause entrepreneurs to seek ever-increasing wealth. But in the market economy, even these motives are put to good work, since it is only by satisfying consumers, and in doing so better than anyone else has done before, that they can be realized.

To be the vehicle of progress, however, the entrepreneur must improve the efficiency of labour by mixing it with *capital*. Present consumption must be given up in order to provide a fund of subsistence and to construct capital goods that will bring greater rewards later on, and it is not just the entrepreneur alone, but the consumers who freely buy the end products, who are benefited. Unfortunately, welfare policies thwart this process in two ways, Mises cautions. First, if the potential rewards to the entrepreneur are artificially lowered by a confiscatory taxation policy, there is less incentive for him or her to give up present consumption for the prospect (never a certain prospect in any event) of greater gain later on. Even if the entrepreneur presses ahead with any particular enterprise, there will be less yield available from it to be ploughed back into the development of the next one. Second, even those on moderate incomes will be more inclined to trust to welfare support than insurance or savings in the bank, so that there is less capital available for entrepreneurs to borrow and work with. Welfare policies lead to capital consumption because they destroy the moderate earners' incentive to save and remove the high earners' *power* to save.

The ultimate absurdity, it seems to Mises, is where banks and insurance companies are obliged to invest in 'secure'

124

government bonds. Because the politicians who control the public budget have, as a result of their limited term of office, a marked preference for current spending over investment in capital goods, the net result is that the capital fund accumulated by the citizens is channelled directly into current consumption. Even though some of the public budget, true enough, *is* spent on capital projects, such as roads and power stations, by far the largest part of the citizens' savings is still being used up on current consumption.[7]

Dynamic nature of the market. Of course, protagonists of the welfare principle retort that in the free economy, much of the wealth of rich people is in fact frittered away on idle luxuries rather than on the accumulation of capital goods; but Mises has an answer for this as well. First, the amount used up in the process is relatively small, and does not substantially affect production, because by definition, rich people are in the minority and much of what they spend will in fact be reinvested in capital projects.

But second, Mises sees the rich not as a group which is able to enjoy luxuries that are closed off to the rest of us, but as people who merely get them first. There is a dynamic element in the market economy: new products might be affordable only for a few at first, but if they are successful, their producers will invest more in order to bring them to a wider public. Thus:

Every innovation makes its appearance as a 'luxury' of the well-to-do. After industry has become aware of it, the luxury then becomes a 'necessity' for all. Take, for example, our clothing, the lighting and bathroom facilities, the automobile, and air travel facilities. Economic history demonstrates how the luxury of yesterday has become today's necessity.[8]

Conclusion. The ability to accumulate personal wealth, then, might lead to inequalities, but they are not pernicious inequalities. In the first place, they are impermanent, with fortunes being quickly made but equally quickly eroded. In the second place, the prospect of personal gain makes it more likely that entrepreneurs will invest their capital in ways that will benefit consumers as much as possible. Third, the benefits of capital accumulation are more direct for individuals, who naturally want to provide for their children as well as themselves, than for the government, where the benefits are thinly spread and where the more highly visible and vote-catching advantages of current expenditure have the upper hand. And fourth, the dynamic power of the market keeps production in constant pursuit of the advantages enjoyed by those at the top of the wealth and income tree.

However, it is doubtful that Mises's bluff presentation of these points would really convince all those whose views he is criticizing. For example, it seems clear enough that wealth in the capitalist system *can* be very permanent. Once an individual has made a fortune, it takes comparatively little skill to invest it cautiously and so maintain it. Indeed, by entrusting it to professional fund managers, with their special knowledge of the capital market, the individual would expect to do much better. Again, large fortunes may well be diluted as they are split between children and then between even larger numbers of grandchildren; but the rule of primogeniture has quite frequently kept fortunes secure and concentrated down many generations. Of course the capitalist community might offer less security to personal fortunes than the rigid caste system of the feudal world; but Mises can be accused of overstating the case if he suggests that the preservation of riches under capitalism requires constant vigilance and special skill.

These objections aside, Mises's restatement of the straightforward point that capital goods improve the productivity of labour is certainly a useful and important one as far as the supporters of the capitalist system are concerned. It reminds us that for labour to become more productive and for prosperity to rise, it must be possible for capital to be accumulated, whoever happens to own it. Whether intentional or not, policies that prevent people building up capital funds (for example, high taxation and low interest-rate policies, both of which discourage saving), and laws to break up fortunes once accumulated, have the effect of depressing the ability of the economic system to provide our needs by dragging down the productivity of our labour.

Insecurity and unemployment

To the charge that it does not help people feel completely secure, the market economy has to plead guilty. It simply cannot live up to the welfarist claim that everyone should have a standard of living they deem satisfactory and the right to enjoy for life the type of job they would most desire.

The market is no respecter of vested interests. Past achievements count for nothing if another producer can offer a better service more cheaply, or if an innovator comes up with a labour-saving device that makes a particular occupation redundant. Yet we cannot blame the capitalists for this problem; it comes from the market demand of consumers, always on the look-out for better and cheaper goods and services. To provide complete security for all workers, it would be necessary to eliminate this consumer sovereignty.[9]

In fact, the welfare propagandists themselves, says Mises, are much to blame. The pressures for government to spend more that lead to credit expansion and inflation, the interventionism which disrupts entire markets, the institutional wage-fixing that causes unemployment, all these are the root causes.

Unemployment. Critics who urge government intervention to tackle economic problems see the market's tendency to produce unemployment as one of their major targets. Mises, for his part, thinks that they are nevertheless greatly mistaken about the causes of unemployment.

In the unhampered market economy, declares Mises, unemployment is only a *temporary* phenomenon. It occurs when working practices or consumer demands change, necessitating a restructuring of production to meet new patterns of demand and new technological frontiers. Once again, the sad fact is that policies inspired by the welfare enthusiasts make the labour market less able to adapt to change and therefore produce greater unemployment. This is because each measure adopted imposes higher costs that are ultimately borne by employees:

If wages are freely determined in the labour market, no raise in wages above the market rate can occur as a result of interventions, such as

127

the shortening of labour time, mandatory insurance of workers at the expense of employers, regulations of workshop conditions, vacations of workers with full pay, et cetera. All these costs are shifted to wages and are borne by the workers.[10]

The unemployment problem comes when these pressures are combined with union rates or statutory minimum wages that prevent the payment of workers below a particular rate. For then, the firm facing a falling market or rising costs but unable to reduce its wage rate will have to reduce its total labour bill by laying off workers or by reducing the hours worked. Far from justifying yet more intervention to alleviate the unemployment (but having the opposite effect because it stimulates inflation), such occurrences should be testimony to the fact that this is one branch of 'economic policy' that kills employment more directly than most.

Doubts. Once again, however, we have to ask whether Mises is right to think that this answer disposes of the problem completely. New production technology can pose a very long-term problem on the labour markets, especially if the changes required are deep and revolutionary, and the effects on particular individuals can be profound. When a coal-mining town is ruined by the advent of nuclear or hydro-electric power, for example, a combination of conservatism, the costs of moving to more prosperous areas, and a simple love of the old community can produce a pocket of unemployment that is far from temporary. New opportunities may be hard to find, particularly for older people. In addition, the relative wealth and high degree of capital ownership that people enjoy today might mean that they are able and willing to stay out of work longer than in previous decades, bumping up unemployment again: but that takes us into issues about how the phenomenon of unemployment should be defined and measured, and whether its presence always indicates a welfare loss.

TAXATION, EXPENDITURE, AND DISTRIBUTION

Given this robust defence of the unhampered market economy, what is legitimately left for the government to do?

The principles of taxation

In the market economy there is still a need for some government activity, and therefore some taxation to support it, argues Mises, because the market society must be preserved in peace. That means it must have institutions for the internal preservation of peace and for the repulsion of foreign threats:

The defence of a nation's security and civilization against aggression on the part both of foreign foes and domestic gangsters is the first duty of any government. If all men were pleasant and virtuous, if no-one coveted what belongs to another, there would be no need for a government, for armies and navies, for policemen, courts, and prisons. It is the government's business to make the provisions for war . . . [11]

Where the government's activities are limited, the need for taxation is therefore small in relation to individuals' incomes. In the liberal economy, taxation is an evil which is to be made as small as possible.[12] In the socialist world, taxation is far more important,[13] being used for motives other than the simple raising of revenue: motives such as promoting equality and breaking up private accumulations of capital. No tax can be neutral in its effect in the real world, but Mises regrets that modern welfare proponents do not in fact seek a tax system that is as neutral as possible, but are drawn to the socialist plan of using taxes to bring about a new pattern of wealth and incomes. Hence, poll taxes and flat-rate income taxes are rejected in favour of 'progressive' taxes that hit high earners hardest. But, says Mises, all measures of that kind once again cause a systematic consumption of capital:

The philosophy underlying the system of progressive taxation is that the income and wealth of the well-to-do classes can be freely tapped. What the advocates of those tax rates fail to realize is that the greater part of the incomes taxed away would not have been consumed but saved and invested. In fact, this fiscal policy does not only prevent the further accumulation of new capital. It brings about capital decumulation.[14]

Because progressive taxation takes away, for current government spending, precisely those parts of incomes and profits that

129

would have been saved and invested on capital accumulation,[15] it works to thwart the development strategies of those very entrepreneurs who are most successful at satisfying the demands of consumers. It presupposes that the government authorities, and not consumers, should have the power to control this part of the nation's wealth.[16] Like the punitive taxation of a person's estate on death, it is not a real tax but straightforward confiscation, and has the same effect of making people consume their capital funds while they still have the chance, instead of saving so as to invest and raise the productivity of labour in the future. And a lower capital invested per worker means a lower income for those very people the confiscation was intended to help.

Public works

What can be said of the functions for which this taxation is raised? Once again, Mises doubts that many of them are necessary. This is partly because much taxation goes simply to support government enterprises that have, on the whole, failed, and are expensive and inefficient.[17] Sadly,

The public firm can nowhere maintain itself in free competition with the private firm; it is possible today only where it has a monopoly that excludes competition.[18]

That deficiency might not be too serious if public resources were conjured up by a magic wand, but in fact they come directly from the pockets of taxpayers; the whole nation loses if they are spent less efficiently by the government.[19] Once again, consumers are being robbed of their sovereignty. Cash is being taken from those individuals and firms they choose to support and spent on inefficient ones they do not.

It would be of little use appealing to Mises that the people have in fact chosen public enterprises for support through taxation, and so they do reflect how people 'really' want to spend their money. Whereas the market gives consumers a daily choice over what things are produced, the political system offers a choice only every few years, and even then for a package of policies and services rather than for any specific one. It is hardly a direct choice. Furthermore, the growth in public services leads to the formation of large groups of administrators and beneficiaries who are dependent on it, and who naturally try to preserve it, whatever the wishes of consumers and voters:

Representative democracy cannot subsist if a great part of the voters are on the government pay roll.[20]

Furthermore, the government is able to exercise strong influence on demand and supply when its budget is large, and it can thus cause the most pronounced disturbances in the market.[21] All these are deficiencies even in that small part of the budget which governments tend to devote to capital projects, making it fair to say that

If taxes grow beyond a moderate limit, they cease to be taxes and turn into devices for the destruction of the market economy.[22]

Confiscation and distribution

Of course, the dreams of welfare protagonists go further than the mere establishment of government industries and public works. They return again to the notion that much of what is raised through taxation or confiscation should be distributed so that everyone receives a more equal share in the available resources.

The trouble, says Mises, is that production and distribution are inseparable in the free economy. There is no fixed pie of resources that can be divided up between everyone. The pie is always expanding – until it is divided in such a way that there is no incentive for entrepreneurs to expand it further. The benefits of capitalism stem from the fact that people *expect* the secure ownership of what they invest and the products derived therefrom. Without that assurance, they cannot be expected to undertake the risks of innovation and production, so the whole driving force goes out of the economic system.

Practical problems. But in any event, the zeal for confiscation and distribution of individuals' resources through central agencies

131

is unrealizable in practice. To begin with, the notion that there should be 'equality' rarely stretches internationally: the comfortable American politics professor may preach equality, but has no urge to divide his or her income equally with the destitute populations of central Africa.[23] And should equal shares be given only to adults, or to children, and those incapable of protecting their allocation and using it wisely? The decision is arbitrary: when it comes to the principles by which wealth is to be confiscated and shared out, the opinions of some authority are what must prevail, for there can be no objective and indisputable arrangement.

If some other distributive principle is being proposed, say allocation in terms of the value of each individual's services to society, according to need, or to merit, who is to decide what value, need, or merit each person displays? And whatever pattern is chosen, there would need to be a large army of administrators and policemen to check the taxation due, raise it, manage the fund, scrutinize eligibility for allocations, make the payments, check the results, adjust errors, and so on. Redistribution does not come free.

CONCLUSION

For Mises, then, government efforts to promote welfare are invariably counterproductive. The taxation that is raised for this purpose unfortunately reduces the gains which people enjoy as a result of their effort and investment, and so has the effect of killing incentives. But without incentives, people will not strive to improve their own position, and that means, in the exchange economy, that others who would have liked to trade with them are disappointed too. The result is a welfare loss.

Just as damaging, taxation takes away from people that very part of their income that would otherwise be saved – that part earmarked for capital investments. But it is on the accumulation of capital goods on which future prosperity is based, because as Mises usefully reminds us, capital machinery and equipment makes labour more productive and allows us to gain more rewards for less effort. And to compound the misfortune, the money that is raised through taxation will be spent to achieve the greatest political effect, rather than the wisest economic one: and that means that it will tend to be spent on current expenditures rather than used to develop and acquire new capital goods. The effect is to consume funds that were intended to be saved, and to squander resources that could have been used to boost output in future years.

Our yearning for a more equal world often blinds us to this delicate principle of capital accumulation on which our future prosperity rests. And it is often the result of a common mistake in economics, that of presuming a snapshot view will give us an accurate description of events that are actually in a state of constant flux. There are rich and poor people in capitalist societies; there have always been rich and poor people in that system. But from year to year, month to month, even day to day, the particular individuals who can be legitimately classified in those groups are different. In the liberal economic order, fortunes can be made, but just as easily lost, and they come only from supplying goods or services that other people demand of their own free will. In the liberal order, the permanent inequality of privilege is abolished. The only inequalities that persist must be earned by contributing to the welfare of others.

However, the common tendency to downgrade the dynamic nature of the market process and make errors based on a snapshot view is only one of many mistakes that are possible when people do not understand the nature of economics. This is a subject on which Mises has much to say.

PART TWO: THE NATURE OF ECONOMICS

CHAPTER SEVEN

Individual Values in Economics

Value is not intrinsic, it is not in things. It is within us;
it is in the way in which man reacts to the conditions of
his environment.[1]

It is remarkable that students today can go through almost the
whole of an economics course without understanding, and often
without even confronting, the notion of value. Frequently, in
fact, the mainstream textbooks use the term 'value' as a mere
synonym for 'price'; and together with other mistakes, the
strong suggestion percolates through that value is an objective
and measurable quality of commodities, something that can be
added and subtracted as different volumes of different commodities are considered in the analysis.

To economists of the Austrian School, these are crass mistakes, leading to a fundamental misunderstanding of the economic process. Value arises only in so far as people value things;
it is not an objective quality of commodities, but something very
personal to the people concerned at the time. Accordingly, all
the things with which economists occupy themselves – the
pattern of exchange and the determination of prices as a result,
for example – are rooted deeply in these personal, *subjective* acts
of valuation. To the Austrians, economics is not about finding
measurable relationships between things, as the physicist
would look for constants linking, say, the volume and pressure
of a gas. Economics is about the relationships between people,
about how people value things, how they react to events and to
the actions of others, about what they *think* of the world.

Some mainstream errors

This conclusion is far from congenial to many mainstream
economists, who have supposed that an admission that eco-

137

nomics is subjective entails that it is consequently unscientific. After all, the target of the natural sciences (in which so much progress has been made) is to eliminate the personal value judgements of the experimenter as far as possible, and to deal only in objective measurement. How can a true science tolerate the subjective?

To the Austrians, of course, this is a misunderstanding of what they are about. Their point is that the very subject-matter of economics is necessarily 'subjective' in the sense that it always deals with human aims and values. But that is not the same as saying that the study of economics is always made unscientific by the 'subjective' intrusion of the experimenter or theorist. We can still deal with the subject-matter of economics in the detached way that is the hallmark of all good science. There is no reason why the personal prejudices of the economist should warp the scientific study of economics.

It may well be a simple confusion on this point that has made the mainstream economists so over-zealous to eliminate any hint of subjectivism from their enquiries. They have supposed that the materials of economics – the prices, costs, money, unemployment figures, exchange rates, expenditures, savings, and so on – are somehow linked by statistical laws, and have devoted a great deal of time and energy to seek out those relationships. They have forgotten that these events have no importance except in terms of what people think about them, and that they emerge as the result of what people think and do, not in obedience to some mechanical rule.

No quantitative predictions. The Austrian School economists, led by Carl Menger, have never pretended that economic events could be predictable – certainly not in the precise and quantifiable way that physical events are predicted by the natural scientists. The subjective underpinnings of economics, the inherently personal character of the individual value judgements upon which all action in the marketplace is based, are enough to guarantee that. The preferences of different human beings are not easy to establish, and impossible to predict with certainty. We might be sure that the volume of bank lending will expand when the interest rate is brought down: but by how much depends upon the personal judgements of those in the market at the time. It depends on how borrowers and lenders perceive and evaluate the opportunities opened up by the availability of credit or the stream of investment income.

From all this it is clear that the Austrian School approach implies a very different view of the purposes and possibilities of economic enquiry than that put forward in the mainstream texts. The principle that economics is fundamentally subjective is therefore of considerable importance, so it will be useful to look at the idea in rather more detail before moving on.

THE SUBJECTIVE THEORY OF VALUE

Economists have long wondered about the principles by which goods settle at the prices they do. The mediaeval notion of the 'just price' supposed that each commodity had an intrinsic, objective, and undeniable value, but still there seemed to be no reason why this should be so, no hard principle from which the 'just price' of any particular good could be derived. Adam Smith made an effort to analyse the problem scientifically by proposing a 'labour theory of value', which equated the relative price of goods with the relative quantity of effort put into their production – a theory which was absorbed, with all its obvious faults, by Karl Marx, who used it to build an equally doubtful theory of capitalist exploitation.

By the nineteenth century, however, theories which credited commodities with an 'objective' value were already seen to be untenable. Prices, after all, did not stay static, particularly in that era of rapid economic development. Price could be depicted no longer as a fixed quality of every good, something as permanent and as measurable as its height, volume, or weight. The more urgent question, on the contrary, seemed to be what made prices *change*.

The subjective nature of values

By the late nineteenth century, the subjectivist answer to this question had been developed, with its fullest and clearest expositions coming (between 1871 and 1874) from Carl Menger, Stanley Jeavons, and Leon Walras. While it was dubbed the 'marginal revolution', it seems to have come from much older ideas, and such was its power to solve some of the insoluble problems of value left by the classical economists that it was soon merged into mainstream theory by Alfred Marshall in his 1890 textbook, *Principles of Economics*. Although a significant victory for the subjectivist approach, this adoption is not considered an altogether happy one by Mises and the other Austrians.

The new view. At the heart of the subjectivist response to the classical economists was the proposition that values are not some objective qualities manifested by different goods, but the subjective way in which people judge those different things and choose with respect to them.

Only the individual can judge whether he or she prefers one thing to another, or would be made happier by the achievement of a particular goal or some other. Values are not part of the objective external world of physical and chemical phenomena – not something that can be observed and measured within commodities. There is no mathematical function linking an assortment of goods with how they will be valued, no way of predicting with certainty which goods each individual will prefer. Values, rather, depend on the personal reaction of the individual to the choices available, upon the needs and outlook of the individual at the time. They are part of the internal psychology of each individual. Echoing the views of Menger, Mises summarizes the process concisely:

Valuing is man's emotional reaction to the various states of his environment, both that of the external world and that of the physiological conditions of his own body.[2]

Values, we may conclude from Mises's statement, are as impermanent as elation, as inaccessible to others as remorse, as unmeasurable as love, as capricious as temper. They are, in short, not the kind of materials from which we can build up a very good predictive science.

Limited agreement. It may well be that there is a large measure of agreement that some things are preferable to others. For example, most people place a high value on life, health, and peaceful co-operation. But it is a fact that there have been and are others who commit suicide, neglect their health, and prefer the solitary life. And we do not know what values will prevail tomorrow. Human values are neither universal nor eternal.

There is not only plenty of divergence between the values of different individuals; the same individuals can put different values on things at different times. Valuation, as an 'emotional reaction' to the world, is not necessarily consistent like the reaction of one chemical to another. An individual's feelings, tastes, and preferences can change, giving rise to changes in the pattern of his or her choices in the marketplace.

Importance for economics

It is this fact of the diversity and unpredictability of individuals that makes the issue of valuation so crucial for economics. For the familiar economic phenomena such as 'demand' or 'saving' and 'investment', must be seen as the outcome of individuals' actions in the marketplace, actions that are not predictable and determinate but which are necessarily rooted in their own particular value judgements at the time.

The Austrian economists, in consequence, warn us not to expect easy connections between economic phenomena without reference to the subjective values of the individuals who are moved by them and who in turn shape them. There is no automatic functional link between the price of a commodity and the quantity demanded, for example; the outcome will depend upon the process of valuation within the minds of the individuals in the marketplace.

And let us not forget that the preferences of those individuals might change. Furthermore, other individuals might enter the market, whose values are very different from those already inside. New products might come into existence, and new production processes might make alternative goods cheaper to produce. Fashions or sociological events might give rise to new demands for new commodities.

Different meanings. Another way of expressing the essential subjectivity of economics and its importance to the prosecution of economic enquiry is the point, made forcefully by both Mises and Hayek, that the same economic phenomena may mean different things to different people. Once again, we cannot escape the subjectivism in which economic events are rooted.

For example, a rising stock market could signify the right time to buy into a boom cycle to one person, a time to sell out and take the profits to another. The same amount of personal wealth could induce one person to retire in modest comfort, while whetting the appetite of another to strive for an even greater fortune. The mass production of a fashion item might make it no longer a desirable status symbol for the rich, no longer a luxury for the poor, producing a marked divergence in their buying patterns. In other words, it is impossible to discuss and manipulate economic concepts without reference to their meaning for the actual individuals concerned, without reference to how those individuals form the subjective judgements they do. As Mises puts it:

Economics is not about things and tangible material objects; it is about men, their meanings and actions. Goods, commodities, and wealth and all the other notions of conduct are not elements of nature; they are elements of human meaning and conduct. He who wants to deal with them must not look at the external world; he must search for them in the meaning of acting men.[3]

Thus, the meaning of economic phenomena for the individuals concerned at the time pervades the whole study of economics. The price of a good might appear to be an objective quantity; but in fact, the sole importance of prices to the economist is in terms of how they result from human preferences and choices, what people think about the prices that prevail, how they expect prices to change in the future, and what they do in response to these and other subjective assessments. Likewise, the 'costs' involved in a production process are a subjective notion, however plainly they might be recorded as balance-sheet figures; for each input might have been used differently, and each producer will perceive and value those forgone opportunities in his or her own way, and so make completely different judgements about the costs that have been suffered.

Values and economic theory. In conclusion, we see that economics must always remain about the meanings which individual attach to things and to events, and that this inherent subjectivism must pervade every study of the subject. There is no objective measure of value, no 'just price' and no fixed relationship between how a thing is valued by anyone and the amount of labour invested in its production. There is no way to measure the 'utility' of a commodity (despite that being a common impression left on students by the mainstream textbook analysis) because that concept too refers only to the personal judgement of a thing make by a valuing individual.

It is easy to become confused on this issue, particularly in view of our eagerness to apply the quantitative methods of the natural sciences uncritically to economics, and thus to suppose that everything it is appropriate for the scientific economist to deal with must be measurable and objective. Prices, for example, are often represented as the measure of value: as the monetary expression of a given quantity of value inherent in a particular good. And, like the classical economists long before them, many today are therefore content to presume that value is objective. But while *prices* are certainly objective, since we can record and measure them without difficulty or dispute, their roots are still subjective, explains Mises. For a price is the rate of exchange between a good and money (or between one good and any other): and that rate is merely the *outcome* of many acts of valuation, many personal choices, by the different individuals in the marketplace. Their subjective origin cannot be ignored.

To the Austrian economists, then – and the view is found at its strongest in Mises's work – there are, in short, no economic 'facts' that can be treated like the facts of physics or chemistry, nothing that can be subjected to empirical tests and given the status of quantifiable 'laws'. Economics is a science quite different in character from the natural sciences.

Economics and psychology

If the study of economics must remain rooted in the subjective values of individuals, it might appear that the whole discipline is no more than a branch of applied psychology. Menger, in fact, certainly seems to have taken a view something like this, although he was careful not to become embroiled in groundless speculation about the human psyche.

Mises, however, took Austrian economics very firmly in a new direction by insisting that economics has a distinctive approach of its own which makes it unnecessary for the economist to enter into psychological questions at all, and which marks the dividing line between the two sciences.

Rules and content. The important distinction made by Mises is between what specific things psychological forces pull people to choose and the rules or logic by which choices are made, whatever specific things might be chosen. The economist, he argues is interested in the latter, in the general principles of how people make choices, but not in the psychology of what the actual content of those choices might be. The economist's position, one might say, is rather like that of the grammarian, who is interested in discerning the general rules of grammar that describe how sentences are constructed, not in knowing the actual content of the millions of sentences that people utter each day.

Thus, the economist's concern is not *why* people have the particular values and motives they do, but how they go about satisfying their purposes, whatever those happen to be. Psychology, physiology, cultural history, and many other disciplines may busy themselves with investigating what natural and social factors determine the actual motives of individuals. The chance of our discovering remains slim:

We do not know why and how definite conditions of the external world arouse in the human mind a definite reaction. We do not know why different people and the same people at various instants of their lives react differently to the same external stimuli.[4]

144

Even if we could discover why, the economist would remain much more interested in the demonstrated *results* of such reactions, in the pattern of their activity in the marketplace and the general principles determining their choices, rather than in the specific psychological causes which ultimately prompt them. Economics, for its part, simply accepts the fact that different people have different motivations and prefer different things. Its purpose is to examine the operating principles behind human actions of a particular kind – the actions of people exchanging goods and services – and not to investigate the human psychology that makes a particular person's scale of values what it is.

For example, economists cannot become interested in why people like to drink alcohol; just in the size and strength of their demand and its consequences in the marketplace. The economist does not know whether it is a thirst for knowledge or simple snobbery that makes particular people buy philosophy books; all that is important for economic theory is that a certain number of books are bought at a certain price. In economics,

It is without importance whether the demand for weapons on the market comes from men who are on the side of law and order or from criminals and revolutionists. What is alone decisive is that a demand exists in a definite volume. Economics is distinguished from psychology by the fact that it considers action alone and that the psychic events that have led to an action are without importance for it.[5]

Meaning of subjectivism. To Mises, then, economics is not so much applied psychology; rather, psychology marks the boundary of the economist's interest. Economics cannot go into the reasons why particular people value particular things more than other things, but must take individual values as 'given' and the actual choices made by individuals as the 'data' it has to work with but cannot explain, just as the natural scientist has to take the existence of gravity as a datum:

The ultimate judgements of value and the ultimate ends of human action are given . . . they are not open to any further analysis.[6]

It is this barrier, says Mises, that makes economics a *subjective* study. Its analysis must stop not at the objective physical events studied by natural scientists, but at the various subjective values, preferences, motives, and aims of human beings.[7] It cannot seek to explain how such values are arrived at, nor even if they are prudent or laudable; it must take people's various purposes and values, their ultimate ends, as given and not open to criticism by any absolute standard. The attention of the economist must be confined to the human events that follow from them – to the ways and means people actually use to satisfy their desires, the choices people make in practice. Those at least we are able to judge objectively on the grounds of their suitability and efficiency with respect to the particular ends at which people aim.[8]

VALUES AND ACTION

To the Austrians in general, then, it must be vain to look for quantitative statistical linkages between economic events, as the natural scientist looks for statistical relationships between physical objects, for economic phenomena depend always on the subjective process of valuation by unique individuals. To Mises in particular, there is also a firm barrier to stop the economist going into the psychological processes which make people value some things more than others. So what principles of action and choice can the economist discern? How can we discover the rules, the grammar, the logic within which human values are formed, and the process by which they are manifested in market activity?

In answer, Mises develops a bold theoretical position which not only marks a crucial stage in the development of Austrian economics, but which is perhaps his most obvious and significant departure from the mainstream approach. He believes that the key principles of economics, the rules by which people choose – regardless of what particular things they do choose – can be deduced logically from the basic concept of action and choice itself.

Demonstrated preference

In making this claim, Mises seems to have moved from an economics based in subjective valuation to one where hard actions and real choices are the key. And to those who accept that economics must be subjective but nevertheless consider that the personal and inaccessible nature of human values makes them a poor basis for any scientific enquiry, this is an important step.

To Mises, however, the step is a comparatively short one. The fact that subjective valuations pervade everything we study in economics, he concludes, does not stop us treating the actions and choices of individuals in the marketplace scientifically. We can still build up a theory of demand and of prices, for example, and make scientific statements about the nature and behaviour of these very evident elements, despite the fact that we know they are rooted in the personal, inaccessible, and subjective values or preferences of the particular individuals who happen to be in the market at the time. For what we call 'values' are really our way of interpreting concrete actions.

A person's actual choice in the marketplace, insists Mises, is a 'demonstrated preference' which reveals something about the nature of his or her scale of values. Thus, it may well be that human values are personal, meaning that we cannot sense directly the preferences of any other individual; but nevertheless, we can and do *infer* those values by observing what choices that person actually makes. The reality of action is our sole guide to the subjective world of other people's values.

We know from examining our own minds that when we choose one thing against another, it is because we prefer it to the other. The thing chosen is more important to us at that time than the thing left behind. So our preferences or values are revealed in what we actually do. Similarly, when we see other people act, we presume quite reasonably that they are not automatons and that their choices also spring from the inner pressure of their values and preferences. By examining their actual choices, therefore, we begin to understand the scale of values which motivates them. To take an analogy, we cannot

147

see nor feel another person's emotions of gloom or pleasure, apprehension or guilt, and have only the outward signs of their behaviour to go on. We know how we would react when stung by these emotions, and presume that when other people react in similar ways, they are experiencing the same inner feelings.

Values as an interpretation. In other words, values, like emotions, are personal psychic events that cannot be experienced directly by outsiders. We can feel or see their bodies, but we cannot see into their minds and feel exactly the same mental events as they. But although we are denied this direct access to their psychological world, it is still useful to talk about other people having certain 'goals' or 'aims' and 'preferences' and 'values'. For what we do is to look at the reality of their actions and then credit them with a scale of values which would explain the result, even though we cannot share or experience those values directly.

To Mises, therefore, the idea that particular scales of values exist within the minds of other people is just a way of interpreting how they really act. It is no more than a construction we devise in order to help us understand why people act the way they do, rather like we would attribute a person's weeping or shunning company to their 'emotional state'. We have no direct access to the inner psychology of an individual's choices, and can understand it only through the operation of his or her decisions on the external world. The hypothesis that the individual is driven by preferences or values is something we construct in order to bring some intelligible order to that endless string of particular choices.

Thus, we *see* an individual do A and not B; we *interpret* such an action by conjecturing that the individual mentally values A more than B. If an individual buys a can of beer instead of a loaf of bread, we say that, at the time, the beer appeared more important, more valuable, or more desirable to the individual than the bread. Under Mises's reasoning, it would be senseless to say that the individual chose the beer but valued it less; values and actions must always be in agreement, because one is simply our way of analysing and interpreting the other.

The crucial result of all this reasoning is that Mises believes it quite legitimate to conclude that a scientific study of economics can proceed from the basis of action and choice and yet retain the essential subjectivism of the discipline. This is possible because values are manifested in action and must always match it.

Scales of value. If we watch such an individual making a large number of choices, it is quite probable that we will detect a certain consistency in his or her actions. An individual might always buy a loaf of white bread even where a brown one is available, for example. With enough observations, we can construct quite an elaborate table of actual choices in which some things are consistently chosen over others. Thus we can infer from these choices that the individual possesses an extended 'scale' of values.

Of course, there exist many different ways of satisfying human wants. For the individual, nevertheless, these diverse possibilities can be arranged on such a single scale – according to their relevance and urgency for increasing his or her well-being. In Mises's words:

The satisfaction derived from food and that derived from the enjoyment of a work of art are, in acting man's judgement, a more urgent or a less urgent need; valuation and action place them in one scale of what is more intensively desired and what is less.[9]

The pure logic of choice

From here, we can begin to glimpse what Mises means when he argues that the principles of economics can be deduced from the concept of action itself. For the very idea of conscious human action implies that the agent has some particular values; it suggests that those preferences will be more or less compelling; it entails that something (the present state) is given up for something else (the anticipated result) that is valued more; and it allows even that combinations of less valued goods can be given up in the pursuit of some preferred outcome.

Already, and without having to know anything about what specific goods any particular individual actually prefers over

149

others, we have begun to reach substantial conclusions about *how* individuals choose, declares Mises. We have uncovered the economic principles of exchange, of marginal utility, and of the use of combinations of producer goods in the pursuit of consumer goods. And all that was implicit in the very meaning of the word 'action'. By following through the logic of human choice, Mises concludes, we can successfully deduce the fundamental theorems that we need to construct a science of economics.

UTILITY ANALYSIS AS AN EXAMPLE

A good illustration of this deductive method at work, which Mises describes in some detail,[10] is the Austrian analysis of marginal utility. As we have seen, this subjectivist analysis achieved prominence through the writings of Carl Menger and others at the end of the nineteenth century and, because of its evident power, was soon merged with mainstream theory to become a staple feature of the modern textbooks. In that mongrel form, it also provides a good example of how mainstream economists have misunderstood the principle of subjectivism and commit serious errors in treating subjective phenomena as if they were measurable and objective things.

Valuation and utility

It was misunderstanding on this point that generated the 'paradox of value' detected by the classical economists. Nothing is more plausible, concedes Mises, than to assume that things are valued according to their *utility* – that is, their capacity to produce some satisfaction. But then a difficulty appeared to the classical economists: they observed that things with very great utility (such as water, which is essential to life and useful for many different purposes) were valued less than other things of smaller utility (such as diamonds, which are inessential and, apart from any limited industrial use, fit only for wearing as ornaments). It was a difficulty the classical thinkers failed to solve.

150

Source of the problem. One source of the trouble, in Mises's view, was that the classical writers were expecting to find some mathematical quantity of 'utility' generated by each particular good, from which an objective measure of the 'value' of each one could be established. But, however we look at it, the benefit, the 'utility' derived from a good by any individual is inevitably a subjective phenomenon, so it remains nonsensical to talk about and compare 'the' utility or 'the' value of diamonds and 'the' utility or 'the' value of water. Values do not exist in commodities themselves, only in the minds of the individuals who are doing the valuing; and utility is not an objective quality but is judged to be greater or less according to the needs and preferences of the individual concerned. Like beauty, these things exist only in the eye of the beholder and are not measurable characteristics like height or weight. When treating the subject of valuation, therefore, we must remember that valuations and judgements about the 'utility' of a particular good are personal and unquantifiable:

Acts of valuation are not susceptible of any kind of measurement.[11]

A solution. But the misunderstanding which generated the classical economists' dilemma goes very much deeper than this, as Carl Menger explained. It was he, asserts Mises, who found a solution to the dilemma (although Jeavons and Walras could certainly put in convincing claims as well), and in the process he made some crucial and important observations about the nature of value.

Menger was aware that choices depended upon the state of mind of the individual at the time, and upon the specific quantities of each commodity on offer. Indeed, it is this latter point that is the key to understanding and solving the problem. For no individual chooses between 'water' and 'diamonds' in the abstract, and is very unlikely to be forced to choose between *all* the water and *all* the diamonds in the world. The only choice is between a particular quantity of water, say a pint, and a particular number of diamonds. Most people have enough water for their satisfaction, or could easily get more, and so would put little value on an extra pint. A man in the desert,

151

however, might sacrifice plenty of diamonds for it, because his special circumstances would colour his decision. In conclusion, we can see that it is nonsense to talk of 'water' in the abstract, or any unit of water, having some absolute value or utility.

Some examples. Mises extends Menger's observations with some of his own examples that show how people really do make choices in the real world, and illustrate how impossible it is to expect human values to conform to neat mathematical analysis. The actual arrangement of the possible means to our satisfaction in a single order of rank, he reiterates, depends on the individual and on the unique conditions that apply at the time. Choices are not based on any abstract 'quantity of value' that exists within commodities, so that when we know the value of one unit we can multiply up to find the value of several. Choices are always between definite quantities on offer and are not subject to mathematical laws. An individual's valuation of the total stock of two things can be totally different from his or her valuation of parts of these stocks, and not in any sense *pro rata*.

For example, two aspirin tablets may be valued greatly to relieve a headache; but a hundred at that moment would probably have the opposite effect, not be fifty times better. Or consider a more complicated choice between different commodities. A man who needs ten logs to complete the roof on his cabin might well exchange his raincoat for ten logs; but if he is ninety logs short, he would not exchange his raincoat for ten, twenty, or even thirty logs, because nothing short of ninety would serve to keep him dry. And examples of this kind form the reality of human choice: people do not perceive a smooth functional relationship between the utility of different commodities, like the gentle slopes of the textbook indifference curves. The individual's choice always depends on the definite quantities on offer and his or her needs at the time. One choice made under a given set of circumstances and at a given time cannot be generalized mathematically so that we can predict how the individual would choose when faced with some other decision involving different quantities at a different time.

A farmer with seven cows and seven horses might prefer to

give up one cow rather than one horse if that is the choice, but to
give up all the horses rather than all the cattle if that is the only
option. Mises concludes:

There is no ratiocinative operation which could lead from the
valuation of a definite quantity or number of things to the determination of the value of a greater or smaller quantity or number . . .
There are in the sphere of values and valuations no arithmetical
operations; there is no such thing as a calculation of values.[12]

Marginal utility

Sometimes we have a stock of some commodity which is
homogeneous, meaning that any part of it can be substituted
for any other part and still render the same services to the user.
If the user is asked to give up one unit of his or her stock, how is
the choice made? The answer is that the unit given up will be
that which was generating least satisfaction for the user in the
employment it was previously assigned. The services generated
by the whole stock do not have to be considered in the choice:
only the value of the least important use. The decision,
therefore, is made on the basis of *marginal utility*.

Similar reasoning applies when we are investigating how the
individual will react to the acquisition of an *additional* unit of a
homogeneous stock. Since we know that the individual will
make sure that his or her most urgent needs are satisfied first –
that is how we define 'urgent needs' – the services generated by
this new unit will be deemed less valuable than those from any
unit already held. A second additional unit will serve even less
urgent needs, and so on. This is the familiar law of diminishing
marginal utility, which Mises calls more generally the *law of
marginal utility*.

A basis for exchange theory. Such analysis comes into its own when
we are looking at how people exchange a unit of one commodity
for another – the action which is at the kernel of the study of
economics. Once again we can see that the choice will be made
on the basis of marginal utility, and that the individual will
volunteer an exchange only if the marginal utility of what is

acquired is valued higher than that of the thing given up. With this analysis, we have begun to understand the principles of exchange: something we will consider in more depth shortly.

At this point, however, it is worth mentioning Mises's caution that the term 'utility' can have two meanings. One, which Mises in his early book on *The Theory of Money and Credit* and his predecessors in the Austrian School called '*objective* use-value' refers to the capacity of a commodity to bring about some effect – such as the 'calorific value' of coal. A quite different notion, that of '*subjective* use-value', is the meaning used in marginal utility analysis, even though it might not be based on true objective use-value – such as when people overestimate the rejuvenating effects of snake oil.

Implications for mainstream theory

The development of marginal utility analysis in its pure Austrian form, as described and refined by Mises, reveals some of the sources of error that are found in the mainstream textbooks.

Real-world choices. For instance, it is plain from Mises's description that marginal utility analysis will work only when the stock in question is homogeneous. For simplicity, the textbooks tend to regard this as the most usual case, but Mises's examples quickly remind us that this is not so. Most real-world choices do not involve the exchange of incremental portions of one uniform stock for incremental portions of another. Practical decisions involve choices between things that are very different in quality, and where the individual might well see no benefit in having a small increment of some good, but discern a major benefit in having a greater one, as in the example of the logs and the overcoat.

Suggestion of measurability. Another mistake in the mainstream portrait of marginal utility analysis is the implication that utility is measurable. At its worst, this is found in those textbooks where 'blocks' of 'utility' are shown as being added up to form a graph of 'total utility'.[13] In fact, as Mises insists, utility cannot be summed in this manner, since human values are not measurable and therefore not additive. The marginalist approach in its correct formulation might talk about the utility attached to a particular incremental quantity of some good, or that the use of each unit given up is the 'least important' one: this is the 'margin' that features in the analysis. But the theory as espoused by the Austrians would never suggest that the importance of different units can be added up to give a measure of the total value gained or lost by the change. There is no smooth, continuous, functional relationship between the volume of a good which an individual holds and how he or she values the total of that stock, as Mises's examples illustrate once again.

Indifference curves. The indifference curve analysis that is another common feature of modern textbooks was originated by Edgeworth in the late nineteenth century, but came into its own under the hands of Hicks and Allen in the 1930s. It can be seen as an abandonment of the traditional utility analysis, a move prompted in part by this mistaken view that it aimed at the cardinal measurement of utility.

The indifference curve analysis avoids any tendency to imagine that utility might be measured and added up by charting the various quantities of a pair of goods to which the individual is indifferent. Thus, it does not discuss greater or lesser utility but the *combinations* of goods which the individual perceives as generating precisely equal benefits. However, in the light of Mises's application of demonstrated preferences and the Austrian insistence that utility is not measurable anyway, this approach seems rather superfluous. To the Austrians, it is also somewhat sterile, because economics deals with choice and thus with action, not with indifference and inaction. Furthermore, in portraying smooth and continuous functional relationships, it prompts the student to make unwarranted assumptions: it suggests that the possibilities on offer to the individual are infinitely small gradations of different goods, not the discrete and finite quantities that are actually proffered in the real world.

155

Preference and practice. But the mainstream elucidation of the indifference curve analysis suffers from a much more fundamental problem, and Mises develops and sharpens a serious criticism of it and of other similar models.

The real problem with the mainstream approach in all its forms is that it assumes that preference scales exist beyond the realm of what has actually been chosen. The smooth graphs of the indifference curves suggest that many combinations of goods to which the individual is indifferent can be extrapolated from a few known observations.

But a reflection, along with Mises, of the nature of choice will dispel any such illusion. For as Menger and he stress, every act of choice is a decision between two or more specific opportunities – between definite quantities of particular goods on offer, for example. What we call the individual's values or preferences are merely our interpretation of those specific choices. We cannot extrapolate from that interpretation, based on those specific and observed choices in the past, to say how the individual *would* have acted had the range or quantities of goods on offer been slightly different. Thus, an individual might gladly buy a can of beer in preference to a loaf; but when faced with the free offer of a dozen cans of beer or of three loaves, the same individual on the same occasion might prudently choose the bread.

The same holds true for attempts to predict the actual choices people will make in the future, on the basis of past experience. For how people have reacted to specific choices in the past is no firm guide to how they will choose when faced with different opportunities in the future. How will the individual's choices be affected, say, by a punitive tax on beer? The textbooks glibly deal with this question by shifting demand curves bodily one way or the other, as if the answer were both predictable and obvious. But in fact, until the new circumstances actually arise, there is no way to predict with apodictic certainty how people will choose. Even the individuals concerned may be unable to say how they would decide until they are actually faced with the brute fact of having to make a choice.

In both these ways, the mainstream economists are liable to

make mistakes because they assume that preference scales exist somehow independently of actual choices. They are presented as abstractions which allow a smooth relationship to be charted between the demand for one commodity and another. Thus, smoothly sloping demand curves are drawn up on the basis of only a small number of observations about past levels of demand and prices; expenditure patterns are predicted into the future on the basis of 'propensities' to consume and invest which are imagined, quite remarkably, to be both measurable and constant; and people are assigned a set of 'indifference' curves that are supposed to describe how they *would* act when faced with choices that have not in fact occurred. All these constructions are arbitrary and unreal. Preference scales can tell us only about actual choices, not about abstract or future possibilities:

one must not forget that the scale of values or wants manifests itself only in the reality of action. These scales have no independent existence apart from the actual behaviour of individuals.[14]

Arbitrary motives. The recent history of mainstream economics has been an attempt to eliminate subjectivism from the discipline as far as possible. To some extent, this is founded on the correct view that the economist cannot become preoccupied with debating the psychological (and therefore inaccessible) events that cause people to choose some things and not others. But, much less creditably, it stems also from the headlong rush of economists to make their study look respectable by dressing it in the clothes of the physical sciences. Thus, they have tried to make it a science of prediction, a subject which, like physics, can boast a whole theology of laws and constants.

But economics must deal with the actions of real people, and real people are not so narrowly circumscribed in their actions as the predictable courses of the physical objects described by the natural scientist. The actual values which people hold are hard to ascertain, impossible to measure, complex in nature, wide in scope, and too changeable to form the basis of a predictive science. To help them make sense of how economic choices are made, therefore, the mainstream theorists have resorted to abstracting a specialized set of explicitly economic motives – a return to the classical idea that individuals possessed a number of 'economic ends' that could be assumed to guide their action. Thus, individuals are assumed to strive to maximize their pecuniary gain, and firms are assumed to aim at the maximization of profit.

To Mises, this is a serious error. It does not give a real answer to the question of how human choices are made, but simply assumes that they are made according to an arbitrarily assigned set of assumptions. It builds theories on a hypothetical family of 'economic ends' which are artificially circumscribed, making the theories themselves less generally valid as a result. We must remember, says Mises, the full richness of human motives: in fact, all conscious action is 'economic', because it always involves preferring one thing over another, a decision or choice between alternative possibilities, an exchange of one state for what the individual expects to be a more satisfactory one. Such actions are not limited to what are called 'economic goods', but may involve the decision to opt for honour instead of financial profit, integrity instead of wealth. How can the textbook model of the 'rational' economic agent pursuing only 'economic' ends be reconciled with this?

DEDUCTION IN ECONOMICS ONCE MORE

With these illustrations of the Austrian method at work, we can now begin to appreciate more fully the principle espoused by Mises that the fundamental theorems of pure economics can be deduced from the very concept of action.

Mises asserts that the concept of *action* is intuitive and universal. The human mind has preferences built into it, just as it has emotions built into it, and so the concept of action – the pursuit of a preferred situation – is a part of *how* we look at the world, not something we know only *through* observation. From this, we can deduce a great deal about how individuals will behave as they pursue their preferences, says Mises. In other words, we can derive the main theoretical principles of economics.

For example, from the intuitive concept of preferences, we

can see straight away that people will act to maximize their satisfaction and minimize their dissatisfaction. To take the example of an individual who has to give up some part of a stock (say, to exchange it for something else), we can thus quite reasonably say that the employment of the unit which the individual *does* forgo is the 'least urgent' and, using this marginal utility analysis, go on to draw conclusions about how people will choose between one good and another, and how they will enter into economic exchange, without any observation being necessary. Nor does it require psychological experience, knowledge, or reasoning: the correct conclusion is found in the nature of human choice itself: people by definition satisfy their most urgent needs first, and give up the satisfaction of their least urgent needs ahead of the rest. Different people may have very different needs, but economics does not have to know what they are in order to analyse *how they will act* to satisfy them.

Ends and means

The same sort of reasoning can be applied more generally to build up a picture of other economic concepts such as ends and means, profit and loss. To Mises, the distinction between ends and means arises straight away when we think about human action, and the difference is obvious:

The result sought by an action is called its end, goal, or aim ... Strictly speaking the end, goal, or aim of any action is always the relief from a felt uneasiness. A means is what serves to the attainment of any end, goal, or aim.[15]

But again we must be careful to recognize the subjective nature of this. Things we find in the natural world, water for example, are just things. They become *means* only when they are employed by human beings to quench their thirst or drive their mills. Economics is not about the physical world, but about people's conduct with respect to it. As Hayek has put it, a hammer is a physical object; but to describe it properly and fully understand what it is, we would have to mention its importance to those people who use it as a tool.[16]

Scarce resources. All economics teaches that resources are limited. Mises derives this from the idea of action once again: if people had a sufficiency of everything, they would have no reason to act. Means must therefore necessarily be limited, because action implies that people seek more of something or another. If some things, such as air, are in such plentiful supply that they do not need to be economized, then people do not need to act to gain them, and they are not *economic goods*, and are outside the scope of a science of action such as economics.

We can now go on to divide means into different categories – categories which, Mises maintains, can still be derived logically from the idea of action. The first set is that of means which satisfy human wants directly, which can be called *consumers' goods*; the second contains goods which can satisfy wants only indirectly when used in co-operation with other goods, and these can be called *producers' goods* or *factors of production*. Some producers' goods may bring about a consumer's good directly, and some may be used to bring about another producers' good which only then makes it possible to bring about a consumer's good.

The Austrian school reminds us, therefore, that it is wrong for the neoclassical textbooks to oversimplify this division as they do. Producers' goods are not all the same: they can be nearer or further away from production, arranged as it were in a series of higher or lower *orders*. And they will be valued according to the part they play in the production of consumers' goods.

Costs and profits

The ideas of cost and profit also follow naturally from the idea of action, explains Mises. Action is an attempt to substitute a more satisfactory condition for a less satisfactory one. What is given up to achieve that end is called the *price* the value attached to the satisfaction foregone is called the *cost*. Again, the Austrian approach reminds us that these concepts of cost and price are not at all objective measures, despite the fact that we normally think of both as definite and measurable amounts of money. Instead, they depend entirely on personal judgements of the value of the things that are given up in the process of acquiring other things.

The difference between the value of the price paid and that of the goal attained is called the *profit*, or gain, or yield. And, once more, one of the crucial and distinctive doctrines of Austrian economics is that there is nothing objective about this either:

Profit . . . is purely subjective, it is an increase in the acting man's happiness, it is a psychical phenomenon that can be neither measured nor weighed. . . . how much one satisfaction surpasses another can only be felt; it cannot be established and determined in an objective way.[17]

Sometimes, of course, the action does not attain the end sought, and might even produce a condition that is less desirable than the previous one; in which case the difference between the valuation of the result and the costs incurred is called a *loss*. This is another concept which defies objective measure.

The understanding that prices, profits, costs, and losses are not objective measures but personal judgements about value by the particular individuals involved can help explain why there seems to be no mechanical link between these and other economic concepts. Recognizing the subjective foundation of apparently objective phenomena is crucially important if we are to discover how people really act, for it reminds us that people will often aim not at the maximization of financial returns, but at other results that will bring them a greater satisfaction, or profit in the subjective, non-monetary sense.

THE EXCHANGE PROCESS

So far, we have looked at Mises's explanation of how subjective values are at the heart of every personal action. All action is the attempt to substitute a preferred state for a present state, says Mises, the exchange of one condition for another. When we

understand the process of valuation, we can begin to understand the very foundation of the process of economic exchange:

All human action, so far as it is rational, appears as the exchange of
one condition for another. Men apply economic goods and personal
time and labour in the direction which, under the given circumstances, promises the highest degree of satisfaction, and they forgo the
satisfaction of lesser goods so as to satisfy the more urgent needs. This
is the essence of economic activity – the carrying out of acts of
exchange.[18]

If ours were a world of isolated individuals, of desert-island
castaways who never had any dealings with other people, this
analysis might be all the economics we would ever need to
know. But in fact, economists are interested specifically in the
exchanges that occur *between* individuals, not just within each
one. And the subjectivist approach emphasized by Mises and
the other Austrian economists shows its true power when
applied to this *interpersonal* exchange process.

Why exchange occurs

The classical economists began with the false idea that value is
an objective quality intrinsic to particular goods, says Mises –
like their colour or weight. But this thesis, he continues, gave a
completely wrong account of the process of exchange. It
supposed that people first established the 'correct' value of the
goods in question and then bartered them against goods of
equal value – since nobody would exchange one good for
another of demonstrably lower worth. The fact that goods were
exchanged implied that they had the same 'objective' use value.

This classical analysis makes it hard to understand why
people should exchange things at all, since they gain no value
from the process. The subjectivist approach, on the other hand,
explains the phenomenon of interpersonal exchange quite
easily by using opposite logic. People buy and sell, says Mises,
precisely *because* they value things *differently*. People have different goals and so attach different priorities to available
commodities. Exchange between two people will occur only

when they place items in a different order on their scale of priorities. In Mises's words:

economic activity has no other basis than the value scales ... constructed by individuals. An exchange will take place when two commodity units are placed in a different order on the value scales of two different persons.[19]

Thus, a person who values bread more than meat will be happy to trade with another who values meat more than bread. Although neither any bread nor any meat has been created by the exchange, human welfare has increased: both parties are better satisfied after the transaction, simply on account of their different preferences. They make the exchange because they both benefit, and they both benefit because they each value what they gain more than what they give up.

It was, concludes Mises, a serious mistake of the classical economists to suppose that the value of a commodity, like bread or meat, was objectively measurable. The fact that these things are exchanged implies that people disagree on their value: the attempt to measure value objectively is vain.

The determination of exchange ratios. If the economist cannot make scientific measurements of values, what is left? Being denied any access to the psychological process of subjective valuation, says Mises, means that the economist's attention must be confined to a study of the actual amounts of various commodities that people are, in practice, prepared to exchange. The study of exchange, which Mises calls *catallactics*, centres not on *use-values* but on *objective exchange-values* – on the mutual exchange ratios of goods and services actually negotiated in the marketplace.

The actual ratio at which people in the marketplace are prepared to trade specific volumes of different commodities – the *price* of one in terms of another – this, certainly, is an objective and measurable phenomenon with which economists can deal. It is nonetheless determined by the particular values of the traders concerned, so subjectivist considerations pervade even this:

even objective exchange value is not really a property of the goods themselves, bestowed on them by nature, for in the last resort it is also derived from the human process of valuing individual goods.[20]

Money and prices. In the modern market society, of course, goods are not usually exchanged against others but against a third commodity, *money,* whose sole function is as a medium of exchange. Thus, all exchange ratios are expressed today not in terms of particular volumes of particular goods but in terms of a particular amount of money – and this is what we normally call the 'price' of an item. However objective the balance-sheet figures may look, the principle that price is an objective outcome based on the interplay of subjective forces, and that the subjective elements in the process are the most interesting and important part of the economist's study, remains untarnished.

Prices, values, and change

Again, it must be remembered that prices are not a measure of value: they are not the product of an equal valuation of things, but of a *discrepancy* in valuation. They are the *outcome* of acts of valuation by a number of individuals, which in the market societies of today can be many millions of people.

It is certainly true that the larger the market, the less the individual can influence the prices of goods on offer. The classical theorists, noting that in a large market, the impact of any individual buyer or seller on exchange ratios would be small, falsely abstracted the phenomenon and supposed that each commodity was indeed endowed with a certain quantity of value that was independent of the appraisal of individuals. They forgot that goods must be *exchanged* by individuals, and supposed that they simply *exchange.* They supposed that the price was inherent in each particular good traded, and that there were 'natural' or 'just' prices for everything. Even today, economics textbooks discuss models in which the individual is seen as having *no impact at all* on prices, which are 'given'. It is not surprising that such faulty reasoning produces crass mistakes.

By contrast, the subjectivist approach which Mises did so much to develop reminds us that there is nothing permanent or 'given' about prices. They are as fickle as the human desires from which they spring:

the exchange ratios which we have to deal with are permanently fluctuating. There is nothing constant and invariable in them.[21]

The market phenomena we observe at any moment represent just one instantaneous position in a kaleidoscopically changing world.[22] They represent only the particular concatenation of actions by a particular group of people in accordance with the values they hold at a particular time:

the conditions which produce them are perpetually changing. The value that an individual attaches both to money and to various goods and services is the outcome of a moment's choice. Every later instant may generate something new . . . [23]

Critique of Walrasian models. For Mises, then, there is little more absurd than the attempts, initiated by Leon Walras, to describe the situation in which all markets are in perfect balance, the condition of general equilibrium. For it is again the unwarranted extrapolation of incorrect assumptions about the nature of markets to what must inevitably be a false conclusion.

The search for general equilibrium might seem reasonable if we accept the mainstream model of smoothly sloping demand and supply schedules which intersect at some equalibrating, market-clearing price. From there it is only a short step to imagine that the balance discovered in one market might work through to others, so that the whole economy could reach a state of equilibrium. To reach this happy point requires the solution of a large number of simultaneous equations, like the attempts to achieve balance in the socialist economy proposed by Enrico Barone and others, for the adjustment of supply and demand in one market will certainly affect what goods are available and in demand in others.

But as we now see, the smooth and continuous supply and demand functions on which this mathematical effort depends are nowhere to be found: real economic choices involve discrete quantities, not tiny increments. Such discontinuity makes the problem insoluble. Furthermore, prices have no importance other than what they mean to the actual individuals involved at the instant in question. The arrival of new individuals, changes in the existing individuals' scales of value, the perception of new opportunities, or the invention of new goods and new production processes will all generate different responses to the prevailing prices, keeping the economic process in a state of continual change, not a state of continual balance.

CONCLUSION

For Mises, then, the classical assumptions that goods exchanged must have the same value, or that 'natural' prices are determined by impersonal forces, leave economics with neither soul nor life. The basis of economics is human action, and human action is *change* – the replacement of one state of affairs by another. One of Mises's most significant contributions to the subject lies just here, in the elucidation of how human values and the changes they generate are the driving force of the phenomena which economists observe. And within that body of theory, he develops a strong critique of the general equilibrium model that occupies so central a place in the mainstream economics textbooks. This is the contribution that forms the substance of the next chapter.

CHAPTER EIGHT

The Crucial Importance of Change

> Human action originates change. As far as there is
> human action there is no stability, but ceaseless
> alteration.[1]

We live in a world of change. Natural conditions, for example, are never constant: there are unforeseen accidents (lucky and unlucky), good and bad harvests, the discovery or emergence of new resources and the destruction of old ones by fire, flood, or tempest. Human conditions too change significantly: human populations grow, old members are replaced by young ones, new production processes are developed and old ones fade into disuse.[2]

In a study of how human beings pursue their particular values, then, change is a vital element. Natural change will give a new urgency to some needs, and alter our valuation of the means for their satisfaction, such as when an earthquake makes the need for shelter and hygiene more urgent and promotes the priority of a supply of tents and medical equipment. Human changes will have the same effect, such as when a revolutionary new production process makes old factories and skills redundant and turns a former luxury into a commonplace good. Indeed, completely new goods might be produced or discovered, their emergence prompting a close examination of how existing production processes could be quickened or cheapened by using the new artefacts or resources.

Furthermore, people themselves change. The pattern of human wants is always changing. It is not just that changing circumstances mean that people alter the values they put on various things throughout their lives: in addition, young generations grow up with values that are often different, sometimes radically so, from those of their parents. They mature, after all, in a different world from that of their parents' childhood, with different social conditions prevailing, different political questions shaping events, and a different economic structure that provides them with different opportunities. The fact that their values are often different should be no great shock. Yet as Mises repeats, economics is not about the mechanical actions of *things*, but the values and behaviour of *people*; the inevitability of change in the population and in the value structures of individuals means that economics, too, is a study of change. How people act to satisfy their desires in a changing world is not a question that is incidental to economics, or a mere subsection of that discipline. Understanding how people adjust to change is what economics is all about.

Mises's impact

Mises's principal exposition of this important point and its implications is found in *Human Action*, although there are traces of it in his earlier writings. It was greatly out of tune with the prevailing approach of economists, which was to search for conditions in which each market, and therefore the whole economy, would be in balance – the 'general equilibrium' analysis popularized by Hicks and Samuelson. To Mises, the equilibrium approach, implying as it does a complete balance between market forces and the absence of any change, is merely a hypothetical abstraction, designed to be *contrasted* with the real world so that the importance of its assumptions could be judged, and not intended as a *portrayal* of the real world. It is a deliberate oversimplification, useful for precisely that reason.

The trouble is that decades of uncritical textbook use of the approach has convinced students, and some teachers, that general equilibrium is an accurate description of the real economy. Mises declares that such a view is not only mistaken, but utterly misleading. The economy is never static, never finely balanced at equilibrium, but always in motion as individuals act in pursuit of their various objectives.

Recent incursions. Mises's critique of the equilibrium analysis took time to have its effect, but in recent years the equilibrium theorists have begun to reappraise the assumptions they have

168

been content to apply for some decades. They have begun to recognize that changes in human values and expectations *do* have an important impact on how markets adjust and what the end result will be – as when the expectation of a falling dollar leads to panic selling that makes the fall even more pronounced, for example – and this 'expectations theory' is a growing part of mainstream economics today.[3] In addition, Mises's followers and other market economists have discovered a powerful analytical tool in his insights. They have produced a completely new understanding of the nature and importance of such concepts as competition and entrepreneurship, and have demonstrated in detail the crucial role of time and information in the process of economic adjustment.[4]

THE USE AND MISUSE OF EQUILIBRIUM THEORY

Mises's critique of equilibrium theory is not easy to follow, partly because he agrees that some elements of the traditional approach are valuable, indeed they are essential, if we are to understand the importance of certain features and workings of the economy. His objection is rather that it is painfully easy to misapply the idea and thus to overlook everything that is important about the character of the economic system.

The state of rest versus equilibrium

What, then, is this concept of 'equilibrium' which has been so useful, but upon which so much poor economic analysis has been based in the past? It was pioneered by Leon Walras and his successor Vilfredo Pareto in Lausanne in Switzerland. Although the theory has become sophisticated and complex in the many decades since then, the idea of equilibrium can be explained quite straightforwardly as the situation in which two or more forces in opposing directions are in perfect balance – a situation in which there is no further tendency to change. In a market, for example, equilibrium is reached when the quantity of the product which sellers wish to supply is equal to the quantity which buyers want to buy.

Textbook errors. The idea that markets can and do reach a state of balance is suggested very strongly in the presentation of demand and supply analysis in the mainstream textbooks, and is reinforced by the graphical portrayal of the Marshallian 'scissors' approach to price determination. In these models, students are asked to imagine the result of a change in one of the variables – a change in the volume of demand, for example – and are informed that the answer is generally a smooth adjustment to a new price level at which supply and demand are once more in balance. Only in the rare case of the 'exploding cobweb' is it supposed that such balance does not return to the market. The balanced situation that is described as 'equilibrium' seems to be not only desirable but commonplace.

If balance can be achieved in any particular market taken at random, so might it be achieved in others, this approach suggests. Of course, what happens on one market will affect what happens on others – a bad grain harvest may bump up the price of bread and generate a greater demand for vegetables and meat, for instance. But after all these changes have worked through, we seem to be left with the prospect of a 'general equilibrium' in which all markets are in balance.

Thus the equilibrium approach suggests that we can go even further than the simple analysis of price determination in one market. The fact that markets are intertwined might make the mathematics a little tricky, but with some elementary calculus and enough computing power to solve large batteries of simultaneous equations, we should be able to see how a single change in one market will work through all the others until the economy is back in general balance, and so to specify the new level of the quantities traded and the new prices that will prevail in each market.

Mises's objections. Seductive though this vision may be, Mises objects that it can be utterly misleading. Markets, in reality, are never in balance, because the forces that operate upon prices and demand are in constant flux.

A source of confusion on this point, suspects Mises, is that, while we never find markets in equilibrium, we often find them in what he calls a *state of rest* – when the stock exchange closes and no further trading is allowed, for example. No buying and selling is going on, so in this case the market can be said to be at a state of rest. Nevertheless, this should not be confused with the concept of equilibrium, because it is not a state of balance by any stretch of the imagination: the forces which are operating on the prices of various stocks are not in perfect balance just because the doors are locked and the market is closed. The forces which were pushing prices up or down may not have achieved their full effect when trading ceased, and prices will thus continue their path when it is resumed.

It is important for the economist, as well as the stockbroker and the entrepreneur, to recognize what forces drive prices in various directions, and how strong each different pressure might be. For the economist, the task is to understand how prices are determined; for the stockbroker and the entrepreneur, it is to predict more accurately how they are moving.

The trouble is that it is hard to see a clear relationship that any one factor might have on prices when many other factors (all with different strength, volatility, endurance, and promptness of effect) are changing as well. How, for instance, can we judge the impact of increased student incomes on the market for denim jeans without being confused by the simultaneous changes in cotton prices, in the supply of copper rivets and blue dye, or in the wages of sewing-machine operators that prevail at any particular instant?[5]

The true purpose of equilibrium theory. The answer, says Mises, is that we resort to a hypothetical fiction to judge the effect, and this is the – very limited – purpose of the equilibrium approach. We take the real prices that were paid today as our starting point, and try to discover where those prices are heading. In the example, we look at the forces operating on wage rates, and on the supply conditions that are likely to alter the prices of cotton, dye, and rivets, and then assess where the price of jeans is likely to settle when all of those effects are fully worked out. Having done this, we can now look at the imagined effect of a particular factor that interests us, such as that of rising student incomes. If it appears that the prices of jeans would settle at a very different value because of this change, then we judge the effect of student incomes to be a strong one.

Thus, we assess the strength of particular factors by moving from the real world to a fictional one where the forces under study have exhausted themselves and prices have settled at a 'natural price' or 'final price' where everything is in balance and there is no further change, the world of economic equilibrium. But we must not forget that it is a fictional world, an oversimplification designed to help us thread our way through a confusing cauldron of changing forces.

Confusion of real and hypothetical states

Unfortunately, however, it is easy to confuse the state of rest from which the analysis starts – today's prices as they are actually quoted in the marketplace – with the equilibrium position at which it finishes – the 'final price' or 'natural price' at which they are presumed to settle once all the market forces have worked themselves through. One is a real state, an instant in which real prices actually exist at observable levels; the other is an imaginary position whose character depends entirely on the hypothetical assumptions we make about how it might evolve.

In reality, no market is ever in perfect balance. It is always somewhere on the path to adjustment as opposing forces buffet one another, like the jerky movement of a ping-pong ball on top of a fountain of water. Today's prices tell us only where things happen to be, not how they got there or how they will move tomorrow. Just as the photographer can take a snapshot of the ping-pong ball, so the economist can produce a 'snapshot' description of market prices at some particular time (at the end of a day's trading, for example). In the photograph, the ball does not move, just as quoted prices do not move when the stock market is closed for the day. But that does not mean that things are in balance. After the shutter has clicked, the ball resumes its erratic motion, and when the market opens in the morning, stock prices will once again demonstrate their obstinate refusal to stand still.

When we seek to understand how prices are determined,

then, we must look deeper than the momentary prices that actually prevail on the market and try to understand the underlying forces that are operating. The snapshot may be useful, but to interpret it correctly we need first to understand what human motives are at work and in what direction they are pulling events – just as we need to know something of the story so far before we can make sense of a still from a movie and go on to guess what happens next. We realize that, whatever prices happen to be quoted at any instant, the market is already agitated by forces that will pull prices to some other position. To work out the direction in which things are tending, the economist tries to calculate what the market will look like when all the present forces are exhausted and have had their full effect – the 'final state' or 'natural price' at which prices will settle (in the absence of any further knocks). But exactly how we imagine the market will settle depends entirely on what assumptions we make about those latent forces; different people may form quite different opinions about where the eventual point of balance will lie. Equilibrium, in other words, is no definite and objective point: it is a state which never exists in reality, only in the mind.

Misleading results

The setting up of a hypothetical end state to which prices are tending and at which all the forces in the market are supposed to be in balance is just one example of a general method that can be a powerful aid to our understanding. Mises calls it 'the method of imaginary constructions', and although his name for it is not widely used, the technique itself is. It works by allowing us to abstract from the buzzing cacophony of the real world a few conditions so that we can explore the hypothetical consequences of their absence or existence. It is indispensable because we cannot experiment freely with real economic conditions as easily as the physicist experiments with real weights or real electrodes; the economist cannot in reality halve incomes at a stroke, say, to explore their effects on prices. The method is indispensable not because it is an accurate portrayal of the world, but precisely because it yields up unreal and

173

hypothetical results which can be compared against others or against reality to judge the presumed effect of an imaginary change in one of the variables.

Spread of effects. In the realm of the imaginary construction, however, it is possible to make grave mistakes by forgetting the limits of its fictional application. For example, says Mises, many economists overlook the fact that the forces which determine prices do not produce all their effects at once. Prices are determined by a succession of events, each of which can influence the outcome of the next, and all of which can be modified by other factors that impinge on them as the process unfolds. Exactly what happens, therefore, is not easily predictable; it depends crucially on the element of time involved in the working out of the various effects. Our imaginary construction may be valuable up to a point; but in ignoring time we have ignored a crucial element of the market process.

The evenly rotating economy

Nevertheless, it is quite common for equilibrium models to ignore the timing problem, and to leave us with the suggestion that prices adjust smoothly and quickly to their final state under the pressure of concurrent forces. In the analysis of price adjustment in an isolated market, this mistake is bad enough; but it is compounded when the broader economy is considered. For in that case it is evident that changes in any one market will take time to influence a second, which will in turn take time before it has an impact on a third, and so on. In the meantime, all kinds of feedback are likely to have sent the market we started with into turmoil again. The notion of general equilibrium, then, is even more rarified and less a description of how the economy actually works than the simple equilibrium analysis as applied to a single market.

Whatever the oversimplifications involved, however, the end result of the general equilibrium approach is the imaginary construction that most economists call the *static economy* or *static equilibrium* (but which Mises, for clarity, prefers to call the *evenly rotating economy*), a world that is without any further change because all forces on prices are completely spent.

174

Using the model. Although it is far from reality, the imaginary construction of a general equilibrium can be a useful tool. It helps us to understand the global effects of an isolated change by supposing that all markets are in prefect balance – have already reached their 'final state'. Once again, the forces operating on prices are assumed to have worked themselves out completely, so that we are spared their complicated influence in our subsequent enquiry. Now we can introduce an isolated factor provoking change and observe its effects under the familiar condition of *ceteris paribus*: that all other things remain equal – this time on the whole economy and not just one part of it.

This method of 'comparative statics' is now commonplace in economic theory. To see the effects of change, we start from an imaginary state of perfect balance and work out what new balance would be struck in the event of some particular factor being changed. By comparing the new equilibrium with the old, we can assess the impact of such a change without being confused by all the other forces that might influence the result in the real economy.

Such results are edifying; and Mises acknowledges that the static method is in fact the only adequate way of analysing some changes, since it allows us to look at isolated developments and to ignore the background agitation that actually exists on the market, the fact that changes may not occur instantaneously, and the problem that changes in other markets might in the meantime jolt the process of adjustment from a smooth path.

Bizarre results. However, when we look critically at the hypothetical worlds that are compared in the static approach, we see that they are strange worlds indeed. In this general equilibrium or 'evenly rotating economy', there is never any departure from perfect balance. If there were to be any disturbances in the market data, it would be instantly absorbed and the system brought back immediately to its former position. The manufacturing processes, the consumption goods produced, the demand for consumption goods and the prices at which they exchange would spring back immediately to exactly where they were before. That is why Mises calls it the 'evenly rotating economy' and avoids the word 'static' used of it by others. It is as if the economy is rotating evenly round a fixed centre: the only effect of any change is to return it to its original position.

Nevertheless, as long as we bear its hypothetical nature firmly in mind, it does not really matter that this construction abounds with insoluble contradictions and absurdities: for it is only an *imaginary* construction that is designed to help us solve some particular problems, not an accurate picture of the world.

Pitfalls of the static model

Sadly, however, the textbooks often suggest that this imaginary equilibrium, or something very like it, is in fact the prevailing state of affairs, or at least a real state to which markets will tend unless they are prevented by some 'imperfection' or other. Thus, students are told that unhampered markets will always find balance through the equilibrating mechanism of price. For example, if buyers demanded more designer jeans that sellers wanted to or were able to supply, the sellers would simply raise their prices until the less enthusiastic buyers dropped out and demand came back into balance with supply once more. Whatever might happen on any particular day, the tendency would be for prices to adjust so that the forces of supply and demand are always kept in perfect balance. And textbook equilibrium theory can go further, since what is true for one market is true for another – suggesting that not just particular markets, but the whole economy tends to equilibrium.

In reality, things are very different, and the search for an actual state of equilibrium is an attempt to grasp a mirage. The economy simply does not work like the abstract models of the neoclassical textbooks. Changes are not instantaneous but take time to occur; people take time to notice market surpluses or shortages, and to act to rectify them; the information they are working with may be more or less accurate, more or less up to date; their adjustment can be derailed by other events that occur in the interim; all kinds of practical barriers limit the extent to which the desired adjustment can be achieved; and this list does not even include the institutional barriers that are normally regarded as the key 'imperfections' thwarting smooth market adjustment. Indeed, there is no justification in our supposing that even a close approximation to equilibrium must necessarily prevail: surpluses, shortages, and unemployment are not only common in reality but may in fact be the normal environment outside the rarified atmosphere of the imaginary construction of the evenly rotating economy.

Free-market view. In the light of this warning from Mises, it becomes possible to see more clearly why many economists who are sympathetic to the free-market philosophy are easily undermined by their interventionist critics. For the perfect-competition models suggest very strongly that markets will gravitate smoothly to some desirable point of balance – in which surpluses and shortages are abolished – if only they are made 'perfect'. To the free-market economist this in turn implies that arbitrary rules and regulations on producers, consumers, and the movement of prices and wages, should be avoided (and indeed, Mises and the other Austrians would share this conclusion, though not the reasoning that produces it).

Unfortunately, if one's advocacy of the free market depends upon the belief that markets generally approximate the conditions of perfect competition, it rests on an insecure foundation. It takes little effort for the interventionist to show that markets are never perfect, that 'insiders' have an imperfectly large share of market information, that buyers and sellers are not all equal because some rich individuals or large suppliers have more market power, that the goods traded are not of perfectly equal quality, and so on. All sorts of interventions, including the nationalization of information services, the enforced equality of incomes, and the prohibition of non-standard goods, could be justified as efforts to restore the very 'perfection' for which the free-marketeers themselves are arguing.

The trouble in this case arises because both sides have fallen into the trap of believing that markets can actually be made to function as they do in the perfect-competition model, and so to achieve the happy state of market equilibrium or general equilibrium. No Austrian economist would make such a mistake. To Mises, for example, the market economy can be either 'unhampered' or 'hampered', but it is never anything like the 'perfect' models of the mainstream textbooks. Buyers and sellers are different; the goods they trade are of variable quality and unique in terms of the time and place in which they exist; and market information is spread neither instantly nor uniformly. Human preferences and the state of technology are not 'given' – innovations arise, accidents occur, new wants are felt. And of crucial importance, things take time to happen.

These are the actual conditions within which markets function, and they must form the starting place for any analysis of the market process. They are no mere 'imperfections' that can be imagined or legislated away. The goal of economic policy should be to allow markets to work most efficiently in the context of these features, not to strive for some mirage in which they are supposed to be absent.

Of course, the existence of such conditions implies that the economy will abound with temporary imbalances and will never achieve the comfortable state of general equilibrium. But then it is only the absence of such perfection which gives human beings any reason to act at all. The economy only works *because* there are imbalances which people can exploit, unsatisfied needs that people can help satisfy.

The neglect of action

Textbook abstractions, then, can lead to grave misunderstandings and a completely false impression of how the economy really works.

As Mises states, in an equilibrium world in which there is no change, there is no reason for action. Action is the attempt to substitute one state for a more satisfactory one. If change is ruled out, as it is in the static world of the equilibrium economy, then action itself is ruled out. Real economic life has ceased to exist in this hypothetical state.

Perhaps the worst danger for a proper understanding of economics is this tendency to forget that the assumptions of the equilibrium model automatically eliminate the motivation for any action at all. Action aims at achieving a preferred state, but in this constant world there can be no improvements. The driving forces of the market economy, entrepreneurship, profit, and loss, are nowhere to be found. In the evenly rotating economy, the same assortment of consumers' and producers' goods are traded every day.

Statics, growth, and dynamics

Some economists, recognizing the artificiality of the general equilibrium construction, have proposed refinements that are supposed to improve it. Mises believes that these efforts still fail to recognize the purely imaginary nature of the whole equilibrium approach.

Dynamics. For example, it is acknowledged quite widely that the static equilibrium model – the 'evenly rotating economy' of Mises – does not describe the real economy very closely because incomes and wealth tend to be growing, not static. Equilibrium theorists have therefore produced concepts of 'growth equilibrium' in which this shortcoming is said to be met.

Yet others have advocated a study of 'dynamics' in the attempt to answer the question of how disturbances to one equilibrium market produce a new equilibrium – just how supply and demand conditions will move before the new equilibrium is achieved.

To Mises, both of these efforts represent a failure to understand where the deficiency of equilibrium analysis is really to be found. If we want to analyse change, it is certainly correct to start from an imaginary static state, so that we can introduce a hypothetical change and observe its impact against an unchanging backcloth. The static method, paradoxically, is the only way of understanding change. However, the equilibrium construct is inevitably unreal, and gilding it with 'dynamics' cannot remove that character. Actually, it serves only to conceal it even further and to make economists believe that the imaginary constructs they are manipulating are actually an accurate picture of real events.

Growth equilibrium. Mises has little to say on the idea of 'growth equilibrium', although this again has featured widely in economics textbooks. Austrians in general have little time for the idea, because it once again assumes away the changes and imbalances that spur human beings into action and overlooks the values and the logic that prompt them to act in particular ways. As we have seen, the static equilibrium model suggests the odd hypothesis that the same assortment of the same goods are traded day after day. In the 'growth equilibrium' world, the only difference is that *growing volumes* of exactly the same assortment of goods are traded every day. In either case, there are no imbalances, no unfulfilled wants waiting to be satisfied by quick-thinking entrepreneurs, no uncertainty about future prices and hence no prospect of making a profit or reason to take a risk – in short, no spurs to action at all.

The idea of the same assortment of goods being traded each day, just in growing volumes, reveals a fundamental mistake about the logic of human choice. In an admittedly oversimplified model, it might be an acceptable assumption; but the trouble is that it has a habit of bursting out of its hypothetical test-tube and infecting the way we think about how markets work in actual reality. Quite simply, the supposition that people with growing incomes would actually buy the same package of goods as before (just in larger quantities) is absurd. Rich people, for example, do not buy twice as many potatoes as those on half their incomes. They might even buy less and spend their money on more exotic foods. The package of goods bought, in other words, is bound to change as incomes change. The growth equilibrium notion that markets all grow uniformly is no more an accurate picture of the world than is the construction of the evenly rotating economy. It might be useful as a tool, but it is not real life.

Real-world adjustment. Another source of error, precipitated by the application of calculus and graphical analysis to these problems, is the strong implication in the mainstream approach that any real-world economic adjustment is likely to be smooth (as the dynamic analysis would suggest) or instantaneous (the idea which statics often leaves us with).

On the contrary, argues Mises, economic adjustment can never be smooth. It derives from the discrete choices people make at every stage, and as such is never a smooth movement from one point to another but more a series of jerky steps. Given this simple fact, it would be misleading to portray economic adjustment – even hypothetically – as a smooth process. Just as a close inspection of an impressionist painting reveals it to be not solid blocks of colour but innumerable separate brush-strokes, so a close inspection of the adjustment process reveals it to be a sequence of interdependent but discrete actions by the participating individuals.

Furthermore, these individual steps on the path to adjustment result from subjective forces: the values of those concerned, their perception of events, and how they react to them. We are dealing with diverse individuals, and should not be surprised, therefore, that economic forces seldom generate smooth and predictable results. The idea of dynamic equilibrium analysis, then, rests on abstractions that are fundamentally different from the actual workings of the economic system. We have only ourselves to blame if it leads us to absurd conclusions.

Overblown mathematics

Even professional economists who should know better, says Mises, incautiously slip into dealing with equilibrium 'as if it were a real entity' and not a 'mere mental tool'.[6] In particular, people look at the imaginary state of equilibrium and attempt to apply mathematical analysis to it while disregarding the motive forces that power the economic process.

The introduction of mathematical techniques is probably an inevitable feature of general equilibrium theory. The starting assumption of smooth supply and demand schedules naturally suggests that a dose of elementary calculus can reveal precisely how any market will respond to a change in the data; and the notion that all markets are interconnected cries out for the use of simultaneous equations that can be solved to reveal the prices and traded quantities in each market that are consonant with the general equilibrium state.

Thus, concludes Mises, general-equilibrium economists find themselves putting numbers on things that exist only in the mind. This is a serious error, because it ignores the reality of how human beings actually choose, and thus misrepresents the entire purpose and practice of economics. The trappings of mathematics might make it look as if the adherents of this approach have discovered the same kind of functional relationships that can be found in the natural sciences; but unfortunately the mathematics is being applied only to a mental construction and not to the real world at all. These 'mathematical economists', says Mises,

deal with this evenly rotating economy – they call it the static state – as if it were something really existing. Prepossessed by the fallacy that economics is to be treated with mathematical methods, they concentrate their efforts upon the analysis of static states ... But this mathematical treatment virtually avoids any reference to the real problems of economics.[7]

Although the mathematics of growth equilibrium and of 'dynamics' might appear to be even more sophisticated, their essential hollowness is just the same.

Different values. No amount of statistics, believes Mises, can get round the essential point different people have different values and that the response of one set of individuals to market changes may not be the same as the response of others. There are no mathematical certainties in economic life. Hence:

The economists who want to substitute 'quantitative economics' for what they call 'qualitative economics' are utterly mistaken. There are, in the field of economics, no constant relations, and consequently, no measurement is possible ... Different individuals value the same things in a different way, and valuations change with the same individuals with changing conditions.[8]

The attempt to attach a figure to the responsiveness of the demand for potatoes to incomes, for example, is an absurdity. Not only does it require the artificial condition of *ceteris paribus* which alerts us to its hypothetical nature right away, but different people, on different incomes, at different times, would respond quite differently in any case. Statistical measures of the 'marginal propensity to consume' potatoes or the 'marginal propensity to save' income might describe how a particular group of people have acted in the past, but they can certainly never furnish us with the sort of 'constants' that the physicist finds in the natural world, because human behaviour is not constant. What we find in the economic data of the past is no indication of how different sets of people, facing different conditions and at a different time, have acted or will act in the future.

Precision or pattern? Statistics and measurement, then, have a limited role in economics, according to Mises. Statistics cannot help us predict with accuracy the effect of economic changes, because all such changes take time, because what happens depends upon the choices of unique individuals facing an array of options that is never again repeated precisely, and because each outcome will be conditioned by intervening changes and by the complex and particular circumstances which prevail in the economy at that moment alone. The attempts of macroeconomic economists to establish statistical relationships between economic magnitudes are therefore misleading in the extreme, and actually cloud our understanding of what is really happening when markets adjust. There are no constants in economics: quantitative measurement is inevitably restricted to historical events only, and tells us nothing about an inherently uncertain future in which the complex intermingling of different and changing human values and actions must decide the outcome.

Mises's thoroughgoing rejection of measurement and statistical methods as practiced in general equilibrium theory raises once again the question of whether prediction is ever possible in economics. The answer which Mises appears to give is that prediction is possible, but only in a rather broad form, and never with mathematical certainty or precision. If the makers of designer jeans raise their prices, for example, we can be fairly confident that demand will fall as the less enthusiastic buyers drop out of the market. Precisely what price rise will produce precisely what effect, however, cannot be predicted and would not be repeated from one situation to the next. Or again, Mises predicts (as we shall see later) that an expansion of bank credit sets of the expansion and later contraction of business that is known as the trade cycle. Mises never suggests that it is possible to predict exactly how deep or how long the cycle will be; but he certainly regards it as an established empirical fact that the link exists.

Mises's student, F.A. Hayek, introduced the notion of 'pattern prediction' to illustrate the limited but important prediction that is possible in the social sciences such as economics.[9] It is, he explains, sometimes possible to predict the general *pattern* of behaviour in a human group, even though the exact behaviour of any individual within the group might be impossible to observe or predict with accuracy. Thus we can accept that the action of any *individual* is impossible to predict (since even the individual concerned might not know how he or she would react until actually faced with a particular choice), but still detect some regularities in human behaviour and thus in the response of markets to events. Mises did not use the phrase 'pattern prediction' himself, and indeed many of his supporters initially regarded Hayek's description of it as a radical departure from Mises's own method. Some still do, arguing that if it is impossible to predict the actions of any one individual, then it must be similarly impossible to predict the actions of any *group* of individuals, no matter how large.

Nevertheless, the concept of pattern prediction has won many supporters, and the fact that we do seem able to detect general patterns in economics has reinforced it, and made many scholars conclude that Mises was too sweeping in his conclusions. However, modern supporters of Mises, who credit him as being the source of so many developments that are only now being 'rediscovered' by economists, have formed the opinion that his work demonstrates an unspoken understanding of the principle that empirical predictions were possible in economics, even though he acknowledged that they could be only *qualitative* in nature, and that it was pointless to search for statistical precision.

THE MOTIVE POWER OF THE MARKET

What is left once we have acknowledged the shortcomings of the equilibrium approach? In answer, Mises proposes that instead of a fruitless search for conditions of stability and balance that must inevitably fail to describe the workings of the economic system, we should instead concentrate on the real forces that promote change and imbalance, and which therefore give rise to the kinds of action we call 'economic'. In place of the concept of equilibrium, we should be exploring the concept of the *market process*, the way in which markets actually adjust. And in so doing, we will discover that the two paradigms yield very different conclusions about what is important in economics.

The market process

It is quite natural that the forces which keep the market in perpetual agitation should be the proper starting-point for economics. Economics is, after all, a science of human action, and

Where there is action, there is change. Action is a lever of change.[10]

The role of the economist, therefore, is specifically to study how and why the various actions of diverse individuals, each pursuing their different goals in the marketplace, mesh together to produce the results they do. In other words, economics studies the *market process* by which people adjust their actions in response to events, including the actions of others. But clearly, the idea that the market is a continuing process of change is starkly incompatible with any notion of a world that is static, balanced, and in permanent equilibrium. And the research strategies suggested by the two approaches are just as divergent.

This is not to rule out the possibility of equilibrating *forces* being at work in the marketplace. Where there are shortages, prices might well tend to rise and so induce buyers to cut back and sellers to produce more. Yet that is not to say that perfect balance can ever be achieved, since the exact responses of buyers and sellers to shortages or higher prices are not mechanical and might even promote further imbalance (as when a shortage of sugar, to take our earlier example, causes people to

185

stockpile it regardless of price), and the return to a balanced market could easily be knocked off course by outside changes in events (such as a government report showing that sugar is bad for health) or in other markets (rising sugar prices inducing entrepreneurs to develop new sugar substitutes, for example). When dealing with markets, therefore, we need to be aware of the forces that keep events in continual motion as well as those pulling them into balance.

One market? For his part, Mises is convinced in the existence of strong equilibrating forces – in the tendency, for example, for local shortages or surpluses to be wiped out by people shifting commodities in or out of the region so as to take advantage of higher or lower prices, a movement which in turn will tend to make prices equal in every part of the market. This 'law of one price' is part of the theory that he says can be deduced logically from the nature of action: action aims at securing a psychological or economic gain, and wherever there are market imbalances there are gains to be made by those shrewd enough to see them and satisfy them.

The existence of equilibrating forces, however, does not mean that equilibrium is anywhere to be found. However straightforward is the 'simple truth' of the law of one price, the actual phenomenon is less easy to detect in practice. Our recognition of it is confused by the complexity of the variables involved – in the costs of information and transport, the non-homogeneous nature of most commodities, the institutional barriers (such as immigration laws, import restrictions, and price regulations) raised against the process, and of course the rich variety of intervening events that make the course of the adjustment uncertain at any moment.

To revert to the analogy of the ping-pong ball: however strongly the force of gravity acts to pull the ball towards a state of rest on the ground, the force of the water keeps it bobbing in the air, never resting as long as the process continues. Likewise, the fact that Mises views the market as a *continuing* process suggests that, however strong the equilibrating forces, the absence of equilibrium and the forces which cause it are in his judgement the more interesting phenomena:

186

On the market agitation never stops. The imaginary construction of the evenly rotating economy has no counterpart in reality.[11]

Thus we can see why the proper study of economics is this concatenation of the actions of many different individuals; how individuals respond and adjust to the continual unfolding of the human and natural events that surround them:

The market is not a place, a thing, or a collective entity. The market is a process, activated by the interplay of the individuals . . . [12]

Or again:

The market is not a place; it is a *process*, it is the way in which, by selling and buying, by producing and consuming, the individuals contribute to the total workings of society.[13]

The critical importance of time

Even though it is hardly mentioned in the mainstream text-books, the factor of *time* must clearly assume a central importance if we are to understand the functioning of this market process.

Following Böhm-Bawerk, Mises points out that all action takes time. While it is in progress, other events can change, and even when the action has achieved its effect, new developments can occur and ruin the result, requiring the individual to take yet further, remedial action to improve matters. The various ends to which people direct their economic actions, therefore, will not all be reached. Some action will fail in its objectives because of unexpected events, both natural and human.

For example, it may take weeks, months, or years to gear up a new production process. Yet the future profits anticipated from this lengthy task can be dashed away even before it is complete. Any number of factors, such as changes in consumer tastes or the discovery of revolutionary and cheaper production methods, could make the whole process pointless. Even where the productive machinery is successfully completed and working, there is no guarantee that things will turn out as its builders

187

planned. A flourishing business looking forward to a bright future can be ruined by a change in the law, by improvements in competing products, by accidents, or a host of other factors. The satisfaction derived from any action may be only temporary.

The passage of *time*, then, must be a crucial element in economic analysis, not a mere incidental. During the time it takes for people to recognize market changes and to adjust their production or consumption to take advantage of them, events may turn yet again and require still further adjustments which in turn are prey to yet other developments. Not just natural phenomena, but *competition* from other individuals, keeps this process in motion; the fact that one individual or firm is known to be setting up a new production process, for example, could induce others to look for cheaper or faster methods that in turn causes the first to review, abandon, or accelerate its plans. The determination of *prices*, similarly, is not a smooth or instant adjustment towards some 'equilibrium price', but yet one more *process* which depends upon changing events and different human appraisals of them. All of this is lost in the textbook world of equilibrium what was drawn up by the classical and neoclassical economists. It is, protests Mises, a crass mistake to underestimate the pivotal role of time in economic life:

The classical economists failed to recognize the essential importance of time, which manifests its effect directly or indirectly in every exchange . . . economic theory has failed to see the importance of the fact that a shorter or a longer period of time must go by before the equilibrium of the market, once it has been disturbed by emergence of new data, can again be established.[14]

The speculative nature of action. In Mises's view, the preoccupation with equilibrium theory has blinded many people to the essentially uncertain world in which individuals go about their economic business. In the static construction, everything is known and certain, and markets return to a predictable point of balance after any disturbance. In reality, the outcome of our actions is far from secure. Some action will succeed, some will fail.

Whether an action will produce a profit or a loss depends on the outcome of a continual *process* in which people form opinions about what is likely to occur, and act on the strength of those speculations. Yet there is no way to know the precise outcome in advance.

Every action is a speculation, *ie* guided by a definite opinion concerning the uncertain conditions of the future. Even in short-run activities this uncertainty prevails. Nobody can know whether some unexpected fact will not render vain all that he has provided for the next day or the next hour.[15]

As we shall see in the next chapter, this speculation and the actions taken on the basis of it is the driving force of the market process.

CONCLUSION

The general equilibrium analysis, then, is to Mises a tool that can be very useful for the understanding of change, but is just as frequently the source of wild misunderstandings about the way in which markets work.

As long as we remember that the equilibrium economy is an imaginary and hypothetical construction, its patent absurdities can be overlooked. When we start to regard it as a description of the real world, however, we become swept up in those same absurdities, to the detriment of our understanding. For the equilibrium world is one of unchanging certainty: there are no risks to be taken, no prospect of profits to be grasped, because it is a world of perfect balance in which tomorrow is just like today. The changes and the opportunities that actually motivate human beings are nowhere to be found. Nor is the recognition that actions take time and might therefore be thwarted along the way, a phenomenon that in reality keeps markets and economies in constant motion.

Yet, very often, the equilibrium model is actually set up as a proper goal of economic policy. It is supposed that this imaginary world of balance, implying as it does the absence of surpluses and shortages, can be created deliberately and

189

should be created deliberately. Unfortunately, the attempt to create that imaginary world would require the destruction of everything that drives real-world markets. The result has been seen many times in the various efforts of governments all over the globe to design a perfectly balanced economy by conscious central planning and the suppression of individual entrepreneurship.

CHAPTER NINE

Entrepreneurship, Profit, and Loss

No 'automatic' and 'anonymous' forces actuate the 'mechanism' of the market. The only factors directing the market and determining prices are purposive acts of men.[1]

In the dead world of the equilibrium model, the profit element has little importance. Textbook explanations of 'perfect competition' suggest that in the marketplace, profit is merely what is left to suppliers after they have paid their capital, labour, and distribution costs: a humble residue in the production equation. Competition, moreover, will ensure that it is similar for everyone, and beaten down to the lowest level that will still tempt suppliers to remain in the market.

So widespread is the use and misuse of this classical framework that much of contemporary economic thinking quite ignores the motive force of profit, the role of entrepreneurship, and the balance of risk and reward facing all who take part in the uncertain business of business. When profit is merely a mathematical residue that can be calculated in advance, and when nobody can expect to derive more than a 'normal' return because of the swift operation of perfect competition, there can be little spur to innovation and improvement. Successful business practice in this classical world boils down to being a careful calculator of costs and revenues; the skill, entrepreneurial drive, and simple luck that produces success in the *real* world are nowhere to be seen.

Mises has made a great contribution to economic theory by reminding us of the *human motivations* that are nowhere to be found in the classical system but which in reality provide the motive power to the market process. To him, profit and loss are not dead mathematical facts like the height of the Empire State building; they have a meaning which motivates individuals to engage in the economic activities which economists seek to

191

understand. His radical departure from the lifeless formalism of the textbooks provided a firm foundation for the vigorous debate on the nature and importance of entrepreneurship that is occurring today.[2]

THE MEANING OF ENTREPRENEURSHIP

The economist who rejects the imaginary constructions of the economics textbooks discovers a world of change and uncertainty. The market in reality is a concatenation of the actions of many and varied individuals. What happens at one instant will shape how people will react the next; and that in turn will raise new opportunities, create new prospects, and provoke people to act in new ways that could not have been fully foreseen at the outset.

Correct anticipations

It is from this uncertainty about the future conditions of supply and demand in the marketplace that Mises's notion of entrepreneurial profit and loss is derived. For an entrepreneur will make a profit only if he or she anticipates future market conditions better than others.

Production of any commodity requires complex choices and procedures; complementary factors of production must be brought together in the right way, a process which might well take some time. To be successful, the producer must be able to sell the final product at a price which, allowing for the time difference, is higher than the cost of the various inputs. This in turn, requires that a number of guesses about the future should be good ones: not an easy task, since during the production process it is quite possible that the costs of inputs might rise, that other entrepreneurs may enter the market and bid for customers, or that new and better products are developed. Even then, when the final product is marketed, it might well not tempt consumers at the proposed price for a variety of reasons: they might simply not share the entrepreneur's high opinion of it, might have by then moved on to newer fashions, or might be having to economize because of the collapse of a large national employer.

Correctly anticipating future market conditions can therefore be in large measure a matter of luck, but it is also something of a skill. The skill to seek out the cheapest combination of inputs and the cheapest sources, to anticipate whether the cost of inputs are likely to rise, and to judge whether consumers will in fact want the product at the proposed price at the end of the day all come into it. Those who anticipate better than others will be able to sell their products at the highest profit; those who incorrectly anticipate market conditions could well make a loss. The fact that future market conditions are necessarily uncertain means that all action, all production, is by nature a speculative venture.

The nature of profit. From this we see that profits are not the 'wage' of the entrepreneur as they are often described in the textbooks. Nor is there any such thing as a 'normal' rate of profit on capital invested, as is commonly suggested. In the real world, profit is not so impersonal. Whether the entrepreneur will make a profit or a loss on the resources he or she deploys depends not upon inevitable and mechanical laws of fate but on the free choices of consumers and other producers. Even if a production process generates profits today, it may not do so in the market conditions prevailing tomorrow; indeed, the fact that one person is making profits will induce others to enter the market and compete for the same revenues. There is consequently a tendency for all entrepreneurial profits to disappear. Far from being the 'normal' return on an investment, entrepreneurial profits are inherently temporary, something dependent on the whims of the consumers:

it is absurd to speak of a 'rate of profit' or a 'normal rate of profit' or an 'average rate of profit'. Profit is not related to or dependent on the amount of capital employed by the entrepreneur. Capital does not 'beget' profit. Profit and loss are entirely determined by the success or failure of the entrepreneur to adjust production to the demand of the consumers. There is nothing 'normal' in profits and there can never be 'equilibrium' in regard to them.[3]

Everyone is an entrepreneur

When Mises uses the terms 'entrepreneur' and 'speculator', we must remember that his definition of them is a technical one and not the same as the ordinary meaning of the word in everyday speech. When ordinary people talk about 'speculators', for example, they probably have in mind a distinct group of bankers, stockbrokers, or currency dealers. When the same people talk of 'entrepreneurs', they conjure up an image of a small group of smart operators who have a keen eye for the main chance, who have more initiative and venturesomeness than others, and who have the power and ability to create new products or develop revolutionary new production processes.

To Mises, however, all action is a speculation, and all people are to some degree entrepreneurs, seeking to use their skills and resources to produce future profits, even if those profits are only psychological and not financial. Entrepreneurship, to him, is a term which signifies a particular *function* in economic life, not one which delineates a particular *group* of people. The entrepreneurial *function* will continue even when today's bankers, stockbrokers, and currency dealers are all dead, and would continue even if such professions had never existed.

Functional overlap. Although everyday language and naive economics often divides the world into discrete groups of entrepreneurs, landowners, or capitalists, the good economist has to be more precise. In the first place, notes Mises, these categories cannot distinguish particular *people* but refer only to different economic *functions*. In the second place, there is considerable overlap and complementarity between each one.

For example, there can be no such thing as a 'pure' entrepreneur. A 'pure' entrepreneur would not own any capital – that is reserved for the 'pure' capitalist – and so presumably must borrow the funds necessary to seize a market opportunity and direct production in a particular way. If successful, the entrepreneur makes a profit and thus becomes a capitalist, owning capital in the form of cash in the bank. If that same venture brings only losses, it becomes evident that it is the capitalists who lent the funds who have borne the real risk of the speculation, for it is upon them that the losses fall. So again, the two functions are inextricably alloyed: there is no such thing as a 'pure' entrepreneur, and no such thing as a 'pure' capitalist either. Similarly, a landowner takes the risk that harvest will continue to be good or that the rents people are prepared to pay for a particular patch of land will remain high, which is another act of speculation. Each worker's training for particular types of work is also a speculative investment, since the wages which can be commanded for a particular job will depend upon the changing conditions of the market at the time; so even the worker is to some extent an entrepreneur and a speculator.

The technical sense in which Mises speaks of 'the entrepreneur' is sufficiently far away from its traditional usage, in fact, that Mises urges a new term to signify those individuals who are eager to profit by adjusting production, and have the power and the initiative to do so: the term 'promoter', he thinks, is a better one for this use.[4]

ENTREPRENEURIAL PROFIT AND LOSS

From this approach it can be seen that Mises's view of entrepreneurship is not just an improvement over the static equilibrium approach that prevailed in his day and is still to be found deeply entrenched as the basis of economics teaching, but a significant departure. For Mises reminds us that there is simply no role for the entrepreneur in a world without change. Not even the dedicated static economist can overlook the actual prevalence and importance of entrepreneurship in the real world, but its very existence implies a crucial defect in the static approach, because entrepreneurship is impossible where the future is fixed and certain.

Anticipation and alertness

Entrepreneurship, says Mises, means acting in the context of the changing conditions of the market. It means acting on the basis of a particular theory about what the future holds, about how people will react to certain events, such as the offer of a new product at a particular price. The entrepreneur's speculation

195

does not have to be completely accurate: costs can be over-estimated, demand can be underestimated, and yet a venture may still prove profitable. But an entrepreneur can profit only if he or she predicts future market conditions better than others. If everyone were to anticipate correctly future prices and demand, the costs of factor inputs would be instantly bid up until there was no profit to be gleaned at the end of the day. If others do not anticipate the future demand, however, they leave the necessary factors still available at a price which allows the entrepreneur to buy them more cheaply than the finished product can be sold.

Mises's student, Israel Kirzner, has developed the theory of entrepreneurship in great depth. In his work, we find a view of the entrepreneur as someone who has a greater *alertness* than others, and who therefore can perceive opportunities for profit, for example, when the arbitrageur makes a profit by buying in one market where a commodity sells cheaply and selling it again in another where a higher price prevails. In that inter-pretation of entrepreneurship, prices are known and the entre-preneur is simply the person who spearheads the process of adjustment.

Although it is primarily a matter of different emphasis, however, Mises's entrepreneur is one who acts not in the context of known prices but against an *uncertain* future. The entrepreneur endeavours to predict the outcome of the various changes that are going on continually in the marketplace; entrepreneurship requires a *choice* between different guesses about what may happen. The motivation to make the guess as good as possible is the prospect of an entrepreneurial profit if it is accurate; and Mises also reminds us that the prospect of making a loss is another powerful motivation to judge the market with care.

The entrepreneur's method. In the real world, the function we generally think of as entrepreneurship is perhaps a mixture of both elements: the alertness to detect opportunities among known facts and the ability to anticipate the future state of an uncertain market.

While certain facts about the conditions currently prevailing in the marketplace can be known, not even the most successful entrepreneur could claim omniscience. Perfect information exists only in the imaginary models of the textbooks, never in reality. What the entrepreneur must start from as the basis for his or her speculation is a set of patchy and incomplete data. Some raw facts such as current prices can be gleaned easily enough, but other things of which the entrepreneur must take account cannot be established so precisely. As we have seen, it is not objective facts, but the subjective meanings people give to facts, the personal values against which they judge events, that determine the course of economic activity.

That subjective element also implies that the conditions prevailing in the market today will never be repeated exactly tomorrow. People and circumstances change, and social phenomena have none of the functional regularity which the natural scientist finds in physical events. Mises has already told us that prediction is impossible in applied economics: so how is the entrepreneur to anticipate future market conditions and grasp the opportunities they present?

The Austrian answer is that successful entrepreneurship is not a matter of scientific knowledge but of insight. The task is to *understand* how people will react to events, to apply one's 'inside knowledge' of how people think in an effort to appreciate what value judgements they will form, what actions they will take, and how they will value the outcome. There can be no scientific certainty, only a conjecture based on the entrepreneur's own appreciation of how other human beings think and act. The Austrians call this process the method of *verstehen*, and it is a principle which is practised by us all as we plan for the future and seek to explain why people acted as they did in the past.

Entrepreneurs and entrepreneurship. Real-world entrepreneurs are often forceful characters and perhaps a vision of the future and the boldness to *make* a certain outcome happen is a necessary part of their personality. Yet we must not confuse this picture of actual entrepreneurs with the *functional* definition of entrepreneurship with which Mises is working.

Nevertheless, Mises clearly believes that some *individuals* have a particular ability to become good entrepreneurs, and the market, in his view, encourages and rewards such people. Those whose anticipations prove correct are rewarded with profits which give them the capital to back more extensive prospects in the next round. Further success reinforces their ability to make more momentous choices in the future.

While this skill is rewarded and reinforced, however, the entrepreneur's success is by no means guaranteed, no matter how much capital he or she has built up. Tomorrow, any entrepreneur can be proved wrong and be ruined. It is the consumers, and not the entrepreneurs, who will decide the outcome.

Profit and consumer satisfaction

We have already seen that 'profit', correctly interpreted, is a psychological phenomenon and not merely a financial one. Every individual acts in order to achieve a profit, meaning an outcome that brings greater satisfaction than the previous state of affairs, not necessarily one which yields simply a financial return. We cannot imagine a world in which people act without the intention of attaining a psychological gain.

In economics, however, we are very much concerned with monetary matters. Catallactics, the science of market exchange, is for Mises

the analysis of those actions which are conducted on the basis of monetary calculation. Market exchange and monetary calculation are inseparably linked together.[5]

It is important to remember, therefore, that the financial gains which accrue to successful entrepreneurs are something more than just a personal gain. The entrepreneur's profits are a *social* phenomenon, expressing the appraisal that others make of his or her contribution to the satisfaction of people's wants. Profits are not necessarily any measure of the happiness which success brings to the entrepreneur, but they certainly reflect others' evaluation of his or her contribution to *their* lives and welfare.

The entrepreneur is the one who decides on the employment of various factors of production, and dedicates them to some specific future product, motivated no doubt by the prospect of financial returns: but whatever the entrepreneur's skill at combining factors of production and correctly anticipating future prices, he or she can succeed only by best serving the consumers. The entrepreneur's profit depends firmly on the consumers' support for the end product.

Profits and progress

Perhaps surprisingly, therefore, a world in which it is possible for some people to pursue financial gain is one where the needs of the general public are more swiftly satisfied. The desire to make financial profits motivates people to act in ways that help the consumers who will pay them:

> thousands of business people are trying day and night to find some new product which satisfies the consumer better or is less expensive to produce, or better *and* less expensive than the existing products. They do not do this out of altruism, they do it because they want to make money.[6]

This is another reason why the imaginary construction of the evenly rotating economy can give us a quite misleading idea of the real-world economy if we take it too literally. In the evenly rotating economy, all future prices are known, and hence the prices of all factor inputs have already been adjusted to that fact; in other words, there are no profits to be made by anyone. Thus, by treating the construction too literally, we completely overlook the driving force of profit and its importance for progress and for the satisfaction of the vast body of consumers. We come easily to the mistaken view that profits are not the motive power behind human advance, but things which occur only because they have been unfairly stolen from other people.

In the related construction of the stationary economy, in which the average level of real incomes never varies, any profit that is gleaned by one entrepreneur can arise only because another makes a loss.

In the real world, the fact that profits are made by one person does not imply an automatic loss for others. To understand why this can be so, one does not need to look much further than the imaginary construction of the progressing economy. In that model, entrepreneurs seize on new capital goods or improved methods and seek complementary factors of production, bidding them up in price and thus adding to the returns or the wages of those who hold or produce them. Inevitably, the benefits of progress are shared by the workers, capitalists, and landowners as well as with the entrepreneurs initiating the change. Profits do not represent the 'exploitation' of any group; on the contrary, the greater the profits to be won, the greater is the increment in general prosperity.[7]

The striving of entrepreneurs for profits is therefore the driving force of the market economy, and the ultimate source of general prosperity, according to Mises. Profits stem only from serving the needs of consumers, and they help *direct resources* by signalling to entrepreneurs where consumer needs are strongest and by giving greater financial influence to those with a proven record of satisfying those needs better than other people.

Entrepreneurial and non-entrepreneurial profits

Mises distinguishes *entrepreneurial* profit and loss from other factors which might affect the entrepreneur's revenues. A loss could arise from the fact that a particular process proved inadequate to produce a commodity, even though the entrepreneur might have been quite right about the strength of the public demand for the good in question. Political events can leave an entrepreneur expropriated. Accidents, such as fires and floods, can bring losses to some entrepreneurs but improve the prospects of their competitors.

Certainly, those entrepreneurs who protect themselves inadequately against technological failures, accidents, or political risks will tend to fare less successfully in the market; but theirs is not an entrepreneurial loss, just as those who benefit from lucky accidents are not enjoying an entrepreneurial gain. The ultimate source from which strictly *entrepreneurial* profit and loss are derived, says Mises, is the uncertainty of the future constellation of demand and supply, and the relative abilities of entrepreneurs to anticipate it accurately.

THE PRICING PROCESS

Success and profit for the entrepreneur, then, require an accurate assessment of the state of the market, and in particular they require a better estimate than others of the price at which consumers will be prepared to purchase a product as and when it can be brought to market. Because Mises's interpretation of the entrepreneur's function and success hinges on prices in this way, his analysis reminds us of another important point that is often concealed by the perfect-competition approach: that prices are not the 'given' outcome of impersonal forces. On the contrary, the determination of prices is itself a *process* which depends entirely on the personal values and the actions of the particular individuals in the marketplace at the time. It is a process in which the entrepreneurs play a leading role.[8]

The leading edge

In the perfect world of orthodox economics, knowledge itself is perfect, with everyone in the marketplace sharing an accurate picture of the state of the market now and in the future. But a moment's reflection reveals the absurdity of this assumption: if everyone were blessed with the same view of the future, prices would adjust immediately to meet it. Any change in the data would similarly be accommodated in an instant as everyone recognized the effect of the change and correctly anticipated how all others would react to it. In the real world, however, such omniscience does not and could not exist.

The adjustment avalanche. The actual determination of prices is very different. Markets in the real world, says Mises, are peopled with individuals who do not have the same information about market conditions, and even if they did, would appraise it differently. Changes in the data (such as the interruption of trading links by foreign wars, new fashions, or the discovery of new mineral resources) are first anticipated or perceived by only a few individuals, who might well come to different conclusions about their importance. The more astute individuals see the ramifications of the changes sooner and more accurately than others, and so succeed better in the actions they base on that understanding. Gradually, more and more individuals will follow, making the adjustment more and more general.

The effect on prices, then, is far from instantaneous or uniform, but more like an avalanche where one falling rock dislodges others which in turn jolt still more into motion. The entrepreneurs lead the process, buying and selling those products which they feel are mispriced as a result of the initial change in the data. Competition between them, and then the competition of those who follow, bids prices up or down. Next, the entrepreneurs will seek to acquire factors of production to take advantage of the new opportunities which the initial change reveals to them, and competition will again bid up these prices a little at first, and then more, until manufacturers of producers' goods perceive the demand and expand their output to meet it. Lastly, the entrepreneurs will promote their products to consumers, but once again competition will bid down the prices of the consumers' goods they sell.

A complex social process

The pricing process is therefore a very complex process indeed. Changes in the data produce opportunities for profit that set entrepreneurs into action and prices into motion. But prices will adjust at different speeds, creating as they do so yet further opportunities and initiating yet further entrepreneurial activity and yet further price movements. In the meantime, changes in other market data will occur, setting off another train of equally complex adjustments. Furthermore, the nature and speed of each adjustment will depend on the individuals involved and how they perceive and evaluate the opportunities presented. To Mises,

The pricing process is a social process. It is consummated by an interaction of all members of the society.[9]

Classical economic analysis, resting on the assumptions of perfect information, identical suppliers, identical consumers, and homogeneous products, entails the logical conclusion that when market conditions change, prices adjust instantly and uniformly. Yet the first result denies the importance of history, while the second says that geography is no good either. In real markets, both time and place are crucial: dealing with local or anticipated changes in market conditions is the foundation of entrepreneurs' success and gives the market economy its driving force.

No firm prices. It is wise to remember that there is no such thing as 'the' price of a commodity. The price of eggs, for instance, will depend on their quality, their size, on the competition between suppliers and consumers, and on the prices of alternative foodstuffs. It depends on when the sale is made and on the conditions of various markets at the time. It depends upon the volume of the sale, since most sellers will be glad to offer lower rates to their bulk customers such as restaurants and hotels. And it depends on where the sale takes place: prices vary not just between the city and the rural areas, but from town to town and even between different shops in the same street, depending on the attitudes of each seller and their appraisal of the market conditions of the hour.

To Mises, therefore, talk of 'the' price of a commodity is simple nonsense, betraying a misleading and simplistic concept of how prices are determined. Similarly, the attempt to treat prices statistically, to compute price averages or explore historical changes in 'the' price of this or that commodity are similarly misguided. Statistical methods, lumping together many different transactions, serve only to disguise the intricate workings of the market process that it is the object of true economics to study.

Prices and individual values

The formation of prices is always determined by the subjective value judgements of individuals, avers Mises. The relationship, however, is somewhat complex. Exchanges, and hence the objective exchange ratios that we call prices, take place because people value the same commodity *differently*: prices are not a *measure* of value but the product of *differences* in value.[10] Although the relationship between individuals' values and the prices of consumption goods is complex, its existence and primacy are both clear enough.

What factors determine the prices of production goods? The relationship with individual values is still strong, but less direct. Production goods are held only for the consumption goods that they engender, and are consequently appraised on the basis the expected prices of their products. So the prices of production goods are still linked to the pattern of individual values, but through the intermediary of consumption good prices.

The process of price determination is the same for production goods as it is for consumption goods. Entrepreneurs, detecting opportunities among the changing data of the market, bid for the land, capital, or labour they need to capture them. They have to compete for these resources with existing users and with their rivals, but what they are prepared to pay is limited by their anticipation of the future prices that can be commanded by the ultimate products. An entrepreneur with an overoptimistic idea of future prices will be prepared to pay more for the factors of production, but will suffer losses when the final product is marketed, and thus will eventually drop out of the competition. An entrepreneur who makes too pessimistic a guess will equally be prized out of the competition because he or she will lose land, equipment, and workers to others who are prepared to bid higher for them on the basis of a view of the outcome that happens to prove more accurate.

Satisfying the most urgent needs

Entrepreneurship, then, brings the prices of production goods into synchrony with the prices of consumption goods, since overbidding and underbidding are systematically eliminated. Like everyone else, the entrepreneurs seek the greatest gain from their actions, and so operate where they perceive the greatest discrepancy between consumer needs and present practice. Thus, they will adjust production to meet the most urgent needs first, bidding factors out of the hands of those who have been applying them to less profitable uses:

To the entrepreneur of capitalist society a factor of production through its price sends out a warning: Don't touch me, I am earmarked for the satisfaction of another, more urgent need.[11]

At the same time, the competition to supply the market with the most profitable products makes the prices of these consumption goods tend to fall. Competition and entrepreneurship, in the end, direct production to satisfy the most urgent needs in the cheapest way. Entrepreneurs may be motivated by the anticipation of personal profit; but when they detect consumer needs and bid for the factors of production necessary to satisfy them, they are effectively acting as mandataries of the consumers. They succeed if and when their actions are in concert with consumer needs.

The entrepreneurial function, then, promotes the general wealth of society. Those still trapped in the static mentality might overlook the fact, warns Mises, but the adjustment of production to the changing circumstances and opportunities of the market is a business that is in constant, daily motion. Entrepreneurs are perpetually on the watch for opportunities in which they can benefit by helping others, and the result of this process is to increase the prosperity of the society as a whole:

The development of capitalism consists in everyone's having the right to serve the customer better and/or more cheaply. And this method, this principle, has, within a comparatively short time, transformed the whole world.[12]

It has, for example, generated a prosperity that has enabled human numbers to grow far beyond former limits.

Entrepreneurs and promoters play a crucial role in adjusting production so that consumers obtain the best products as cheaply as possible. If we fail to recognize this, we find it hard to explain the profits that accrue to actual entrepreneurs and promoters in the marketplace. Trapped in the static mentality, we suppose that the market does not change and that production therefore never needs to adjust, or we imagine that the market's response to any change in the data is instantaneous and automatic. Since entrepreneurship has no function in the static world, people are likely to side with Marx when they meet real-life entrepreneurs and promoters, and to explain their profits as derived from the 'exploitation' of other, genuine workers. What other explanation can there be than that their wealth is stolen by way of their superiour power? But in fact, the recognition that the market is in constant motion, and that the adjustment of production to deliver consumer goods in the cheapest way is a continual and complex task, must quickly remind us that the entrepreneurial function is not only an important one, but one that consumers reward in a quite open and voluntary way.

Entrepreneurship and society

Entrepreneurship, then, is a social process. As such, it is affected seriously by other social events. This is a subject upon which Mises himself says little, although it has now become a topic of deep debate among his followers.

If entrepreneurship is such a valuable function, the question is how the supply of entrepreneurs can be boosted. The right social conditions will plainly influence the matter; for example, a postwar economy where rationing has just ended might provide a wide range of opportunities for entrepreneurship, and so encourage sizeable numbers of people to enter the field.[13]

Education might be another factor which influences the prevalence of entrepreneurship. Mises argues that poor education does not in fact hold back entrepreneurs, and that the uneducated individual can become rich just as the well-educated person can become poor. Nevertheless, attitudes of educationalists towards entrepreneurship, the degree of self-confidence encouraged by teachers, and even how the workings of the economic system are taught in schools, could all have importance consequences.

In the wider context, an intellectual environment in which attacks on business practice are common is likely to have a dampening effect on entrepreneurship. If this leads to controls on prices and profits, the depressive effect will be even more pronounced. If 'competition' is thought of as a distasteful alternative to planning and if its social function is overlooked, still more damage is done. For this reason, it is essential to break out of the neoclassical mould and understand the true social importance of entrepreneurship, competition, and the profit motive.

CHAPTER TEN

Competition, Co-operation, and the Consumer

> There is nothing automatic or mysterious about the operation of the market. The only forces determining the continually fluctuating state of the market are the value judgements of the various individuals and their actions as directed by these value judgements. The ultimate factor in the market is the striving of each man to satisfy his needs and wants in the best possible way. Supremacy of the market is tantamount to the supremacy of the consumers.[1]

For Mises, competition is something that is possible only within the context of market changes. It is part of the process of entrepreneurship, and its nature determines how entrepreneurial activity shapes the nature and direction of production.

The chimera of perfect competition

Once again, the nature of competition is often misunderstood because of the prevalence of static approaches to it. In the 'perfect competition' model of the textbooks, all suppliers are identical and consumers are therefore indifferent between them, knowledge of consumer tastes and preferences is shared equally by suppliers, the goods being traded are homogeneous, and the market is freely open to everyone. Consequently, any change in the market data leads to an instant adjustment of prices and profits back to the 'perfect competition' level which is just sufficient to induce suppliers to remain in the market.

Generations of scholars and their epigones have presumed on the basis of this classical analysis that any differences between suppliers, any natural obstacles to people freely entering markets, and any large profits enjoyed by entrepreneurs must represent market 'imperfections' or 'failures'. But in fact, competition is meaningless in a world in which there are no differences to be traded on, no obstacles to be overcome, and no gains from superior service. Competition does not exist at all where, for example, prices are uniform and the goods traded are identical, market competition is *all about* suppliers continually trying to outdo one another by supplying better goods at cheaper prices, not the same good at the same price. It is a *process* which promotes continual advancement and change, not a lifeless form that inhabits an imaginary world.[2]

COMPETITION AND THE CONSUMERS

The role of competition in the market economy is therefore closely connected with the role of the entrepreneur. It is part of the process by which entrepreneurial activity prevents the persistence of a production structure that cannot serve the consumers with the products they want in the cheapest way. Entrepreneurs must compete against one another in the effort to win the resources they need to structure production according to the opportunities they recognize and the market demand they perceive as coming from consumers. The greater the scope for competition, the more imaginative do entrepreneurs have to be in assessing the needs of consumers and adjusting production to meet them. The more active the competition, the quicker and shrewder do entrepreneurs have to be to succeed in their activity, and thus the quicker and better are the needs of consumers met.

Mises's successor, F.A. Hayek, has built on this view to characterize competition quite explicitly as a *discovery procedure*. Under the stimulus of competition, entrepreneurs approach consumers with different ranges of products, and quickly learn from the result where the needs of consumers really lie. Similarly, competition forces entrepreneurs to seek out the cheapest production processes so that they can fulfil consumers' needs in the cheapest possible way.[3]

Consumer sovereignty

Mises agrees that competition is a process of selection, but argues strongly that we must remember who does the selecting.

To him, decisions are not made by the entrepreneurs, but by the consumers. Ultimately, it is their choices that will decide what production processes will be expanded and which will shrink, who will become rich and run the big factories, who will end up scrubbing the floor.

Because Mises has reminded us many times that the entrepreneurs are the real 'driving force' of the market, and that it is they who arrange for the factors of production to be combined in new ways to execute their particular anticipation of future prices, it would be easy to get the impression that he assumes them to be the real powers behind the market economy. His intention, however, is quite otherwise. Entrepreneurs might steer the ship, he declares, but they are nevertheless subject to the orders of the captain in the shape of the consumers.

The process by which the consumers give their orders to the entrepreneurs, promoters, and capitalists is straightforward and familiar. But Mises insists that it is more powerful than people commonly suppose, and that if businessmen do not 'strictly obey' the orders of the public, they suffer losses and are superseded by others at their eminent position at the helm.[4]

Consumers, naturally, patronize those shops in which they can buy what they want at the cheapest prices. Those who gain their business will succeed, those who do not will have to drop out of the market; and the same is true for the farmers, wholesalers, and manufacturers who supply the retail outlets. Manufacturers too will be looking for the best and cheapest source of supply, and so the orders of the consumers are transmitted through them right back to the suppliers of production goods such as land and capital equipment. Thus, the consumers ultimately determine not only the prices of consumers' goods, but the prices of all factors of production and the income of everyone involved in the productive process. They make people rich or poor, and determine what is to be produced and in what quantities. They are hard bosses, not caring about past merits or expensive investments if new suppliers can better satisfy their whims. Entrepreneurs and capitalists, nevertheless, must simply obey; any deviation or mistake means that they will be quickly supplanted by competitors.

Sources of imperfection. As Mises sketches this process in *Human Action*, it looks rather like a smooth, automatic, and supremely efficient mechanism. But this interpretation would be discordant with his more general view of the market process as something which is decidedly not perfect and mechanical. The information upon which entrepreneurs act, for example, is of course neither perfect nor complete. Their estimate of what the consumers really want and what they will still be wanting at the conclusion of what might be a fairly lengthy production process is essentially a matter of conjecture, not a question of fact. They must try to anticipate the subjective preferences of consumers as they are and will be, to put themselves into the minds of others and try to guess intelligently how they will act: and to do this against the backcloth of changing prices and other market conditions.

It is evident, then, that entrepreneurs can make mistakes about what consumers need most urgently and would be willing to pay for, that accidents can happen, and that changing events can make existing plans useless. So the competitive, entrepreneurial process does not guarantee that consumers' needs are instantly and automatically satisfied. Mises's description of the process, if it implies that the exact wishes of consumers are always met, would therefore be overdrawn: his wider belief that there is nothing automatic about market adjustments must outweigh his enthusiasm on this point.

Inequalities among consumers

Mises's picture of consumer sovereignty, with ordinary buyers in the marketplace giving the 'orders' to direct how capital and human energy should be applied, looks very democratic, and he does in fact refer to the analogy of an election.[5] Thus, the market is seen as a referendum that is repeated each day, one in which every penny spent by consumers goes to determine the structure of production and who is to remain at the helm of each element within it. This has subsequently become a favourite theme with free-market economists, who contrast the rather weak and sporadic opportunities people have to vote for a package of many different policies in political elections with the daily opportunity consumers have to 'vote' with their money for individual goods in a varied marketplace.

Unequal democracy? But Mises was conscious of the fact that some critics, agreeing up to a point with this election metaphor, were turning it into the argument that incomes should be deliberately equalized and not left to the market to decide. For they concur with the merits of an equal 'democratic' say in deciding the structure of production, but object that this is not in fact found in the present operation of this market 'election' system on the grounds that different consumers have different purchasing power, and therefore a different ability to affect the structure of the production process. Thus, they insist, it is rich people and not the mass of consumers who really control the market economy, since in the referendum to decide what should be done, the rich have more votes than the poor.

Mises answers this criticism by observing that the analogy, although it makes a useful point, is far from perfect. Actually, people on modest incomes have a much greater leverage than they could enjoy in a political election between different packages of economic planning strategies and social policies. The reason is that in the market, each money ballot has its effect, and those who want to spend their income on minority tastes are free to do so, whereas in the political arena the minority must put up with what the majority decide, and their votes count for nothing. Even those of modest means, therefore, exert a direct effect on the allocation of productive resources, and their influence is not simply swamped as the influence of political minorities can be. The analogy, like all others, has limits that must not be ignored, or we will be misled into overestimating the power of the wealthy.

Even so, argues Mises, the analogy of the election obscures the fact that the market is a continuing process in which today's position has been determined by previous events. Some consumers being more wealthy than others does not undermine the power wielded by the general mass of ordinary people, since

to be rich and to earn a higher income is, in the market economy, already the outcome of a previous election. The only means to acquire wealth and to preserve it . . . is to serve the consumers in the best and cheapest way.[6]

Thus, wealthy consumers with more power to cast their ballot in the daily decision-making process of the market have become wealthy only because they in turn have obeyed the orders of other consumers. More important still, they will not, says Mises, remain wealthy if they do not *continue* to serve their fellow consumers. When we trace the source of any individual's economic power back in this way, we find that it lies firmly in the hands of the consumers.

Business power

Mises alleges that it is possible to make similar mistakes about the apparent power enjoyed by large enterprises. A cursory view certainly suggests that it is the leaders of big business, and not the general body of consumers, who have the real power and make the important economic decisions. It might seem that business leaders alone have the power to make people rich or poor, depending upon where they assign them on the ladder of production. But once again, Mises reminds us that even large businesses are utterly beholden to the desires of the consumers. Only if they do what is necessary to induce consumers to continue patronizing them will they continue in business; it is consumers who ultimately decide how they operate. For example,

It is *not* the Hollywood film corporation that pays the wages of a movie star; it is the people who pay admission to the movies.[7]

From this point of view it strikes Mises as remarkable that big business should be the object of bitter attacks from those who regard themselves as spokesmen for the general mass of society. It is a characteristic feature of big businesses that they have grown big by addressing their production specifically to the mass market – by serving that same mass of the people.[8] They make large profits because large numbers of people purchase their products voluntarily, but they will continue to prosper only if they continue to do so. Far from being opposed to the interests of the general public, they exist to serve them.

Competition in operation

Competition in the marketplace, what Mises calls 'catallactic competition' is unlike many of the other things we call 'competition', and careless use of the terminology can lead us to mistaken views of how it operates. Its function is not to find the best, like a prize fight to find the strongest boxer, rather to stimulate continuing improvement and to promote the best satisfaction of the consumers given the conditions prevailing at the time. It is a continuing process in which sellers continually try to surpass one another by offering better or cheaper goods and services to the public, and bidding higher prices for the factor inputs they need to advance their ideas. Market competition is not a contest in which only one person can win at the expense of everyone else, but a continuing process of adjustment in which entrepreneurs benefit by benefiting others, until their contribution is surpassed by another.

Competition is necessarily 'imperfect'. In order to accomplish this function of advancing the material progress of mankind, competition does not have to be 'perfect' in the sense used by the neoclassical textbooks, and in fact it could never work if those conditions were met. It works by sellers offering consumers a choice of *different* products, by continually improving what is on offer, not selling the same product at the same price as everyone else. As Mises expresses it:

Freedom of competition does not mean that you can succeed simply by imitating or copying precisely what someone else has done.[9]

Innovation, improvement, and change in the products on offer is what real-life market competition is all about. Similarly, we must depart from other assumptions of the mainstream textbooks and remember, for example, that free entry to markets is an absurd assumption. It is rare for entry to any market to be perfectly open to every individual; only a few people can compete in the labour market as opera singers, for example. Yet competition still operates, despite such natural limits on the actual numbers of service providers who are able to compete in any sector.

Technical innovations, suggests Mises, have the tendency to throw up new opportunities that did not previously exist, and therefore to increase the scope for wider numbers of individuals to become involved in the competitive entrepreneurial process. It might be added to Mises's remarks that technical innovation is often one of the *results* of entrepreneurs' competitive urge to serve the consumer better than others, so the activity might be regarded as self-perpetuating. On the other hand, licensing, protectionism, and other efforts to reduce competition in particular sectors tend to stifle the beneficial social effects of competition along with the competition itself. Mises has no doubt that:

The sharper the competition, the better it serves its social function to improve economic production.[10]

Competition, profits, and wealth

The ability of consumers to assign people to different positions in the social system, and the struggle of entrepreneurs to rise to the top of that system by providing consumers with what they need, are what give competition its driving forces and makes the process work to the general benefit of the society. Once more, however, it is important to remember that the incentives offered in market competition are not the same as those in a fight. Less successful competitors are not eliminated, Mises points out, but they are removed to a more modest place in the economic system. Those who succeed, by contrast, are awarded a better position. The consumers, in buying some products that are offered and rejecting others, are ultimately the ones who determine each individual's position.

It is pointless to rail against the 'injustice' of large profits and large incomes, therefore, because those are the incentive which induce individuals to compete actively to serve the public, and because those rewards are decided not by any elite or accident of birth but by the general mass of consumers. Controls on the level of profits that a successful entrepreneur can retain as a result of his or her service to the public have an effect similar to that we have seen when controls are put on prices: the effect of dampening the enthusiasm of suppliers and potential suppliers to see that consumers get the goods they need.[11]

No lasting wealth. The absence of controls means that people can make sizeable fortunes by successful entrepreneurship. Such wealth is often the target of egalitarian attacks, but Mises is insistent that high earnings and large profits are not granted in perpetuity by the market system. The consumers are hard bosses, and if another individual or firm serves them better or more cheaply tomorrow, their allegiance will switch straight away. Suppliers must therefore be constantly on the watch for changes in the market data that will affect how they are able to serve the consumers; even brief inattention or a mistaken assessment of the importance of changes will erode profits, and could cause entrepreneurs to lose the precious capital they have built up. Large companies are just as susceptible to this effect as small ones: in the competitive market economy, no capital is safe forever.

Even inherited wealth is much less secure than people assume it to be, asserts Mises. Arguments along the lines that one penny invested in the time of Jesus Christ would be worth a huge fortune today ignore the fact that the penny would have to be invested in the right place, secure from bank failures, political uprisings, spendthrift descendants of the investor, and all the other things that can erode a fortune. Only a consistent record in supplying the needs of consumers can be the foundation of lasting wealth.

The abolition of elites. There are, similarly, no lasting elites under the capitalist system. Before the arrival of modern capitalism, economic systems were run on caste or tribal lines. Usually, social status was impossible to change and an individual had to be content with the lot that was assigned by his or her more powerful peers. A significant feature of capitalism, however, is the social mobility it promotes. Individuals who start poor can, by shrewd anticipation of the conditions of the market, become rich. It does not depend on education or social status, only on the ability to see and grasp the opportunities that unfold.

CO-OPERATION IN THE DIVISION OF LABOUR

It may still be difficult, rooted as we are to non-economic ideas of competition, to understand how market competition is simultaneously a form of social *co-operation* in which everyone seems to benefit. To resolve the apparent contradiction in this, it is helpful to examine the co-operative structure which Mises says is the very 'essence of society',[12] namely, the principle of the division of labour. For it is upon this foundation that are built the exchange economy and the trading relationships, entrepreneurship, and competition that we find within it.

Origins of the exchange economy

The division of labour comes about, explains Mises, for a variety of reasons. First, differences in individual ability make it sensible for people to combine to share tasks. Thus, everyone does what they are best at, rather than trying to be completely self-sufficient, and then people exchange what they have produced that is in excess of their own requirements. Second, the unequal distribution of natural resources throughout the globe explains a part of the phenomenon; those close to mineral resources, for example, can co-operate by exchanging what they mine with those who live too far away for easy access to the mineral. Third, there are some tasks which are simply impossible for a single individual to do alone, so that for the task to be accomplished requires different people to take on different parts of it.

These needs and solutions are manifested in the very minute division of labour we have in the market economy today. People have different vocations and specialisms, areas have become predominantly urban or rural, and the use of machinery has allowed complex production processes to be split into a variety of smaller tasks that can be undertaken by different people.

217

Improved productivity. Such specialization allows people to co-operate in their activities and thus to improve the standard of living of everyone. Labour which is divided is more productive than the attempt to be self-sufficient. It means that resources can be exploited that would be forever beyond the grasp of single individuals, and this enhanced productivity, estimates Mises, has produced an increase in wealth that has enabled human society to expand to ten times what was possible before it arrived on the scene.[13]

This greater productivity helps reduce the conflict over resources that would occur in the world of self-sufficiency, since by co-operation, people can expand the production of the commodities they need. As Mises puts it,

where there is division of labour, there is no longer question of the distribution of a supply not capable of enlargement. Thanks to the higher productivity of labour performed under the division of tasks, the supply of goods multiplies.[14]

Competition in exchange

If all individuals could see immediately the best way of co-operating to enlarge the product of their joint labour, and were unanimous in how to divide the product, then it would indeed be a socialist paradise without conflict. However, Mises believes the actual workings of society are quite unlike this. To him, there is no perfect knowledge of what is required nor perfect agreement on how to achieve it. So if the principle of the division of labour is not embarked upon in the pursuit of agreed overall objectives (except in the case of goods that can *only* be produced by co-operation), what *is* its motivation?

Critics of the capitalist system often suggest that the division of labour in the context of private ownership is essentially self-regarding. In that analysis, individuals choose their position in the production structure as best they can, in the hope that they can subsequently wring a profit from other people in the process of exchanging their surplus. Is this capitalist world not one in which conflict and self-interest are in fact the ruling principles? Is personal gain not being pursued at the expense of society?

218

Mises dismisses such criticisms. Society, he reminds us, 'is nothing but the combination of individuals for co-operative effort'.[15] It is mistaken to talk in terms of the interest of a particular individual who offers goods for exchange, being opposed to the 'interests of society'. The principle of exchange is part of the co-operative system. Exchange is voluntary; nobody has to purchase goods they do not want. A profit for the seller does not automatically mean a loss for the buyer. On the contrary, because each person values the commodity traded differently, they both derive a psychic profit from the exchange, and the exchange would not take place unless both sides regarded themselves as better off for it. Exchange implies a mutual gain, not a one-sided attempt to cheat someone else.

To Mises, therefore, the tendency to dismiss the capitalist society based on the division of labour as self-regarding springs from a blindness to the social interdependence of individuals and the position of voluntary exchange in furthering it. As he puts the point:

In the society based on division of labour and co-operation, the interests of all members are in harmony . . . [16]

The means of production

A part of the principle of the division of labour that has caused most concern among socialist critics of the market order is the ownership of the means of production. Mises agrees that under the division of labour, the ownership of land, factories, warehouses, distribution vehicles, and all the other items necessary to produce goods and bring them to consumers is vested in private individuals. Yet, he goes on, this is simply a part of the process of specialization.

It is not sensible for us all to be farmers, the self-sufficient manufacturers of all our needs, and retailers, so we let different individuals take on each separate function. The function of operating a particular productive process is undertaken by only a few specialists, just as only a few individuals become teachers or carpenters. Such a division of tasks improves the overall productivity of everyone's effort.

Nevertheless, Mises reminds us, the control of these means of production cannot and does not rest exclusively with their nominal owners. Productive machinery is built with the sole purpose of bringing particular goods into being; those who buy or do not buy the end products are really the ones who decide whether the process should be expanded or shut down. Ownership means nothing without control, and in the capitalist economy, that control rests ultimately with those at the end of the co-operative structure of which each productive process forms a part. Thus it is true in a real sense to say that:

ownership in a society which divides labour is shared between the producer and those for whose wants he produces . . . He does not decide the purpose of his production; those for whom he works decide it – the consumers. They, not the producer, determine the goal of economic activity. The producer only directs production towards the goal set by the consumers.[17]

Although it might seem that the very tools of production are concentrated in the hands of those who might not necessarily use them for the benefit of the public, therefore, the reality is that:

In the society that divides labour no-one is exclusive owner of the means of production . . . All means of production render services to everyone who buys or sells on the market.[18]

COMPETITION AND MONOPOLY

Marxian critics in particular doubt this rosy view of society in which competition and the division of labour produce a society without conflict. To them, this specialization and private ownership in the means of production is the origin of the very *un*co-operative practice of monopoly. Effective control will not rest with the public, they say, but with a small band of very wealthy individuals who have the power to decide what will be produced, and at what price.

The Marxian view

The theory that the division of labour under private ownership would lead to progressive industrial concentration and the emergence of giant monopolistic firms might have seemed evident enough when Marx wrote in the nineteenth century. At that time, new sources of power (especially steam and water) allowed the establishment of much larger factories and mills in which the economic advantages of large-scale production could be captured. In Marx's view, the superiority of larger manufacturers would lead to the ruin of smaller ones who could not produce so cheaply, and to the absorption or merger of enterprises into larger and larger units. Each sector would eventually be dominated by a single firm or a small number of firms that could easily form a cosy cartel arrangement.

This horizontal concentration would also be supplemented by vertical integration, according to the Marxian view. Instead of buying in supplies and selling on to distributors, for example, large firms would find it cheaper to perform those processes themselves, taking advantage again of the benefits of large-scale operation. The inexorable rise of industrial concentration into monopoly units would be complete.

The Marxists cited the enormous fortunes amassed by industrial capitalists in the nineteenth century as clear evidence of this trend to increasing concentration and economic power. Marxian theorists even today continue to cite multinational corporations and multimillionaire businessmen as evidence that economic power is becoming increasingly concentrated into the hands of a tiny minority who must get richer and richer because of the natural tendency of fortunes to grow larger and larger by the simple expedient of investment.

Mises's critique. Mises, as one might expect, rejects this as nonsense. Part of the problem, he argues, is that the rise of large companies and the acquisition of large fortunes is easy to see: the famous names glare out from our newspapers every day. It is far less easy to detect the *decline* of large industries that have once been market leaders but have now lost their competitive edge, shrunk in size, or even gone out of business altogether. So we tend to overlook this natural attrition, and seeing only the large firms of the moment, assume that they will continue to grow and become established as dominant in the market. (It is instructive to follow Mises's point by looking through old magazines of a few decades ago in order to see the advertisements for products and companies that have fallen out of the competition and have been forgotten for years.) For his part, Mises expects that the need for increasing specialization in the society that divides labour will bring about larger numbers of small firms that can take on specific functions more efficiently than larger enterprises,[19] and there is some evidence that in the economy of today, he is right.

If horizontal integration is not an unstoppable feature, the same is true of vertical integration, according to Mises. Again, the question must be asked why we should assume that enterprises will take on other stages in the production chain wherever possible. The very principle of the division of tasks rests on the breaking down of separate activities between different people or groups of people, because that specialization and that breakdown is more efficient than everyone trying to be self-sufficient. The same is also true of the firm: often, companies can buy in their raw materials from suppliers who could be far more efficient and cheaper than the firm could hope to be itself because of the suppliers' ability to specialize.

Again, Mises will not let us forget that, whether they are visible or not, there is nothing inevitable in the rise of fortunes. As before, we tend to see the obvious wealth of famous people, but do not hear much about those who were once wealthy but have now lost their fortunes. That constant turnover of wealth, however, does exist and gives the lie to the Marxist notion that capital accumulations must necessarily become increasingly concentrated in fewer and fewer hands. To conclude, investment mistakes and the risk of loss for any number of reasons mean that

there can be no question whatever of a tendency for fortunes to grow bigger and bigger. Fortunes cannot grow; someone has to increase them.[20]

The idea of monopoly

If there is no natural tendency for the enterprise economy to descend into monopoly, why is everyone so concerned about it? Partly, explains Mises, because we have a confused idea of what a monopoly is. In common usage, the word often signifies control over the conditions of human survival. While a global socialist state might have this power to starve to death those who do not obey it, however, such total monopoly fortunately has no relevance in a market economy.[21]

The second usage of the word implies control over a particular commodity, which is seen as a disagreeable corruption of the principle of market competition. But once again we are easily confused, says Mises, because the exclusive control over particular commodities is in fact perfectly compatible with the principle of market competition. Market competition works *because* people differentiate their products – and so each lawyer, physician, or manufacturer markets a slightly different good or service from everyone else. They each control their own product exclusively, and have a personal monopoly – but the competitive principle still operates.

Monopoly prices. For economics, the most pressing problem is not who controls particular products, but what happens to prices because of it. Thus, Mises warns us to remember that monopoly control and monopoly prices are not the same thing. A poet enjoys a monopoly over his output, but nevertheless might well be unable to command any price for it all (as many disappointed poets have found). What happens to prices depends not just upon the actions of suppliers, but upon also upon the nature of demand.

A monopolist (except one like the socialist state that controls the necessities of human life) cannot charge *any* price for his or her product.[22] The existence of monopolies might lead to higher prices and higher revenues for the monopolist, but the tendency is not unstoppable as the Marxians suppose. Market competition means that consumers can turn to other suppliers who offer a similar product or a substitute. It does not need the 'perfect competition' assumption of an infinite number of suppliers selling perfect substitutes to make this competitive pressure work: small numbers, or even a single competitor, can be quite sufficient to bid down the monopolist's prices, and so can the emergence of a tolerable substitute. The existence of airlines and bus operators may have a very noticeable effect on the fares that can be charged by monopoly train networks.

Size and power. Because people often assume that the (impossible) conditions of textbook competition are necessary if monopoly practices are to be prevented, and fail to see that real competition is about a limited number of unique suppliers each offering a different product, they often make serious mistakes in their discussion of monopoly. It is a common error, for example, to suppose that because a firm is large, it must be in possession of monopoly power. In some industries, large-scale operation might indeed be an advantage, and might therefore tend to predominate. But even big businesses face competition from other big businesses, observes Mises. We might add that they also face competition from large numbers of smaller ones which might be just as effective.

Furthermore, entrepreneurs are always developing new products that can undermine existing monopolies. People used to complain about the anticompetitive power of the rail monopolies, for example, but in fact the development of air travel and other forms of transport has undermined this position, argues Mises. Monopoly power is limited because of the wide choice available to the public in an enterprise economy; denied one product, they can turn to many others, since

competition takes place among producers and sellers not only within each individual branch of production, but also between all related goods, and in the final analysis between all economic goods.[23]

The person with exclusive control over a certain commodity, therefore, cannot be said to have 'control' over the market or to be able to 'dictate' prices, although commentators often talk as if this is so. The monopolist, remember, can never have perfect foresight about how people will react to any price increases that are attempted. The effect might be to encourage the exploitation of other sources of supply, to turn the public to the use of other products, and to sacrifice market share to the suppliers of close substitutes.

True sources of monopoly

When we recognize the power of these market processes to erode the privileged position of the monopolist, says Mises, we are left with only two possible sources of monopoly power. One is the control over natural resources of a particular kind and the other is through legislative enactment that grant special privileges to particular groups or industries.

Resource monopoly. The ownership of a mine or a piece of property that is the sole source of a certain useful mineral would be an example of the first sort. To Mises, this is a genuine monopoly, and the owner is able to extract a higher rent for the property or a higher price for the material mined because of that exclusive control. Yet the result is not altogether harmful. Higher prices, for example, will cause people to be more sparing in their use of the commodity, which helps conserve something that is already in limited supply. Furthermore, it may still be possible for consumers to find substitutes. A monopoly in petroleum, for example, would increase the demand for coal and hydroelectric generators. Such monopolies, in other words, might be a source of some inconvenience, but they are hardly important:

The bugbear of monopoly, which is always conjured up . . . need cause us no disquiet. The world monopolies that are really feasible could concern only a few items of primary production. Whether their effect is favourable or unfavourable is not easily decided.[24]

Government sources of monopoly. The second lasting source of monopoly is the imposition of deliberate controls backed up by the power of government agencies. The obvious mechanism here is the restriction of entry into a particular market through the requirement for suppliers to possess a licence of some sort, granted by the government or one of its agencies. Thus, the right to supply the market is granted only to selected applicants, or even to only a single applicant.

Why should a government impose such restrictions? One reason might be the political desirability of controlling a particular market activity that is thought to be undesirable, a waste of resources, or in need of regulation and scrutiny in the form of preconditions that must be met before a licence to practise is granted. As so often when politics is involved, however, the actual pressures working in favour of licence arrangements can be far less laudable. First, the sale of licences may bring in a healthy revenue for the government, which legislators can then use to curry favour with the broader electorate. Second, because the restriction on competition is of particular value to those already selling in the market, it is commonly they who instigate the political pressure for licensure. Self-interest must be a prominent motive of those who have the political muscle to gain such a shelter, although proposals to introduce licences are commonly dressed up and presented as being 'in the public interest' to exclude 'cowboy operators' and bring 'order and stability' into the market.

Another mechanism is for the government to grant itself the exclusive power to deal in certain commodities. In the past, this technique has been applied to salt, telephones, broadcasting, and much more; and is still active today.[25]

Mises seems to suggest, however, that the principal government source of monopoly is through the nationalistic effort to protect domestic industries by the erection of tariff walls or quotas against imports. This is done under the guise of boosting competition by the encouragement of strong domestic industry; but in reality it excludes competition and allows domestic cartels to flourish behind the protectionist controls, immune from the prospect of competition that would surely undermine their might if it were allowed to operate. Whatever justification is cited, the fact remains that it is the deliberate obstruction of free competition by legislative measures that is the origin of the monopolies and cartels we find in manufacturing industry:

Most cartels and trusts would never have been set up had not the government created the necessary conditions by protectionist measures. Manufacturing and commercial monopolies owe their origin not to a tendency immanent in capitalist economy but to government interventionist policy directed against free trade . . .[26]

226

(It is an important side issue that the only way to increase the profits that are generated by this shield of protection is to make the shield even stronger, making the prospect of aggressive nationalism or imperialism that much more likely.[27])

CONCLUSION

When one looks closely at monopolies, therefore, one finds that they exist more rarely and are more restricted than is commonly supposed by socialist writers. Where they do exist, they are either of little significance or are the product of deliberate efforts to thwart competition, not the natural evolution of the market process:

Such is the true story of modern monopoly. It is not an outcome of unhampered capitalism and of an inherent trend of capitalist evolution, as the Marxians would have us believe. It is, on the contrary, the result of government policies aiming at a reform of market economy.[28]

In fact, the natural tendency of capitalism, according to Mises, is to prompt entrepreneurs to supply the goods and services that consumers want, and to do so in the most efficient possible way. Entrepreneurs' rewards come from serving the public well, and are given freely by those who are served; they cannot be dismissed as a pointless injustice. Controls serve only to kill the benefits of the system.

Nor can controls be advocated to bring greater 'perfection' to an imperfect mechanism. In fact, competition could not work if all sellers and products were the same: its motive power comes from the desire of sellers each to differentiate their wares and to serve the public better than the rest. It takes only a few sellers in the marketplace (and as some modern economists such as Baumol would say,[29] only the *threat* of competition) to achieve this effect.

The conditions under which entrepreneurs work as they attempt to reap the rewards of this process by serving the public better than others, and the forces that shape the structure of production and determine the pattern of prices, are therefore a

227

subject of key concern not only to entrepreneurs but to political theorists and economists. The next section will turn to a discussion of these issues.

PART THREE: TIME AND MONEY

CHAPTER ELEVEN

Capital and Interest

> . . . all the policies of a country that wants to improve its standard of living must be directed toward an increase in the capital invested per capita.[1]

One of the Austrians' most important contributions to economic theory is their integration of the theory of capital and interest into a more general theory of time preference. Both phenomena spring from the decisions individuals make as to whether they prefer to act for the attainment of present consumption or are prepared to postpone consumption in the expectation of greater rewards at a later time. A second conclusion of major importance is that the economic role and effect of capital depends on *what* capital goods exist, *where* they are located, and *how* they are used or can be used in the future. Capital goods are not a homogeneous commodity, and public policy should not be directed as if they were. Although this point about the importance of the structure of the capital network was made by Austrian economists before Mises, his outline of it remains a particularly pungent one.[2]

TIME PREFERENCE AND PRODUCTION

Mises begins by noting that the attainment of nearly all objectives takes *time*. Our goals may take many steps to achieve, and each step is likely to take a certain time to accomplish. Even then, the result we achieve may be temporary, and require yet more effort if it is to be maintained or restored. In economic life, we face the limitations of the time taken to achieve some end (the *period of production*) and the duration of serviceableness of the end achieved (the *period of provision*).

Immediately we embark on action, therefore, we face choices in which time is an important factor. In selecting how to employ the various means available for the attainment of a certain goal, we have to make a choice about the time we are prepared to spend on it, because each different strategy, each different production method will take a greater or lesser time to achieve its end results. Similarly, we have to choose whether a product which is more durable but takes more time to produce is preferable to one which gives a shorter period of service but can be attained more quickly. It is not an objective question: different people, depending on whether they are provident or more concerned with the present instant, will come to different conclusions on the matter.

Even when it has been decided to acquire a particular good that provides a given satisfaction, there arises the question of whether that satisfaction should be sought *sooner* or *later*. In the answer to this question lie the origins of Mises's theory of capital and interest.

Time preference in action

Mises reports that it is impossible to imagine a mode of action in which satisfaction sooner is not preferred to satisfaction later, all other things being equal. Indeed, the fact that someone consumes a nonperishable commodity at all reveals that he or she values present satisfaction more than future satisfaction. It is impossible to imagine a person who always prefers satisfaction at a later period to satisfaction at a sooner one, since such a person would never consume anything, always postponing consumption for a later day. And each new day would bring the same choice and the same postponement. But within this limit, it is plainly possible for human beings to have different degrees of preference for sooner or later consumption.

In the market economy, changes are always occurring, of course, so other things are never equal, and people have to make daily decisions about whether to consume or accumulate what they receive in income. Some people consume everything they earn, others save part of their income, and still others sell part of their possessions to boost current consumption. There is no escaping the expression of time preference in everything people do:

The value of time ... is an essential element in every action. It determines every choice.[3]

A simple illustration of the universal validity of time preference, suggests Mises, is that not everyone is prepared to invest money in order to receive a larger amount back at the end of the year. A person consuming 100 dollars today plainly values that consumption more than the 104 dollars, say, that would become available in a year's time if the money were put into a bank account. Were time not to matter at all, the individual would always opt for the higher but later sum. Human time preferences are the key to understanding the phenomenon of interest.

The acquisition of capital goods

When people have satisfied their most urgent wants, they have the opportunity to save the remaining supply of consumers' goods for use at a later time. This makes it possible for them to embark on new production processes which are longer than the old ones, but worth the investment of time because of their greater efficiency.

Mises gives us an expressive example. The primitive fisherman might take longer to catch a fish by first making a canoe and a net than by simply stunning one with a rock or plucking it by hand from a stream. Yet the longer method is far more productive. By going more hungry than he would like and devoting his time to making nets and building canoes, or by building up stores to last him during the construction period, he can reap the advantages of this superior method. His *postponement of consumption* has opened the way to a more ample supply in the future. It might even enable him to enjoy new varieties of fish which he could not catch by hand. Whether the fisherman will embark on this course of action or not depends on his time preference: whether he thinks the current consumption sacrificed is worth the expected future reward.

In time preference, then, we have the origins of capital. Capital accumulation begins with the surplus of current production over consumption. These surpluses can be integrated into production (for instance, stocks of food that have been accumulated can be used to sustain the workers who make nets and canoes), in which case they are used up, but are replaced by the intermediary goods made by the workers in the new processes (the nets and canoes) and finally by the final consumers' goods so produced (the new supplies of fish).

Capital goods, concludes Mises, are intermediate stations on the way to the final goal of production, consumers' goods. *Time* is the key element they encapsulate. The person who has made the sacrifice and postponed consumption in order to acquire capital goods is at a great advantage over others, being nearer in time to the desired target of producing a sufficiency of consumers' goods.

Of course, the accumulation of capital goods allows people to embark on new production processes of all sorts, not just those which involve a greater number of stages and therefore take longer. Having satisfied their most urgent wants, they might decide to apply their spare resources for the purpose of attaining a new range of goods that take only a relatively short time to produce, but which were previously regarded as something of a luxury.

THE CAPITAL STRUCTURE

Technology and time

Non-Austrians tend to assume that the techniques used in production are determined entirely by the technology that is available at the time: that more advanced scientific knowledge means more sophisticated production processes.

Mises and his Austrian School colleagues demonstrate how this view is mistaken. Advanced technology might well be feasible, but whether it is deployed or not will depend upon people's choices between present or future consumption. The fisherman might know how to make a canoe and nets, but might not bother if he is not prepared to make present sacrifices in the anticipation of a reward that may be greater but is more remote. Quite often we find countries which are too poor to sacrifice the time and resources needed to build up the advanced technology that they know would benefit them. What is called a 'capital shortage' is in fact, says Mises, a dearth of *time*.

The employment of capital goods, then, is a much more complex phenomenon than is normally understood. Where they are used, and by whom, depends crucially on the time preferences of the people concerned. Different people may have different time preferences, either because of natural differences in temperament or because they have been able to accumulate different stocks of consumers' goods and are thus able to attend to needs of different urgency. The employment of capital goods depends not only on how people view the future, in other words, but on what has happened in the past.

The importance of the past

Capital goods, as mentioned above, are intermediate stations on the way to a definite goal. They can be more or less specific to that goal: for example, a hammer can be used for many tasks, but a pottery mould is good for only one. If the goals change, the employment of the capital goods used in the process will have to be reconsidered, and what happens to them will depend upon their precise nature.[4]

Inconvertible capital. If producers change the targets of their production for some reason (due, for example, to technical improvements elsewhere, to changes in time preferences, or to new consumer fashions making the old products no longer in demand and the old production processes no longer profitable), some highly specific capital goods will become utterly useless. Some other capital goods might still be used in some way if a little more effort is put into adapting them. A third group will be useable without adjustment, but could have been manufactured more cheaply if the new goal had been known about at the outset. And finally, some capital goods can be employed on the new process without any loss at all.

The producer's response to a change in the market data, therefore, will hinge critically on the *convertibility* of the capital goods employed. It will depend also on the duration for which the capital goods were designed to serve; scrapping a redundant factory or transportation network is a more momentous decision than scrapping a roll of unfashionable fabric that could have been used only once in any case.

The same sort of problems arise when given market data have simply been misjudged by the entrepreneurs and capitalists. If the final product of a particular process cannot be sold, the capital goods used in the process must be scrapped, adjusted, or applied for new goals. Depending on the nature of the capital goods themselves, this will involve larger or smaller degrees of waste.

Past capital and present consumption

When we look around any industrialized country today, we see what might be a depressing picture. Large factories lie disused, old buildings are still in use, people continue to live in crowded towns, and production centres are found in places that are far from their resources or markets. Is this a crisis of capitalism that could be cured by a dose of rational planning? Could we not, with our modern knowledge of technology, natural resources, and environmental health, reorganize and modernize the whole world, given only the political will so to do?

To Mises, these are no more than 'utopian fancies'.[5] When we and our ancestors manufactured the capital goods we are using today, technology might have been less advanced and market demands might have been different from today's. But does that mean to say that we should instantly scrap, abandon, or adjust the capital goods we have inherited? The answer must be firmly negative, because the old capital goods can still provide useful services, and the question is whether the superiority of new capital goods would outweigh the waste of the old. People do not throw out their cars and vacuum cleaners just because new models become available; it depends on how they judge the services rendered by each in the light of the costs of scrapping one and acquiring another.

Consumers, ultimately, will decide the issue of which capital is replaced and which retained, argues Mises. Tenants might still choose to live in an old building, rather than see it replaced by a new high-tech structure which burdens them with higher rents that in turn require them to reduce their consumption of other things. Similarly, businesses might remain located in old towns that are now distant from their markets, rather than go to the expense of moving to new factories and having to recruit new managers and workers in an unfamiliar town. The capital we are using today might not be the best possible in technological terms; but there is a big difference between technological perfection and economic common sense. The economic decision as to whether new capital goods should be introduced will depend on their cost and the cost of those replaced, on the time taken to make the change, institutional barriers (such as trade union objections to new working practices), and the relative improvement in services made possible. And there is nothing objective about the issue, as the technological view seems to suggest: how the costs involved and the gains anticipated are judged depends on the value scale of the person making the decision.

Some results from the theory

This elementary understanding, that it is wasteful to abandon some existing capital goods even when better ones are developed, explodes many widespread fallacies, argues Mises.

Protectionism. For example, trade barriers to protect 'infant industries' are often urged on the grounds that such new industries can outperform those abroad which have a historical advantage but which are less efficient technologically. In fact, however, the establishment of a new industry cannot be justified economically unless the superiority of the new location is so great that it outweighs the losses due to the abandonment of the nonconvertible capital goods invested in the old one. Yet if that superiority exists, the new industry will be able to compete without governmental protection in any case. Political arguments, not economic ones, explain the establishment of trade barriers in so many places.

Patents. Another argument which Mises says we can dispose of with his analysis is the one that large businesses systematically buy out patents and suppress new inventions to protect their products. In fact, he argues, the adjustment of production to take advantage of a new invention is neither costless nor straightforward; it depends on the economic significance of the innovation being recognized, on the (often huge) costs of replacing existing production processes, on the relative productivity of the old and new systems, on the willingness of the workforce to operate new equipment, and so on. Companies spend very large amounts to research and develop new processes and so keep ahead of their competitors, but the costs of abandoning nonconvertible capital goods act as a restraint on the instant application of everything new.

Capitalism. The analysis which causes us to reject the technological view incidentally undermines the source of many of the attacks on capitalism. Socialist writers, says Mises, have often just *assumed* that socialism would bring an immediate replacement of old equipment by new, and the planned restructuring of industries into their most efficient sizes and locations. But this cannot be; capital goods are scarce and valuable, and it is absurd to suggest that they should be abandoned or that new ones should be installed without regard to the waste generated by the change.

Not 'friction'. Some economists describe the actions of industry in sticking to existing production processes even though better ones are available as a 'friction', slowing the smooth operation of the market. But, says Mises, it is not a friction but a perfectly rational decision to retain older capital goods where the superiority of new ones is insufficient to outweigh the loss of the old. The capital structure that has been laid down in the past may not be the best we could imagine today, and might even have been less than perfect at the time. Yet it influences every economic decision we make and modifies our ambitions to start up new processes and abandon old ones. In a very real sense, then, our past inheritance is a key determinant of how the future will unfold.

'Investment' policy. A remarkable number of politicians and commentators suggest that a simple increase in the capital

inventory, a larger amount spent on 'investment', would always bring beneficial results. Thus, they propose the tearing down of old plants and machinery and their replacement by new ones of higher value, as if the fact of the cost increase alone was enough to promote economic growth.

Again, the Austrian analysis in general, and Mises's explanation of it in particular, shows that this is a mistake. Capital is not a homogeneous good that exists in interchangeable stocks that can be built up or run down, nor is it a flow that can be diverted without loss from one branch of production into another. Capital exists only in specific capital goods. More important than the inventory value of those goods is now they are linked and used – a shipyard, a steelworks, and a coal mine, for example, might be utterly dependent on each other's products and unable to survive on their own. So the *structure* of existing capital goods – what they are, where they are, how they are used – is the key policy problem, not their total book value. No measure of the totality of capital goods leaves us with any understanding of how the productive process is actually working. For instance, it is possible to accumulate capital goods at great cost which, because of mistakes or changes in market conditions, bear no relationship in their output to the effort expended in their accumulation.

Malinvestment

Because the capital structure of the present influences the economic decisions of near future, which in turn influence the decisions of the more distant future, it is important to ensure that our choice of which capital goods we want to invest in should be as rational as possible. A mistake today can have lasting consequences. Still, malinvestment is possible and common, and Mises cites the following causes, at least some of which can be prevented.

Technology, tastes, and mistakes. In the first place, changes in production methods or favourable locations could make a capital investment a bad one. But the future is not completely predictable, and such events do occur despite the best of

planning. Similarly, there might be a marked change in consumers' preferences during the construction of the capital
goods or during their period of service, and this again might
lead to the unfortunate waste of capital. Finally, the investment
could be a simple mistake: that the entrepreneur wrongly
assessed the costs of the capital goods or the level of demand for
the final products.

Inflation and intervention

Turning to causes which are less excusable, Mises cites inflation and intervention. Intervention in the form of special
protections offered to some industries (such as tariff barriers,
subsidies, and so on) induce people to invest in certain capital
goods which would not be such a profitable investment in the
absence of the policy. Economically, the result is a loss. Likewise, government inflationary policies cause rises in prices and
changes in the relative prices between different goods,[6] and
make it harder for entrepreneurs to see whether the returns on
their investments are real or illusory. Hence, inflation spawns
malinvestment, which means not only losses today, but the
possibility of losses and distortions continuing for many years
because of the influence of present capital structures on future
economic decisions.

Once more, what is important is the capital *structure*, the
exact assortment of capital goods that exist and the working
links between them. During inflationary periods, people may
well devote a larger portion of their wealth to the purchase of
capital goods, but if the production processes to which they are
directed prove to be unsustainable when the inflation subsides,
serious distortion and disruption of the economy can occur.
Much of the investment undertaken by individuals under an
inflationary government 'dash for growth' policy could turn out
to be a complete waste.

CAPITAL, WEALTH, AND POVERTY

The idea and mythology of capital

It is noteworthy that Mises talks very specifically in terms of
'capital goods' at the places where many contemporary econo-

mists would talk more simply of 'capital'. This is because he believes it is crucially important to recognize the difference between what are two very different things if we are to avoid errors and absurdities and escape the mythology that has built up around the concept of capital.

Capital is an idea. Mises explains that 'capital' is just an *idea*. It is the monetary value which people put on the package of capital goods they own. That value, of course, is necessarily subjective, because it depends upon the individual's assesssment of market conditions and of how other people will value the output of the productive processes in which those capital goods are used. Capital, therefore, is just a mental tool which we use for calculation, and not a physical thing like the capital goods themselves. As he puts it:

Capital . . . is a product of reasoning, and its place is in the human mind.[7]

A little thought will illustrate the validity of the distinction between capital and capital goods, argues Mises. It is not to hard to see that the accumulation or loss of capital is not the same as the creation or extinction of capital goods. All capital goods must be created at some time, and all are eventually extinguished, whether they simply wear out or are eventually consumed. An individual might hold a capital fund that he or she considers to be of a steady size, therefore, while at the same time the assortment of capital goods which make up the fund might be changing from year to year and even from day to day. People can increase, preserve, or run down the inventory value of their capital fund, but the overall figures still give us no indications of what particular *capital goods* are being created or destroyed.

In stressing this distinction, Mises was echoing the sentiments of Carl Menger, but goes a good deal further than some other Austrian economists. Böhm-Bawerk, for example, sought to make the concept of capital more empirical and less subjective, and accordingly defined it as the aggregate of the intermediate goods in the economy, those goods prior to consumption goods. But the idea of defining capital as an aggregate of physical goods will not do, according to Mises. Like other attempts at aggregation (such as the Keynesian measures of 'consumption' or 'national income'), it lumps together things that are very different, and so disguises more than it reveals. Worse, it suggests that capital is an objective quantity and forgets that the important issue for economics is not the existence of physical objects but their *meaning* for acting individuals. Lastly, it confuses real and mental things and no matter how carefully it is deployed, always harbours within it the germ of critical mistakes.

Sources of error. The sharpest distinction must be made between this idea of 'capital' and capital goods, because as we see in other walks of life, it is a serious logical error to confuse an abstract idea with a real thing. For example,[8] we can form the mental image of a unicorn without unicorns actually existing, and we speak of 'largeness' even though it is obvious that 'largeness' is only a concept and as such can not exist on its own, independent of the *things* that we describe as being large or small. Similarly, 'capital' does not exist independent of the capital goods in which it is manifested. To suppose otherwise is to fall into the trap of assuming something to be real when it is in fact only an idea, a mental tool, an interpretation of events. In the words of Mises once again:

Conceptual realism has muddled the comprehension of the concept of capital. It has brought about a mythology of capital. An existence has been attributed to 'capital' independent of the capital goods in which it is embodied. Capital, it is said, reproduces itself and thus provides for its own maintenance. Capital, says the Marxian, hatches out profit. All this is nonsense.[9]

While it might be useful to use the term 'capital', therefore, its nature is easily misconstrued. Its growth is not automatic, nor does its possession guarantee future profits, because the wrong capital goods and the wrong production processes can be chosen by the investor. And it does not come out of thin air: capital funds can grow only as a result of the deliberate action of

individuals who forgo present consumption in order to manufacture and accumulate capital goods. It can be lost by mistakes, and can even be consumed – an individual can dip into
stocks of food or money laid aside, and a business can sell
perfectly good capital equipment in order to pay current bills,
for example. Equally, improvements in production (caused by
better harvests, better productivity, or more settled civil affairs,
and so on) can help people to save and thus to accumulate it.
Capital is not a self-perpetuating physical thing that has
existence outside the realm of conscious human action.

The myth of capital flight. Another example from the mythology of
capital will underscore the distinction further. Some commentators, says Mises, talk in terms of a pool of 'circulating capital'
which can 'flee' from one industry or one country to any other.
The attempt to control this capital flight and to preserve its
residence in domestic industry is often the background to
exchange controls or other interventionist policies. The apparently selfish nature of this capital flight and the movements of
capital investment in the stock market have given such dealings
a bad name.

Yet, Mises argues, it is not the actual flight of capital goods
which is being talked of in this analysis. Capital goods are often
inconvertible and will stay where they are; but if they are
considered to be unsafe investments, their owners will certainly
be prepared to sell them at a loss and use the proceeds for
investment elsewhere. That is a quite rational reaction and no
amount of interventionist controls will prevent it. The real
question is why some investments are considered unsafe, which
will usually boil down to the changing demands of consumers
or the unpredictable or expropriative policies of governments.
They are the root of falling capital goods prices, not the
capitalists.

Kinds of capital

People who forget that 'capital' is only an idea often fall into the
trap of treating it as a homogeneous thing. It is this that
generates the mistake that the amount of capital used by a

society can be usefully measured, and that a larger amount is necessarily better than a smaller amount. A great deal of public policy today is directed to that end and therefore rests on that shaky foundation.

Inventory and structure. The use of the term 'capital' suggests something that it homogeneous. In reality, however, capital is manifested only in specific capital goods, and those can be of a very diverse nature indeed. True, each capital good exchanges at a certain price (depending, ultimately, on the prices of the final goods it helps produce), and these prices could all be added together to give an overall total. But what would be the use of that figure? It is merely an inventory of capital goods, and says nothing about how they are applied. The price of a specific capital good might well be of the keenest interest to an entrepreneur, but the totality of those prices is of interest and use to nobody.

For Mises and other Austrians, the *structure* of a nation's capital is of the utmost importance, its overall monetary value is not. Capital is not a homogeneous stock that yields a homogeneous income; it resides only in highly diverse capital goods that yield many different services and which can be brought together in many different ways to produce many different outcomes. In economic analysis, a knowledge of how goods are used is more important than adding up the prices of each good in the inventory.[10]

Capital is personal. Equally erroneous, according to Mises, is the distinction between *private capital* and *social capital*. Once again, the individual entrepreneur can make calculations on the basis of the price at which a particular capital good exchanges. But the capital goods owned by governmental authorities, the 'means of production' held by the socialist commonwealth, are never traded. As Mises's analysis of socialism makes clear, economic calculation is only possible where things exchange. So the notion of capital makes sense (that is, provides a useful tool for calculation) only where it is bought and sold: where there is no market, the concept of capital is merely academic, not something with practical application.[11]

An understanding of the subjective nature of capital and the importance of the capital structure presents enormous problems for socialism. The first thing that become clear is that capital is not free; it has a cost, and requires a diversion of resources to accumulate. No instant transformation of the economy is possible. Nor are capital goods identical, so there must be a decision on what sort of capital goods should be acquired. In the market economy, the consumers ultimately decide the latter question; under socialism, it is left to planners whose views are unlikely to be consonant with those of consumers and who in any event have no mechanism to make choices because they have no yardstick of value. Also, capitalism favours the accumulation of capital because it is the thrifty individuals who decide to forgo current consumption in favour of accumulating capital; under socialism, the balance is decided by everyone, including those who are more spendthrift.[12] It might be added to Mises's insight that the ultimate decision-makers, the politicians, tend to be the most spendthrift of all, sacrificing the opportunity to accumulate capital for the political gains of current spending. It is no surprise that publicly owned industries tend to be the most seriously undercapitalized. As Mises himself points out, taxation has the effect of removing resources from thrifty individuals for current spending by thriftless governments, and the more paid in taxation, the less accumulated in capital:

The destructionist policy of taxation culminates in capital levies. Property is expropriated and then consumed. Capital is transformed into goods for use and for consumption. The effect of this should be plain to see.[13]

The causes of poverty

When people fail to recognize that capital accumulation is a very subjective business, depending crucially upon the time preferences of individuals, and on their personal assessment of the risks and potential rewards involved in investment, they can kill off the process of capital accumulation with effortless speed.

Comparative prosperity. What is the reason for the poverty of particular countries? It is not a lack of natural resources, says Mises, since some countries without any resources have made themselves wealthy. Nor can it be something inherent in the character of the people themselves; immigrants to Western countries often show remarkable entrepreneurial effort and drive.

The answer is, Mises insists, simply that it takes time to build up capital, and although capital makes labour more productive, some nations have not yet been able to accumulate it. To use the previous analogy: the fisherman who owns nets and canoes has to spend less time fishing and can catch more fish than one without, but it takes time and effort to build canoes and make nets in the first place. That requires time off from fishing – and going hungry for a while, or using up stored reserves of fish and other food. Likewise, for any country whose people have few reserves or cannot manage on much less than they presently consume, it is a slow and hard effort to acquire capital assets.

Where capital has not been accumulated, labour is less productive and relative poverty is the result, particularly where the population is rising:

There are no means by which the general standard of living can be raised other than by accelerating the increase of capital as compared with population.[14]

Mises's position here may not be completely consistent with his view that the *type* and *structure* of the capital goods employed are more important than their simple inventory value. It is quite possible for a developing nation to acquire large volumes of capital goods that are of little effect in reducing poverty: a common problem in countries whose leaders have chosen to emulate the West by building expressways and steel mills in the midst of a rural population that has no use for them. But if we allow this aberration to be left aside, we can probably agree with Mises that there is certainly some rough relationship between the capital acquired and the productivity of labour, and hence a relationship between a nation's capital per head and incomes per head.

Capital is always imported. To illustrate his point, Mises points out the importance of foreign investment from rich countries (whose population can spare it because of the excess of their income over consumption) to poor countries. Britain, the home of the industrial revolution, was the only country to built up its capital unaided, he argues, but all other countries have relied on others to provide the capital for their development:

in all countries except England, foreign capital investment played a considerable part in the development of modern industries.[15]

The developed countries of Europe, America, Canada, Australia and many others all owe their start to foreign investment which provided capital at a time when they could not do so themselves, thus unleashing an improvement in the productivity of labour.

The lesson for less developed countries today is that foreign investment is something to be welcomed and not regarded with suspicion. If the government of the recipient nation has a habit of confiscating foreign-owned assets out of a misguided nationalism, it can hardly expect foreign investors to flock to its aid in future. And thus, being denied the access to foreign capital, the only way its people can accumulate capital is by saving: not always possible in the poorest of nations. Similarly, the other political conditions which make investments more risky, such as unstable monetary policy or unpredictable interventions in foreign trade regulations, will reduce the amount of capital available for development by making investors more reluctant to commit their resources. Mises seeks the free migration of capital as the best means of aiding economic development throughout the world: but such migration will be possible only through the demise of government-inspired barriers and confiscatory of fickle economic policy.

THE PHENOMENON OF INTEREST

Mises's explanation of capital hinges on *time*, that factor which it is all too easy to forget when reasoning starts from the traditional classical analysis. The related phenomenon of interest, as we have seen, also depends crucially on how individuals perceive and value time.

Time preference and interest rates

The rates of interest one finds in the marketplace are complicated things. The rate of interest paid on a loan, for example, includes the entrepreneurial profits of the lenders (their reward for observing that people want to borrow money, and having the ability to give them what they want), a margin for the risk of default, and probably other elements. However, there is a very important and fundamental sort of interest which can be distilled out from this confusing agglomeration, the phenomenon which Mises calls 'originary interest'.

It is this element which reflects the fact that people value the satisfaction of wants today more than the satisfaction of wants at some time in the future, the phenomenon that is manifested in the market economy as the discount of future goods against present goods – in the language of the earlier example, the principle that a person would be willing to give up 100 dollars of consumption today only in return for, say, 104 dollars or more a year from now. It is from such time preference, says Mises, that originary interest derives.

The sources of interest. The traditional view of interest, once again overlooking this time element, can lead to crass mistakes about the nature of interest and public policy regarding it. In the extreme, it leads people to suppose that interest can be abolished, and indeed that it should be abolished because it boils down to exploitation of those without capital by those with it. But once we recognize that time preference inheres in every action – whatever people do, they have to decide when to do it and how long to take over it, how valuable their time is – we see that interest too must pervade every aspect of economic life.

Traditional analysis often pictures interest as the 'price' commanded by capital goods, derived like any other price from the interplay of supply and demand in the marketplace. But, says Mises, interest is not determined by this capital supply and demand. On the contrary, it is people's time preferences which drive them to accumulate larger or smaller capital funds, so it is from these and the rate of originary interest implied in them that the supply and demand conditions in the market-place are derived. Interest reflects the mutual valuation of present goods as against future goods, and so explains the extent to which people are prepared to divert goods from current consumption into capital. Interest, in other words, determines the supply of and demand for capital, not the other way around.

Trees and fruit. Often, people regard capital as something which automatically produces income like a tree produces fruit. And since, in this traditional interpretation, the capital fund and the income it generates are linked directly through the rate of interest – a higher rate of interest generating a greater stream of income, a lower rate generating a smaller one – the phenom-enon of interest is regarded as something that reflects the productivity of the capital concerned.

As one might expect, Mises can find no sense in this idea of capital as a self-perpetuating fund or in the conclusion that the rate of interest reflects the productivity of capital. To him, the whole notion is based on the mistake of treating capital as an aggregate of capital goods instead of the abstract mental accounting tool that it is. Originary interest stems from the time preferences of individuals, not from the productivity of capital goods. There is nothing automatic about the stream of income generated by capital goods: what happens depends crucially on how individuals use those goods, and on the particular time preferences that colour their opinions of them. Treating capital goods as undistinguished elements in a general fund only obscures the particular plans, motives, and actions of those who use them, and so leads to such errors.

The productivity of capital goods is not manifested in in-terest rates, argues Mises, but in prices. He endorses Menger's point that production goods are held only for the value of the consumption goods that they are expected to produce – that it is the value of their output which makes people value capital goods. The productivity of the capital goods, the stream of consumer products that they are expected to generate, is already taken account of in their prices. If time preferences did not exist, the prices of productive factors would equal the sum of the marginal values of the services they were expected to generate, with nothing extra, no residuum that would explain interest. Interest arises only because people prefer consumption sooner and so discount those future products. Interest stems from time preferences and is prior to the accumulation of capital goods.

Abolition of interest. People's time preferences set the rate of originary interest. Those preferences are not so low that anyone would willingly sacrifice one apple today in order to get two apples in a hundred years' time – and the question certainly has nothing to do with the productivity of apple trees in any event. But still, says Mises, some people retain the illusion that interest is some mechanical outcome of a capital fund, and thus fall into the trap that the economy can continue to work under such absurd conditions. They demand, in short, that interest should be abolished completely.

This is, of course, an impossibility: laws might prevent the payment of interest, but not the actual valuation of present goods higher than future goods. Such philosophies overlook the critical point that the acquisition of capital goods depends wholly upon the motivations and perceptions of individuals, and thus would have no qualm in abolishing the system of incentives that are, in fact, necessary if people are to be tempted into the sacrifices needed to accumulate capital goods. Without any reward, the individual would see no reason to build up a fund, and the capitalist might as well simply consume his or her capital:

such decrees would bring about capital consumption and would very soon throw mankind back into the original state of natural poverty.[16]

It is perhaps legitimate to add to this point of Mises that policies designed to manipulate interest rates and depress the payments which individuals have to make on loans or capital goods, policies which are certainly far more common, would also produce the phenomenon of capital consumption, albeit more slowly than a complete ban on interest payments. If the policy were adhered to, however, the result would no doubt be the same.

The entrepreneurial component

Part of the desire of governments to manipulate interest rates is because people still talk as if high or low rates of interest 'stimulate' capital formation. This, says Mises, is a senseless view: differences in the rate of originary interest *are* changes in the degree to which people are prepared to save and divert income into capital. The existing supply of capital goods therefore has no effect on the rate of originary interest nor the amount of further saving.

Lenders as entrepreneurs. But originary interest never appears in unalloyed form, cautions Mises, and market rates *will* take into account the existing supply of capital goods and other factors besides.

One major element of market interest rates, for example, is the entrepreneurial element. Capitalists are also entrepreneurs: when they lend capital to those who believe they can make a profit on it, they are making a speculative decision and taking an entrepreneurial risk themselves. After all, the success or failure of the ventures in which the borrowers are involved hinges on the precision with which they anticipate events. Consumers' values change, and some goods will turn out to be valued more highly, others less highly, than entrepreneurs expect, and it is in the better or worse anticipation of the outcome that the source of entrepreneurial profit and loss resides. In the granting of credit, there is uncertainty about the future, since the debtor or guarantors might become insolvent, and so might be unable to repay all or some of the loan. Originary interest and entrepreneurial profit are inseparable elements of market interest rates.

This point shows how Mises does not treat originary interest as a discernible measurement that can be observed empirically. To him, originary interest is a basic principle that can be derived logically from the concept of human action – which, because human beings do not live forever, necessarily contains the concept of time preferences. It does not need to be established empirically, nor could it be, since it never appears on its own. Yet in thinking about interest rates logically and recognizing the various components that they always contain, Mises would argue, we might begin to understand why their behaviour is never so tidy as empirical economists' predictions.

Government intervention. An important factor affecting the risk on market loans is the likely incidence of government intervention. Most directly, there could be a change the legal conditions under which loans may be extended and held, but a more common and perhaps more potent part of government policy which can seriously affect the market rate of interest on credit transactions is monetary policy, which disrupts the purchasing power of the monetary unit.

Thus a lender who has agreed to accept repayment of a certain sum at a particular future date will be impoverished if that sum of money has become worthless in the meantime. Lenders who anticipate such an inflation would be rational to consume their capital, which as Mises has already observed, leads to lower productivity and worsening poverty. From that simple observation, one can begin to realize that real and momentous economic events depend upon the nature of money and the consequences of monetary policy.

CHAPTER TWELVE

The Nature and Value of Money

> All consideration of the value of money must obviously
> presuppose a state of society in which exchange takes
> place and must take as its starting point individuals
> acting as independent economic agents within such a
> society, that is to say, individuals engaged in valuing
> things.[1]

Most of what Mises had to say about money appeared as early
as 1912 in his book on *The Theory of Money and Credit*. It
emphasized that what people accept as money, and the value
they attach to it, is essentially a matter of individual valuation,
and as such depends upon the whole complex of economic
activity in which individual valuations come to be made.

Sadly, this approach, for all its merit, was not what the
economists and politicians of the day were searching for in a
theory of money. They preferred the more straightforward view
of Georg Knapp that the choice of a monetary standard was a
matter for governments alone (an approach which excised the
Austrian principle that how people subjectively judge such
institutions could be of the keenest importance); and they
rallied around the mechanistic approach of Irving Fisher's
almost contemporaneous work, *The Purchasing Power of Money*,
which revivified the old 'quantity theory' of money and argued
that the purchasing power of the money so supplied could be
predicted according to a simple formula in which the principal
variable was the volume put into circulation. And Mises's
contemporaries were attracted by other mathematical techniques[2] which seemed to offer a scientific way of cutting
through monetary questions which Mises's work characterized
as extremely complex and not soluble by simple equations.

The conduct of monetary policy this century came to be
based very largely, therefore, on such abstract mathematical
reasoning, lacking as it does the Austrian insight of the critical

importance of the motives and values of the individuals affected. The subsequent (or consequent) inflations that have peppered the historical record since Mises wrote, demonstrate that his doubts and warnings were fully justified. It has now become more clear that the quantity of money cannot be glibly controlled by the authorities according to the recipes of the textbooks. And the results of monetary policy have been much more subtle and have demonstrated a number of serious side-effects not predicted in the mechanistic neoclassical analysis. Even those who, with Milton Friedman, have stressed the power of monetary policy have failed to explain the full diversity of the results convincingly with their macroeconomic models. Only now, with the world seeking a more sensitive theory of money, are economists returning in great numbers to Mises's subjectivist masterpiece on the subject, and even Friedman has at last been drawn to respond to it.[3]

THE PURPOSE OF MONEY

What kind of a good is money? A somewhat unusual one, according to Mises, since it is not a production or consumption good, but is acquired by people to facilitate the *exchange* of production or consumption goods. Money does not produce things: indeed, the entrepreneur must give it away in exchange for production goods before any output can be generated. Nor can money be consumed: a rare exception might be the miser who wants to accumulate money for its own sake, but as far as most people are concerned, its sole function is to be once again given away in exchange for consumable goods and services. The sole purpose of money, oddly enough, is to be given away, to be exchanged.

A medium of exchange

The emergence of money in the economic system is easy enough to understand. The production and consumption goods which people want to acquire have different degrees of marketability: for some it is easy to find customers, while others have a narrower appeal that makes it difficult to find customers willing to offer (or vendors willing to accept) a mutually agreeable compensation at the right time and in the right place. So what is the hungry barber to do? It is a waste of time to search round for bakers in need of haircuts: but perhaps there are plenty of bakers who would be prepared to accept something else. The more marketable that 'something else' is, the more likely are bakers (and for that matter, butchers and candlestick-makers) to accept it as payment even when they do not want the specialist services of the barbers. So even the bald baker will accept a commodity that he knows can be readily marketed against the meat and candlesticks and other goods that he might want in future.[4]

To be more technical about it, Mises observes that the person who cannot instantly acquire what he or she needs because of this difficulty in finding a ready market can nevertheless improve matters by exchanging a less marketable good he or she wishes to trade against a more marketable one. The more marketable good can then be traded, more easily, for whatever is needed. Similarly, a person who wants to dispose of some commodity quickly (because it is perishable or expensive to store, or because a fall in its market value is anticipated) acts wisely to trade it against a more marketable good, even if this good is not suitable to satisfy his or her own needs directly.[5]

Importance of exchange media. This system of *indirect exchange*, says Mises, becomes much more important as the division of labour grows. In the advanced economy which is reaping the gains of very extensive specialization, individuals might well find themselves engaged in the manufacture of goods that are aimed at a very small and very specific market and which have no interest or value for anyone other than those few buyers. It is not surprising, therefore, that the greater the division of labour, the more important is it to seek out intermediary goods that are more readily acceptable in the widest range of markets and so able to act as a medium of exchange that facilitates the very widest range of transactions:

A medium of exchange is a good which people acquire neither for their own consumption nor for employment in their own production activities, but with the intention of exchanging it at a later date against those goods which they want to use either for consumption or for production.[6]

Eventually the competitive use of different intermediary goods will sort out one or a group of commodities which prove most acceptable as a medium of exchange. When an intermediary good becomes generally accepted, so that it operates as a common medium of exchange, we normally call it 'money'.

Exactly what will be used as money and how generally acceptable it is will depend upon the individual valuations of those in the marketplace at the time. Today, we often imagine that only the government chooses what will act as money; but while the state has the power to decide what will be the legal medium of payment, only the fact of what people are prepared to accept will decide what is the common medium of exchange. If the government's own banknotes have become worthless, people may deal illicitly using cigarettes, or brandy, or any other acceptable commodity as their money. The government cannot make something the common medium of exchange if people will not accept it as such:

even now the state has not the power of directly making anything into money, that is to say into a common medium of exchange.[7]

Money as an economic good

The essential characteristic of money, which must colour all our discussions on the subject, is thus that it is a good acquired for the purpose of exchange. It is not a factor of production, acquiring its value like other production goods from the value of the goods it produces; it is not a consumption good because the value to its holder consists in its being exchanged away, not in being consumed; it is not even capital because it produces no benefits until it leaves the holder's hands. Its only function is as a medium of exchange, and all the other functions which are popularly ascribed to it are just particular aspects of this its main function.[8]

Mises's insistence upon this characteristic of money puts his view in stark contrast with the traditional textbook description of the subject. While the mainstream economists emphasize the need for media of exchange to be durable and divisible, and talk of money as a store of value (in reality a store of purchasing power), these are, to Mises, incidental qualities. They might help particular commodities such as gold and silver to become the common media of exchange. When we are considering the economic issues surrounding money, however, we should not be diverted by these incidental qualities. The key characteristic of money is that it exists to facilitate exchange.

Although it is unusual, money is nevertheless an economic good. It is scarce, and there is a demand for it. People want to own a store of it, larger or smaller depending upon their personal decision, to exchange for the goods they will need in the future. Like all commodities, it can be traded against other goods at certain exchange ratio – a 'price'. In the case of money, its 'price' is normally expressed a little differently – not in terms of the volume of goods or services that will exchange for a unit of money (how many eggs to the dollar), but in terms of the number of units of money which exchange against another good (how many cents for an egg). In other words, a rising 'price' of money means that what we call its purchasing power has increased. Despite the terminological differences, the principle is the same for money as it is for other goods.

And to complete the identity, the demand people have for money – whether they choose to hold greater or smaller amounts of a medium of exchange – will affect its purchasing power, just as changes in the demand for any good will have a bearing on its price.

KINDS OF MONEY

Before tackling the detail of what induces people to hold larger or smaller quantities of money and from there to answer the question of how the purchasing power of money is determined, however, let us look more closely at the nature of those things which are commonly called by the name of money. In reality, Mises reminds us, these things are very varied and not all of them should be described in the strict sense as money nor treated by monetary theorists as if they were similar.

The broad concept of money, Mises informs us, includes not only things which are genuinely money, but other things, such as banknotes and token coins, which are merely convenient substitutes for money. By isolating the different kinds of money, it becomes possible to understand more of the detail of their effects on the economic system than would be possible when they are all lumped together.

Money in the narrower sense

Let us consider money in the narrower sense first, the sense that excludes what Mises calls 'money substitutes' like token coin and certain other things. We know that the characteristic feature of money in the narrow sense is that people are prepared to accept it as a common medium of exchange. So what kinds of commodity will suit this purpose?

Components within the narrow definition. Mises identifies three kinds of thing that will serve as money within this narrower definition. The first and most important is *commodity* money, something which is not only money but at the same time a commercial commodity. Gold and silver, for example, can be made into consumers' goods such as spoons, ornaments, and wedding rings, and can be used for a variety of industrial processes; yet still they have for centuries served widely as money.

A second sort of money is what Mises calls *credit money*. These are claims against an individual or legal entity such as a bank or a government. They arose as definite claims, secure and payable on demand, which came to be passed from hand to hand as a medium of exchange. In modern times, variants have emerged which are much less certain as claims, with no redemption date specified and so some doubt about the willingness and ability of the debtor to pay and a consequent fall in value from their face value. Yet, still being found useful as a medium of exchange, they retain a value higher than they would have if they were merely claims.

258

It is reasonable to suppose that credit notes could remain in use as a medium of exchange, even if their status as claims on a bank or a treasury faded completely. They would then become examples of the third category, *fiat money*, in which mere tokens that have no industrial value are given the status of money just because they bear the mark of a particular authority.

A digression on fiat money. In Mises's discussion of this point, it is possible to see how he departs radically from much of the conventional wisdom about the nature of money. He does not accept theories that the state can and does decide what the common medium of exchange will be, nor that something with no commodity value can become money just because it has a government stamp on it – the 'nominalist' conception. In his view, while the state can, by its stamp, *permit* such objects to be distinguished and used as money and can pass laws to encourage their common acceptance, they will never *become* money just because the state commands it, only through their common usage by those who take part in commercial transactions.

It is an open question, suggests Mises, whether such fiat money has ever in fact existed, because all government and bank notes have their origin in some commodity or some earlier form of currency. After wars or other events that cause a collapse in the monetary system, governments often issue new currency systems, but although the paper and base metal on which the new face values are printed are worthless in themselves, it is never fiat money, because it is always linked by some formula to the old currency, or to some commodity such as gold or land. Without that link, people could never establish the purchasing power of the new paper, and so could not accept it as a medium of exchange.

Monetary and nonmonetary demand

This distillation of the different qualities of the various types of money helps avoid a number of confusions that are of great moment in monetary theory and policy.

For example, some economists have endorsed the apparently commonsense view that the value of a commodity money stems only from its industrial and commercial uses. Thus, the value of gold and silver is said to derive exclusively from their use as personal and household ornaments or in industry. Mises's analysis demonstrates that this is mistaken. The exchange value of a commodity money derives both from the industrial *and* the monetary uses for which people demand it: as a factor of production or an elegant ornament *and* as a medium of exchange. Plainly, the fact that people want a good because it can be exchanged widely will certainly have a bearing on its market price (what, in the context of money, we call its purchasing power), and this effect will be supplemental to the effect of its demand for consumers' and industrial uses. The monetary theorist, nevertheless, is interested only in the commodity's character as a medium of exchange, and so must attempt to distinguish these two effects:

The value of commodity money is of importance for monetary theory on in so far as it depends on the peculiar economic position of the money, on its function as a common medium of exchange.[9]

The same recognition of the monetary and nonmonetary elements in the demand for commodities is what also helps us to understand why a piece of metal or paper can come to have a value quite different from the industrial value of the object and from the value decided and stamped upon it by officialdom. The 'nominalist' doctrine says that it is the official stamp on a coin which gives it its worth, regardless of the amount of gold or silver it contains. This is not so: official stamps were originally put on metal coins to guarantee that they were of a certain weight and fineness – that what was exchanging was a particular amount and quality of a commodity itself. When governments, seizing the opportunity to gain, started to append the same stamp to coins that were of lesser weight or fineness, people started weighing and testing the coins used in transactions. They were interested in the amount and quality of the real commodity which the coins contained. This, not the nominal amount stamped on by the authority, decided their value. When the reliability of the official coinage became uncertain, ingots or other forms of money were used instead.[10]

Money substitutes

There are other things which are normally thought of as money, but which are in fact money substitutes. These are

claims to a definite amount of money, payable and redeemable on demand, against a debtor about whose solvency and willingness to pay there does not prevail the slightest doubt . . .[11]

Because they are as good as money, they can fully replace money in an individual's cash holdings. They can be embodied in *banknotes* or in freely accessible *demand deposits* with a bank. *Token coins* are also money substitutes if they are instantly exchangeable for money. (In this case, it is not necessary that the government should be bound to redeem them: if their supply is limited, the demand for small change gives them an exchange value and makes them easy to exchange against real money.)

These secure and liquid *claims* to money are often confused with money, warns Mises, but that confusion immediately poisons the well from which any sound reasoning on the theory of money could be drawn. The problem is partly that the inaccurate legal terminology surrounding monetary matters obscures the genuine economic distinctions, as when, for example:

What the law understands by money is in fact not the common medium of exchange but the legal medium of payment.[12]

That is, the law is concerned with what people should be obliged to accept in payment (usually the currency managed by the state's own legislators), not what they want to exchange or, in the case of a national currency that has become worthless as a result of wars or inflation, what they *do* in fact exchange.

It is important to remember that these money substitutes, such as banknotes and token coins, stand in relation to money as bread-tickets stand in relation to bread, whatever the law might say on the matter. Bills and coins are not money themselves – although in ordinary language we talk of them as if they are. They are simply drafts on the treasury for a certain quantity of money.

Two types of money substitute. There are two main categories of money substitutes, says Mises, *money certificates* and *fiduciary media.*

Money certificates originated when people offered and accepted warehouse certificates for certain amounts of precious metals, rather than having to physically carry round large quantities of gold and silver to pay their debts. Because each warehouse certificate was a claim to a specific piece of the metal, they were perfect substitutes for money.

Fiduciary media arise where the money reserve kept by the bank or government is less than the total amount of money substitutes issued. It is rather like increasing the number of bread-tickets even though the amount of bread remains the same. Because these claims can be passed from hand to hand indefinitely, those accepting the substitute may not be fully aware of the fact that not all claims could be redeemed if they were presented at the same time. Only an examination of the bank's balance sheet would reveal that. So in fact a proportion of the total volume of money substitutes issued comprises money certificates, since that proportion could be redeemed against money; the remainder, which could not be redeemed if all claims to money were presented at once, comprises what are called the fiduciary media.

Advantages of substitutes. The use of money substitutes, as has been noted already, is very convenient, because they can be easier to carry than the commodity money itself. And it needs only a simple clearing-house mechanism to allow credits and debits to be offset against each other without metal money actually having to be moved at all, since the claims circulate *as if* they were money, and for the most part, people see no reason actually to exchange them for money.

In terms of convenience, warehouse certificates for a commodity money are useful enough, of course; but if people are prepared to accept fiduciary media, it brings not only convenience, but a great saving to everyone involved, since it eliminates the need for at least part of the production or extraction of real commodities such as gold and silver – processes which of course divert effort and capital and make the commodity more expensive for industrial purposes. The cost of producing money is, in fact, a major concern for metal money systems.

Banks, governments, and notes

Although of more questionable benefit, the issue of fiduciary media also confers significant advantages on the bank or government concerned. Instead of being tied to lend borrowers only up to the amount of money in its vaults, it can increase its lending (and thus its income from lending) out of the new issue. The more notes it issues, the more credit can it grant to borrowers.

Limits under free banking. However, there are limits to this, since a large expansion of this sort of credit could make the holders of fiduciary media suspicious and cause them to insist on exchanging the notes for money. If enough people did this at the same time, the bank would be unable to meet its obligations and would fail. Where banks worked in competition, any suspicion would cause people to accept the notes only at less than their face value, or to flock to patronize other banks where they felt more secure. Either event sets a limit on any bank's ability to increase its fiduciary issue.

Latitude of government. If (as is common nowadays) the bank concerned is a central bank with the sole right to issue notes, there might be more leeway than that available to commercial banks facing the pressures of competition from others, because people are reluctant to give up the currency of the nation, and might also be temporarily held back by the legal tender and other laws that force people to pay and accept payment in the official medium. Nevertheless, a serious lack of confidence in the official currency would cause the failure of the system as people switch to using other media that are more trusted vehicles for exchange.

The analytical separation of these different kinds of money substitutes is important for the theory of money and in the understanding of inflation. Money itself cannot be created at will, and thus the credit granted to borrowers on the basis of the amount of money available from investors – what Mises calls *commodity credit* – is limited. However, money substitutes in the form of fiduciary media *can* be expanded, and it is in the expansion of this *circulation credit* that we find the seeds of modern inflations.

THE VALUE OF MONEY

Thus we have dealt with the supply of money, which as is now clear, is very much more complex than most 'monetarists' would imagine. Accordingly, it should come as no surprise if variations in the quantity of one kind of money or money substitute, or changes in the relative volume of the different elements, produce highly distinct results that could not be predicted under the mechanical view that lumps all these separate elements together under one aggregate measure. Under Austrian analysis, there could never be any reason to suppose, as some versions of the quantity theory suppose, that an increase in the quantity of money would lead to an equiproportional decline in its purchasing power.[13] Certainly, Mises accepted and expounded the logical elements of the quantity theory, and warned that monetary policy had the most profound effects on the economy, including on prices. But he recognized that there can be no automatic linkages when human values intervene at every stage. Mises's views on the treatment of money in applied economics is just one example of his general objection to conflating very individual things and events into statistical aggregates and then imagining that these arbitrary measures are somehow linked.

The demand for money

So we are left well aware that the supply of any commodity is only half the story, and demand conditions have to be examined as well. Like all other commodities, there does exist a demand for money, however odd the notion might seem. People want to keep with them, or in their tills and bank accounts, a certain amount of money that they can use to exchange for other things in the future. So we must look at the factors which influence this demand as closely as we must understand the subtleties of its supply, if we are to discover how the price of money, its purchasing power, is determined.

Demand for exchange purposes only. The demand for any particular medium of exchange depends, such as gold or silver, depends both upon its monetary *and* nonmonetary uses. It might be demanded because it has qualities as a production or consumption good, as well as because it is a commonly accepted medium of exchange.

The monetary theorist, however, is interested not in the production or consumption qualities of the commodity, but in its *value in exchange.* In examining the desire of individuals and firms to hold certain stocks of money as such (what is known as the *demand for money*), the monetary theorist's attention must remain confined to the *monetary* aspects of the medium of exchange, not its industrial uses.

To understand Mises's analysis most clearly, then, it is perhaps best to think of money as being in the form of pure fiat money, with no nonmonetary use at all. Since it has no other uses, what would induce people to hold stocks of this item? They must derive some benefit, since the holding of cash requires sacrifices: every penny kept in a pocket, a cash-box, or a bank vault is a penny that is not spent on immediate consumption. So why do they hold it? The answer is because it has a value to them as a medium of exchange.

Values, of course, are subjective and not measurable. All we can measure are the actual quantities of one thing that are exchanged against others, the *price* of one good in terms of another. This balance will depend upon how each good is valued.

The purchasing power of money

Money itself is an economic good, a scarce commodity that is valued and appraised on its own merits as a medium of exchange, and so its price too (or as it is commonly said, the price of other goods in terms of money) will hinge on how it is valued as much as on how other goods are valued. Changes in the money prices of goods in the shops and the services which people supply to each other can have their roots in people changing their attitude to money, in valuing *money* differently (such as when uncertainty about the future induces them to hold larger stocks of cash) as much as in people changing their attitude to the goods and services which are bought, that is, from people valuing *goods* differently (such as when new production processes make certain goods more plentiful). As Mises puts it:

money plays the part of an intermediary between commodity and commodity. But money is an economic good with its own fluctuations in value. A person who acquires money or money substitutes will be affected by all the variations in their objective exchange value.[14]

From this understanding, drawn from Mises's Austrian School predecessors and reinforced by him, it become plain that money is not a standard of prices, and certainly not a standard of value. Money is *itself* valued for its purchasing power. How it is valued might change from year to year and from day to day, and depends entirely on the individuals concerned. The precise rate at which it exchanges depends, as it does for other goods, on how people assess the market conditions at the time.

Determinants of demand. When we are discussing the question of why people want to hold money, it is an interesting point that *all* money is held by someone or other. Economists today often speak of the 'circulating medium' or 'notes and coin in circulation', but there is no such thing, asserts Mises. The media of exchange are always in the hands of somebody, never in a limbo between persons.

Those who hold stocks of money in their pockets, vaults, or cash registers, may decide to hold greater or smaller amounts of money, depending on their view of market conditions. Prices, of course, are always fluctuating, and their future progress is uncertain. Consequently, most people will want to hold a stock of money so that they can grasp bargains and other opportunities which might present themselves in the future. And again, the demand for money might be influenced indirectly by many things, such as the distribution of business activity and the settlement of accounts over different seasons of the year, the spread and efficiency of banking institutions, and so on. But the effect of these factors is not mechanical, of course: they do not determine the demand for money clearly and precisely. Different people may assess them and the other conditions of the marketplace differently, and conclude that it is desirable to hold larger or smaller amounts of cash at any instant of time.

The circularity problem. People hold money, therefore, because it provides them with a stock of purchasing power. Naturally, a prominent concern when people form their value judgements on this matter will be the question of what the future purchasing power of their stock of money are likely to be. If individuals anticipate a decline in the purchasing power of money, they might be inclined to hold less of it, and spend it today when they can get more in exchange for each unit of it.

The Austrian theorists had reached this point long before Mises began writing *The Theory of Money and Credit*, but could get little further in the application of their value theory to monetary questions. For they were apparently faced with an insuperable circularity.

In short, the problem is this. Individuals want to hold consumption or production goods for the subjective satisfaction they expect from them. Those goods are demanded because they have the power to satisfy, and that demand is one of the elements (along with the supply of the goods in question) that in turn explains their price. But money is different, because (in its pure form) it has no value as a consumption or production good: its ability to bring satisfaction to the individual depends on its use as a medium of exchange, on its purchasing power. People decide how much money they want to hold at least partly on the basis of what they can buy with it now and what they expect it will buy in the future.

Now that is equivalent to saying that the demand for money

depends on its exchange value, on its price; but going back to the supply and demand analysis, it is clear that a major factor in the explanation of price is demand itself. So the older Austrians seemed to be stuck in an unbreakable circle.

While the application of value theory to other goods was simple enough, therefore, and the marginal utility analysis built by the Austrians became popularly infused into mainstream economics, it seemed to founder on the monetary reef. As a result, the whole subjectivist approach was called into question because of its apparent incompleteness.

Mises's solution. Mises's solution to this circularity problem is undoubtedly one of the most important and most radical innovations in *The Theory of Money and Credit*, and also one of the most controversial. It has come to be known as the *regression theorem*.

In deciding how much money to hold, he says, individuals look at what money can be exchanged for at current prices (or more accurately, at prices which prevailed in the moment just passed) As he expresses it:

The individual must take into account the objective exchange value of money, as determined in the market yesterday, before he can form an estimate of the quantity of money that he needs today.[15]

So it is true that the demand for money proposes an existing rate of exchange between money and other goods, an existing 'price' or purchasing power of money. But while the exchange value that emerges today is determined by today's supply conditions and the demand which is manifested today, it is not that same exchange value which is used by individuals in deciding their demand. That decision is made on the basis of the exchange value of money in the immediate past, in the purchasing power of money as determined by the market 'yesterday'. The demand decisions that led to that result yesterday, in turn depended upon what each unit of money would purchase the day before, and so on.

Against the charge that this theorem simply replaces the problem of circularity with the fresh absurdity of an infinite regress, Mises argues that the backward path ends when the commodity just began to be used as a medium of exchange. At that point, its value in the previous instant derived only from its consumption and industrial uses, not from its value as a medium of exchange. Thus, the demand for it stemmed from its ability to satisfy directly, and was not based on its prior purchasing power. So the chain is ended, and the regression is not infinite.

This conclusion, of course, not only breaks the Austrian circularity problem, but it gives us another insight into the nature and value of money. For it indicates that before anything could come to serve as money, it must always have had some nonmonetary function and value:

Before an economic good begins to function as money it must already possess exchange value based on some other cause than its monetary function. But money that already functions as such may remain valuable even when the original source of its exchange value has ceased to exist. Its value then is based entirely on its function as a common medium of exchange.[16]

That point, Mises thought, explains the emergence and persistence not just of commodity money but of credit money and fiat money. Credit money obviously has its roots in real commodity transactions, and so is easily explained by the regression theorem. Fiat money might come from the suspension of convertibility between paper and the hard commodity (paper pounds and lirae once represented those quantities of silver, for example, but no longer), or from the introduction of a fresh form of currency: but the first is, and the second must be, still rooted in some commodity or in some prior currency system that was itself rooted in a commodity. Such money can remain valuable even though its origins are clouded by time.

Objections to Mises's view

This latter point about fiat currency was not perfectly understood by those who read Mises's analysis, and he returned to state it at greater length in *Human Action*. In that same work, he was able to answer other objections to the regression theorem. For example, some economists rejected Mises's way out of the circularity problem on the grounds that it was merely a historical description, and with the argument that events today must be explained by forces in operation today, not those of yesterday.

Both criticisms, replied Mises, have missed the point. His description, true enough, does describe events which must have happened in history: but the analysis itself is a purely logical one, and it is on the logic, not the history of the matter, that it must be judged. And it is perfectly legitimate to argue that people's values (and therefore, demand) today take into consideration things that happened in the past.[17]

Alleged irrelevance. The debate, however, did not end with *Human Action*. Don Patinkin, in his 1956 *Money, Interest, and Prices*,[18] while agreeing that individuals could not make a judgement about the exchange value of money unless its purchasing power was first known, nevertheless argued that this information was not necessary in order to derive the demand function for money. Thus the circularity problem did not exist and Mises was wrong that only by reference to historical prices could utility analysis be applied to money.

This objection is important, though difficult to state simply. It begins by imagining that all commodities are lumped together, so the only choice facing the individual is between the amount of cash he or she wants to hold and the volume of 'goods' he or she wants to consume – a traditional indifference curve model. Next it asks the individual to consider various prices of the goods in terms of money and asks the individual how many units of money he or she would demand at each one. That gives us a relationship between prices and the demand for cash balances that, when added up for all individuals, constitutes the demand for money.

At this point, we have derived a demand function without assuming any *particular* value of money, the Walrasian calculus of simultaneous equations has given us a general theorem to do the job. Next, we can bring down this kite by introducing the supply of money, which together with that demand curve, determines its actual market value, its purchasing power. That allows us to determine the specific quantities demanded by individuals (and thus takes us back to being able to discuss the marginal utility of money without any reference to historical prices).

Assessment of the critique. Such reasoning has convinced many economists, including those in the Austrian School,[19] Mises was wrong to assert that a particular prior value of money *must* be known before the demand for money can be established. Walrasian methods can achieve the same end.

Mises, for his defence, would probably say that the Patinkin argument falls at the first hurdle, because the alleged indifference curve between goods and money could not exist unless people knew the value of money beforehand. Only when we have an idea of their purchasing power do the pieces of paper we commonly call 'money' have any meaning for us. The purchasing power of money must be prior to any indifference analysis. Patinkin, on the other hand, argues that a series of different hypothetical purchasing powers can be used to derive a demand function, which together with the supply function will determine the actual value.

Elegant though Patinkin's approach might be, Mises's analysis still seems to have the edge in terms of providing a causal explanation of how people actually think and behave, instead of a sanitized abstraction. Where new currencies are introduced, they invariably *are* linked to some historical currency, and for good reason. People simply *do* refer back to their experience in assessing their future demand for money and other goods. Market activity *does* take place in the context of what has happened before, and is not an unconnected succession of discrete instants.

CONCLUSION

Perhaps we should concur that the circularity problem was a red herring, but that it has been so in an unusual way. Whatever the rights and wrongs of the argument, the Austrian formulation of the problem, and Mises's attempt to solve it, have unfortunately diverted a great deal of attention from other issues of equal or greater moment.

It is a misfortune when attention is diverted, for example, from Mises's extraordinarily powerful analysis of the different kinds of money and money substitutes. For in this can be detected the source of the practical problems that have been experienced in applying a doctrine that is in essence sound, the quantity theory of money. And the tragedy is no less when monetary theorists fail to look at the *meaning* which money, and the different kinds of money in existence, can have to individuals – and then expect to discover simple mechanical formulae explaining monetary relationships, upon which future monetary policy can be based. It is a dangerous pastime: as the next chapter will show, Mises's reintroduction of subjectivist principles into the theory of money, and thus into the conduct of every transaction in the exchange economy, credits monetary policy with a power that even committed monetarists scarcely comprehend.

CHAPTER THIRTEEN

Inflation and its Effects

> There is no justification whatever for the widespread
> belief that variations in the quantity of money must
> lead to inversely proportionate variations in the
> objective exchange value of money, so that, for
> example, a doubling of the quantity of money must
> lead to a halving of the purchasing power of money.[1]

Thus far we have examined Mises's view of the demand for
money, and his insistence that the amounts demanded by
individuals depend upon their own value structures, formed in
the context of the entirety of their economic circumstances,
rather than upon a few straightforward variables that can be
expressed in simple formulae. Like other prices, the purchasing
power of money can be expected to fluctuate depending upon
the state of individuals' assessment of the market conditions at
the time.

Yet this is only half the story. In the same way that the
available supply of any commodity also has a bearing on how
its price is determined, so does the supply of money have a
bearing on its eventual purchasing power. So we must trace the
possible sources of changes in the supply of money if we are to
explain the evident changes in its purchasing power (usually,
erosions) that do in fact occur.

The supply of money

The supply of a *commodity* currency tends to be rather stable.
True, innovations such as new extraction processes, new
discoveries of currency metals, and the tendency of rises in
purchasing power to provoke people into greater production of
the monetary commodity, will all tend to boost supply. Yet
these are rarely the source of the most significant increases.

The largest changes are generally found not in money strictly

273

defined, but in money substitutes. Banks, as we have seen, may not be able to expand *commodity credit* beyond the amount of the commodity currency their investors entrust to them. But they are nevertheless able to expand *circulation credit* by increasing the volume of the fiduciary media they issue. This expansion might be limited by the pressures of competition, but there are no *natural* limits on it, because fiduciary media are cheap or even costless to produce. Often, it has been deemed desirable to set some legal limit to the amount of paper not covered by money that banks are empowered to issue, that is, to invoke deliberate banking policies. Where only the central bank is empowered to issue fiduciary media, however, there is usually less willingness among the authorities to impose such self restraint.

Scope for expansion. Laws aimed to control the issue of bank paper, says Mises, have proved to be only a modest restraint upon the growth of circulation credit, because other methods of expanding it have been devised. Thus, a banking system based on the fractional reserve principle, where only a proportion of the total credit extended to borrowers has to be matched by money in the banks' tills and vaults, has allowed the issue of fiduciary media to continue, but in a more disguised form. In his words, the laws controlling bank paper

have limited the issue of fiduciary media in the form of notes, but have set no limits to their issue in the form of deposits. Making the issue of notes more difficult was bound to promote an increased employment of deposits; in place of the note, the deposit account came into prominence.[2]

It is quite common for people to speak, perhaps figuratively, of increases in the quantity of money being due to the government (or where they exist, the issuing banks) actually 'printing' more money. In fact, Mises is saying, the main vehicle for monetary expansions is not printed paper at all, but the creation of new credit. When we speak of an 'increase in the supply of money', therefore, it will be more likely to take the form of an increase in government or deposit account credit, rather than the issue of physical bits of paper or metal. And Mises believes that the exact nature of the expansion is of the greatest importance in deciding its outcome.

The quantity theory

This Austrian School position is somewhat contrary to the quantity theory of money, which was accepted quite widely before its validity was challenged in the eighteenth and nineteenth centuries, then rejected completely in the mid-nineteenth century, only to be resurrected as the doctrine of 'monetarism' in the late twentieth. Mises argues that there is a large kernel of truth in the quantity theory approach, but that it does not provide a complete explanation of events and therefore overlooks some of the key questions and problems.

The quantity theory applies a straightforward supply and demand analysis to the question of the price or purchasing power of money. If one imagines that the demand for money is stable (and quantity theorists see no reason to doubt that this is usually the case), then the price of money is determined by changes in its supply. Thus, quantity theorists (or 'monetarists') hold that an increase in the supply of money leads to a lowering of its purchasing power, just as any other commodity is cheapened by an increase in its supply. As a refinement, many adhere to the strict 'proportionality theorem', that a doubling of the supply of money will lead – perhaps after a lag, and assuming that all complicating factors could be filtered out of the picture – to a halving of its purchasing power, and so on.

Mises's refinements. Mises sees the insight that an increase in the supply of money will tend to depress its purchasing power as a correct one, but insists that, once again, the classical analysis overlooks the motives of the individuals concerned and is therefore drawn into a mechanistic view that is completely inappropriate. The ultimate folly in this regard is the belief that the increase in supply leads to an inversely proportionate effect on purchasing power. Thus, the quantity theory is correct only to the extent that it includes all the factors which motivate people to buy and sell, and gets away from mindless aggregates

275

of 'demand' and 'supply', since the final outcome of any change will depend on subjective valuations and not some mythical connection between gross quantities:

From the economic point of view, a quantity has no other relationships than those which exercise some influence upon the valuations of individuals concerned in some process or other of exchange.[3]

In other words, people have different personal reactions to increases in the supply of money and money substitutes. The amounts of cash or money substitutes that they end up demanding in the light of these differences is hard to judge, and it is certainly illegitimate to suppose that there is a 'community' demand for money that is predictable, still more illegitimate to imagine that it is stable. Thus the effect on prices is more difficult to characterize than the mechanical monetarist model would have us believe.

THE EFFECT ON PRICES

The quantity theory presumes that the effect of an increase in the supply of money and money substitutes upon the prices of the various commodities traded in the marketplace is uniform. It may or may not be portrayed as an exactly proportionate change, depending upon which theorist is arguing the case, but whatever change is produced is assumed to be spread equally across all prices. Money, according to the quantity theorists, has an impact on the *price level*, but it is *neutral* in its effect on the relative prices of particular commodities, at least in the medium to long term after any initial but temporary effects have worn off. Changes in the supply of money therefore have only a *nominal* effect, an effect on prices, but do not affect relative prices and therefore do not influence or upset the real structure of production within the economy. This, says Mises, is not only misleading, it is wrong.

The non-uniform effect on prices

The monetarist model starts from the theoretical assumption that the supply of money is increased (or decreased) uniformly across all individuals. In fact, objects Mises, it is 'confessedly difficult' to imagine how every individual's stock of money could be increased by an equal proportion, so that each was left in the same position relative to other holders of money as they were before.[4]

Even if such a uniform change could be imagined, its effect on prices would be far from uniform. It does not require any deep understanding of Austrian subjectivist principles to see that the various individuals concerned would undoubtedly value the increase differently: some would welcome the addition, while others would prefer to dispose of it by spending it immediately. If the latter group of individuals tend to buy different sorts of goods from the former, the effect of the increase will be to bid up the prices of the particular assortment of goods bought by the spenders while the prices of the goods bought by the savers remain unchanged.

A further hitch is that the same individual's spending patterns may change as a result of the new money at his or her disposal. To illustrate Mises's point, would a doubling of a person's money stock cause them to double their purchases of potatoes and also their purchases of caviare? Normally, one would expect the recipient of such a windfall would cut down on potatoes and increase caviare consumption radically. The differing pressures which this puts on the prices of the two commodities is plain enough.

The most favourable (and confessedly difficult to imagine) assumptions, therefore, cannot save the hypothesis that a monetary increase leads to a general increase in prices. It will always generate changes in relative prices, and those in turn will attract resources away from some parts of the economy and towards others. There are, in other words, always *real* changes following disturbances in the nominal quantity of money.

Spreading effect. The monolithic view of prices common in the work of the quantity theorists disguises the fact that relative prices are always in motion, says Mises. The image of a global price level that moves up or down depending upon the amount of money injected into the system is one which conceals information and gives an entirely false impression of what really happens in the marketplace:

When people talk of a 'price level' they have in mind the image of a level of liquid which goes up or down according to the increase or decrease in its quantity, but which, like a liquid in a tank, rises evenly. But with prices, there is no such thing as a 'level'. Prices do not change to the same extent at the same time.[5]

In fact, the effect of a change in the quantity of money is not to raise or lower prices suddenly and uniformly, but to *spread* gradually from one sector to another.

An increase in the supply of money is not dropped evenly across the whole economy from helicopters: it has to start somewhere, and an increase in the quantity of money available to the whole market system can only arise initially as an increase in the cash holdings of certain individuals. Typically, an increase will come from the government: let us say through the issue of additional quantities of paper money. With this at its disposal, the government can buy extra goods and services. This new demand causes the prices of what the government buys to rise immediately, while the prices of other commodities remains unaltered for the moment. Those selling goods and services to the government are the first to benefit, in terms of higher sales receipts and wages, and so the prices of the assortment of goods which they buy then rise. Their suppliers are next to benefit, and their spending bids up other prices, and so on. Thus the boom spreads from one market to another, benefiting one group of individuals after another. The rise in prices is neither uniform nor synchronous.[6]

To take an analogy from F.A. Hayek, the effect is not so much like water poured into a tank, but like honey poured into a saucer: it forms a mound of higher relative prices where it first enters the economy, and only gradually does the effect spread more generally.[7]

Non-neutrality and distribution effects

From this analysis, it can be appreciated that the effect of monetary changes could not possibly be uniform across the whole economic system, and must inevitably produce relative price changes that benefit different groups of people at different times.

For the effect of a monetary change on prices to be uniform, it would require each individual to react both simultaneously and similarly. Each would have to take precisely the same view of the value of the various kinds of money and money substitutes which are kept on hand, and of the new totals that followed their windfall, and to adjust their consumption of all commodities by an exactly equal amount. If we were to believe the additional presumption of *proportionality*, it would require spending on each commodity to increase uniformly in direct proportion to the increase in money so that the pressure on prices is exactly in line with the monetary boost. It does not take much insight to realize that

we may not conclude . . . that a doubling of the quantity of money must lead to a halving of the purchasing power of the monetary unit; for every variation in the quantity of money introduces a dynamic factor . . .[8]

Non-neutrality. This dynamic factor changes the relative positions of prices and of individuals. Some prices rise and some people gain at first, other prices rise and other people gain later on. And naturally, both resources and personnel are attracted to those sectors where prices are rising relatively to the general trend. So there is a marked movement towards those markets where the initial monetary stimulus was felt and away from those where it is not discerned until later. There are, in other words, powerful distributive effects following an increase in the quantity of money.

The quantity theorist, Mises acknowledges, would be inclined to assert that whatever these 'first round' effects might be, the eventual outcome is the same. New money quickly flows from group to group until the income of each has been improved and prices have been bid up uniformly. The initial imbalances were only transitory.[9] But, insists Mises, the adjustment will not in fact be complete. People value new money in different ways, and their spending patterns *will* change, causing more permanent changes. The relative prices of commodities after the effect has petered out will not be the same as those before. There will be *real* changes. Money is not neutral.

Welfare effects. Nor is the effect of monetary increases always desirable. Loans, for example, will generally be repaid in fixed monthly or yearly amounts, especially where no major changes in the purchasing power of money have been foreseen. Consequently, price rises benefit debtors, who can now repay their obligations in a currency that is devalued. Indeed, all transactions which require payment at a later date will be affected by the price changes; some more than others, depending on which prices change and when. Trade, in other words, becomes a much riskier business, and that can hardly have a stimulating effect on the process of production and exchange. Wage rates too will be eroded when prices rise, causing increased problems for the settlement of wage contracts. All such difficulties impose a cost on the individuals and firms in the market, since they have to make provision for such contingencies, and the distribution effects of monetary changes give windfall gains to some at the cost of unexpected losses for others.

In the course of such a monetary disturbance, complains Mises, it is always those in the markets that are last in line to receive the stimulus, those last to adjust, who fare the worst. The groups which are first in line to receive the boom's effects (typically, those nearest to the government's purse) do well: they enjoy heightened incomes while the prices of the commodities they buy remain sticky for a while. Those last in line, however, face increased prices for what they buy long before their own income is uplifted by the boom tide.

It depends also upon whether people correctly anticipate the course of events, whether they will fare better or worse. Some people might expect the increase in prices to be temporary, and not alter their way of life, biding their time until the anticipated fall. They might wait years. But if the increase in money persists or accelerates, as is often the case, eventually even the least perceptive people will recognize that it is better to spend their cash stocks rather than see their value eroded yet further.

A new boom is suddenly unleashed, and spending will rise dramatically. Unfortunately, so will prices: and in fact the boom becomes a crack-up boom as people feverishly attempt to spend their devaluing currency until the monetary system breaks down under the pressure.

Price indexes

A great many economists overlook these crucial relative changes in prices. This tendency is reinforced by the problem of measuring the purchasing power of money.

The objective exchange value of a unit of money can be expressed in terms of what it will buy – a number or volume of goods or services. However, there is no such thing as 'the' price of a good or service, since different suppliers will undoubtedly be prepared to accept different prices depending upon local conditions and upon their individual assessment of the market. Furthermore, individual prices will vary against others: the price of vegetables varies depending on the season, for example, while the price of overcoats might move in exactly the opposite direction.

How one measures the purchasing power of the monetary unit, therefore, depends very much on what that unit is actually used to buy, and when. Attempting to eliminate all the ups and downs in prices, theorists have consequently resorted to lumping together the prices of a large number (or 'basket') of commodities, so producing a 'price index' that is intended to be some sort of measure. But Mises does not regard this as a completely satisfactory procedure.

Inevitable shortcomings of indexes. The trouble, says Mises, is that whatever we lump into an index, the problem remains that different individuals in fact purchase different baskets of goods, and so may face different degrees of change in the purchasing power of their income when relative prices fluctuate. An index might be based on a selection of goods and show no overall change at a particular time: but within that stable global average, food (for example) might be rising in price significantly while the prices of other goods are falling. Households whose budget goes largely on food will find themselves much worse off than wealthier households to whom groceries form only a small part of the family budget.

If we believe that monetary policy should aim to keep prices stable, as many monetarists do, this problem of measurement can be a serious one. For over the years, different goods are traded, in which case the choice of our basket of commodities on which the price index is based becomes impossible. To take an extreme case: how can we compare the purchasing power of the monetary unit today with that of the tenth century when a completely different array of commodities changed hands?[10] The problem facing those who construct price indexes year by year is exactly the same, only different in degree. In Mises's support, however, it might be noted that in a period of rapid technological change, the assortment of goods traded on the marketplace can turn over quite quickly, so the problem is no less important.

A common belief among governments is that rising prices can and should be reduced by a restriction in the supply of money, while falling prices indicate an insufficiency of media of exchange which can be cured by a boost. The trouble is that index numbers actually give us a rather poor idea of what is happening in the economy. They tend to obscure the relative price changes that occur, and make us think that price changes really do appear uniformly and that monetary changes produce only uniform effects. In this, they obscure the data on which the empirical version of the quantity theory of money is formulated, and introduce similar confusions into any policy based on that theory. They do have some usefulness, but it is limited:

Under certain conditions, index numbers may do very useful service as an aid to investigation into the history and statistics of prices; for the extension of the theory of the nature and value of money they are unfortunately not very important.[11]

Political issues. What basket of commodities is chosen, how prices are found, which areas are surveyed, how changing balances in the supply of goods are accommodated, will all affect the index numbers chosen. As Mises expresses it:

There are many ways of calculating purchasing power by means of index numbers, and every single one of them is right, from certain tenable points of view; but every single one of them is also wrong, from just as many equally tenable points of view. Since each method of calculation will yield results that are different from those of every other method, and since each result, if it is made the basis of practical measures, will further certain interests and injure others, it is obvious that each group of persons will declare for those methods that will best serve its own interests.[12]

Monetary policy, therefore, immediately plunges us into political, rather than purely economic, arguments. For it does not affect everyone to the same degree. So, mindful of the serious changes in the relative positions of individuals that are generated following changes in the quantity of money, what should be the policy of the monetary authorities with respect to the supply of media of exchange?

The goals of monetary policy

According to Mises, monetary policy should not aim at fixing prices or pegging any of the other targets at which it commonly aims. The first duty of the authorities, he proclaims, should be to affirm and support the choice of monetary commodity that is reached by individuals in the marketplace.[13] Various forms of money have, after all, emerged quite naturally in the process of exchange, and some, such as gold and silver, were accepted for many centuries. A wise policy for sound money would therefore incorporate a second element, namely some restraint which would prevent the money chosen by economic agents from being corrupted by the political objectives of politicians and the pressure-groups who influence their deliberations. The free operation of the market, rather than the attempt to restrict and regulate it, is likely to be the best bet in this regard, according to Mises:

Unfortunate experiences with banknotes that had become valueless because they were no longer actually redeemable led once to the restriction of the right of note issue to a new privileged institutions.

283

Yet experience of state regulation of banks-of-issue and clearing banks has been incomparably more unfavourable than experience of uncontrolled private enterprise.[14]

Government benefits from inflation. As a matter of experience, inflationary policies have proved powerfully attractive to governments, and Mises believes that there are many reasons why governments lean towards inflation rather than sound money. Indeed, the problem might be worse, says Mises, without price indexes, which at least give some indication that prices are rising and so help to deter the monetary authorities from even worse excesses. The most prominent incentive for governments to inflate is that they are first to benefit from its effects, and so they experience a gain from the distributional changes that Mises has charted. The simple gain to the government as the first beneficiary in the boom processes is a clear inducement to keep the supply of fiduciary media expanding. More issue means that the government can buy more goods and services.

The siren call of inflation. But some economists believe that, even without this mercenary motive, inflation has beneficial effects and is necessary for progress. The stimulating effect of a monetary increase is clear – at least, as long as it lasts. Also, a fixed quantity of money would actually produce *falling* prices because of the tendency for productive efficiency to increase, which means that a growing volume of goods and services must be traded against the same unchanging quantity of money – driving money prices down. This, people imagine, has a depressing effect on entrepreneurship and innovation. To Mises, however, such a conclusion is merely a result of our inflationist psychology, which makes it hard for us to think of falling prices without supposing that they indicate depression and stagnation. In fact, he argues, entrepreneurs are not interested in *nominal* prices, but in whether the goods and services they supply are able to command a price higher than the trend. Progress is all about products becoming *cheaper*, although large inflations in recent decades have often disguised that fact.

However, against Mises's view, we might cite Lord Keynes's doctrine that a modest dose of inflation is beneficial because some prices, especially wages, are notoriously sticky downwards. Rising prices, says Keynes, may give people the illusion that they are standing still even when their incomes or receipts are falling, and so can help the smooth adjustment of the economy to relative price changes. Nevertheless, it remains doubtful that the workers who had been fooled by this device would regard the process as beneficial, whatever its attraction to politicians.

Investment. Other arguments could be marshalled on the side of inflation. It is acknowledged to benefit debtors, and therefore, say its supporters, it benefits entrepreneurs and others borrowing money for productive purposes more than it benefits the thrifty who contribute little to production. Mises doubts that borrowers are in fact more likely to generate wealth (some are borrowing just to consume, not to build factories), and points out the cost and risk that uncertainty about future price movements brings into the loan market – which would actually make funds for business expansion *more* difficult to obtain.

Employment policy. Full employment policy is another major element of inflationism, says Mises. A stimulus to prices might give people in retail trades the illusion that a real increase in demand has come. So they employ more workers, order more goods, and generally boost employment. When the stimulus has worked through their group and moved on to others, however, the stimulus is seen to be transient. Employment will be cut once again. So no lasting gain has been achieved (and, as we will see in the next chapter, expenditure on inconvertible capital assets that must be discarded as the inflationary stimulus subsides may leave us with a net *loss*). The only way to improve employment, says Mises, is to scrap the labour market regulations such as wage minima that price people out of jobs and interventions that induce them not to work.[15]

Mises cites other pressures causing governments to inflate, but the basic problem is that inflation has illusory effects that make it, quite simply, more popular than a deflationary world in which prices and incomes appear to be falling (albeit only in nominal terms).

Rules or commodities?

Milton Friedman, for the quantity theorists, agrees with Mises about the awesome power of monetary policy, but doubts the likelihood of any return to commodity-based currencies in which no fiduciary expansion – and so no abuse of the system by governments – is possible. To his mind, governments are likely to remain as the authorities which determine the quantity of money. So we must ask what principles should guide their actions in this respect.

Friedman concurs that monetary policy should not be used in a futile attempt to peg real magnitudes such as interest rates, foreign exchange rates, or employment. He is nevertheless reluctant to give up the target of stable prices. Thus, he would not stop the growth of the quantity of money cold, because that would produce falling prices; and he believes that governments should aim to increase the monetary aggregates according to a fixed rule that expands them roughly in line with the expansion of output, which would generate roughly stable price levels.[16]

Mises, on the other hand, believes that even if a government were completely honest and above reproach in its attempts to keep the purchasing power of money stable and avoid falling prices, there is no simple rule it could follow to achieve this effect. Price indexes, as we have seen, simply disguise relative changes and so cannot provide any guidance. The actual assortment of goods traded varies from month to month and year to year, making it impossible to devise any basket of commodities that will yield sensible price figures at which to aim. Leaving any discretion to the government would undoubtedly draw us into inflationism once again:

In employing any means to influence the value of money, we run the risk of giving the wrong dose. This is all the more important since in fact it is not possible even to *measure* variations in the purchasing power of money.[17]

The gains and losses in gold

What is left? If we seek a monetary arrangement in which the power of the government to upset matters is minimal, it will have to be one in which all future fiduciary issues, either in notes or in bank deposits, are curbed. It will be one based on a commodity standard, such as gold.

Certainly, admits Mises, a commodity standard is not ideal. It might cost a significant amount to extract the commodity, to store it, and arrange the accounting and money certificate system necessary for its efficient use. Its value still will not be stable, but will depend upon innovations and changes in the cost of extraction, storage, and management, and on variations in its demand for industrial purposes. The prices of other goods in terms of a unit of the commodity currency will still be subject to variations because of this, and the relative difficulty in expanding the commodity in line with the increasing number of transactions in the market economy will probably lead to prices tending to fall more than they rise.[18]

Although a commodity standard such as gold is far from ideal, however, it is in Mises's judgement nevertheless the best available. In fact,

the gold standard has one tremendous virtue: the quantity of the money supply, under the gold standard, is independent of the policies of governments and political parties.[19]

In other words, it is independent of doctrinaire inflationists, politicians seeking to buy popularity, and the pressure groups to which they appeal and which force their hand.

The deficiencies of a gold standard, or any other form of commodity currency, including the drawbacks of its production cost and inevitable price fluctuations, concludes Mises, are not immoderately great. However,

even if the effects were greater, such a money would still deserve preference over one subject to state intervention, since the latter sort of money would be subject to still greater fluctuations.[20]

The result of those fluctuations, as the next chapter will describe, are even more profound than the effects described so far.

CHAPTER FOURTEEN

The Tragedy of the Trade Cycle

> What is needed for a sound expansion of production is additional capital goods, not money or fiduciary media. The credit expansion is built on the sands of banknotes and deposits. It must collapse.[1]

Economists have long speculated about why the economic system seems to swing cyclically from periods of boom to periods of recession and depression. Before Mises, the Austrian School economists, particularly Böhm-Bawerk, had joined the discussion with an explanation in the subjectivist tradition. Mises greatly refined this explanation and added new elements to it, but it was left to his co-worker F.A. Hayek, who became the director of the institute for research into business cycles which Mises founded in Vienna, to explore the details and publish a comprehensive version of the theory. One result is that Mises has received little recognition for his seminal contribution to the subject.

Mises's approach, characteristically, tackles the phenomenon of business cycles from the point of view of the individual business investor, instead of proposing glib, mechanistic, macroeconomic explanations. It is made even more convincing, and certainly very neat, because it integrates several other versions of business cycle theory which, according to Mises, each explain only a part of the overall pattern. Thus, the concentration on money and credit issues found in Ricardo, the effect of the restructuring of production processes found in Böhm-Bawerk, and the forces affecting prices and interest rates found in Knut Wicksell, are all drawn upon by Mises to form a unified theory of economic booms and slumps. Although Mises's interpretation paints a blacker than average picture of the waste caused by business cycles, it does at least offer us some policy prescriptions for preventing them in the future.

MONEY, INTEREST, AND CYCLES

Money, in the broad sense which includes the fiduciary media of government notes, token coins, and uncovered bank paper and deposits, is the root of this particular evil, according to Mises. It can cause serious economic disturbances.

Real effects. In the first place, changes in the supply of money and fiduciary media are not neutral as traditional theories suppose, but bring real changes to the balance of individual wealth, the relative prices of different goods, interest rates, and (as a result of all this) the pattern of investment and the structure of production. It would not be surprising, therefore, to discover that monetary changes lie at the heart of the booms and slumps in production that make up the trade cycle.

Secondly and, Mises hypothesizes, more profoundly, changes in the quantity of money and fiduciary media often show up in the loan market, where they make borrowing cheaper or more expensive and thus encourage or discourage the purchase of capital goods. Thus, monetary changes can have a fairly direct and general impact on the world of production, and once again we are able to trace the roots of the trade cycle from monetary disturbances.

To do so, we must look at the two effects in more detail. And we will find that not only do they depend largely, as Mises is fond of reminding us, on the individual aims, motives, values, or time preferences of those concerned, but that they to some extent work in opposite directions. The real economic disturbances brought about by changes in money and fiduciary media are therefore doubly difficult to predict, and doubly impossible to control. The policy implications of that discovery will become clear later on.

Money, prices, interest, and miscalculation

The first group of effects produced by monetary changes are those on prices and the distribution of wealth, which have been described already in the previous chapter. Changes in both the supply of money and in the demand for it might initiate roughly similar disturbances of this sort, but Mises's main attention goes on changes in *supply*, which he suggests are more pronounced. Further than that, he chooses to examine the roots of trade cycles by looking at *expansions* in the supply, which he indicates are likely to be much more of a threat than contractions, given the temptations offered by fiduciary media with which the banks and the government live.

Whatever its origin, the point is that changes in the money relation, that is, in the interplay between the supply of money and the demand for it, bring about changes in prices and wages. But for consistency and ease of illustration, let us consider once again Mises's classic case of an expansion in the quantity of money and fiduciary media, examining not only the spread of price rises but the additional effects on interest rates and wages, the fundamental elements in every business calculation.

First affected are those markets near to where the new money enters the economic system, often the prices of goods and services bought by the government and the wages of those who supply them. Entrepreneurs who sell in markets where prices are rising and buy in those as yet untouched by the effects of the expansion will gain, and will be prepared to pay higher interest rates for the loans they need to expand their business. Similarly, they will be prepared to pay higher prices for their other inputs, and so the markets which supply them will be stimulated in turn, and entrepreneurs there will enter upon the same course of business expansion. The result is that changes in the money relation precipitate a series of small booms in business, spreading from one market to another and then another. However, the stimulus is temporary, and when prices start to rise more quickly in other sectors, it is lost. Business activity falls back down again, expectations become more pessimistic, the demand for loans declines, and interest rates fall.[2]

Uncertainty of redistribution

The effects on production might be more lasting than this, however, depending upon exactly how the new money is distributed, and on the the new distribution of wealth in society that follows the change. The process of inflation will shift the distribution of wealth, leaving some individuals (principally those who were first to benefit) relatively better off than before, and others (principally those who were most remote from the stimulus) relatively poorer than before.

If the principal gainers from this process are those who tend to save and accumulate capital rather more than those who lose are inclined to do, there could well be a net swing of the balance of economic resources towards capital projects and away from immediate consumption. The structure of production will tilt towards more sophisticated and lengthy processes than before. This in itself implies a lowering of the underlying rate of interest – people being more prepared to forgo present consumption and undertake long production processes means that they are discounting future consumption at a higher rate. And the larger the subsistence fund accumulated by the fortunate group which benefit most from the inflation, the lower is the rate of interest prevailing in the market likely to be pushed.

Already, then, we can see that inflation is causing serious changes in the economy. If the principal gainers from the inflationary episode are those who save and accumulate capital more than the losers, then there will be a pressure to channel the structure of production into more sophisticated processes than before. The greater the accumulated subsistence fund, the lower is the rate of interest likely to be. If, on the other hand, the gainers are all spendthrifts, present goods will be preferred to future goods, loan funds will be harder to get, and the rate of interest will rise.[3]

Policymakers are often urged to expand the supply of fiduciary media in an attempt to push interest rates down and thus encourage business creation and expansion. But this insight from Mises reminds us that there is in fact no straightforward relationship between monetary changes and interest rate changes: it depends on how the monetary changes affect the balance of wealth in the community and on the particular values of those involved.[4] In Mises's words:

One thing must be clearly stated at this point: there is no direct arithmetical relationship between an increase or decrease in the issue of fiduciary media on the one hand and the reduction or increase in the rate of interest which this indirectly brings about through its effects on the social distribution of property on the other hand.[5]

The implications for business decisions which hinge upon interest rates are similarly difficult to predict.

Prices and the price premium

Gross market rates of interest, as shown in Chapter 11, include elements in addition to that of originary interest. The entrepreneurial element, reflecting the lender's anticipation of future prices and of the risks of the loan, is one. The price premium is another, and it is particularly relevant to the discussion of monetary changes.

The price premium. The price premium is the element which reflects anticipations about the future level of prices. Where prices are expected to rise, the gross market rate of interest must be higher if lenders are to receive the same real return. To take a hypothetical example, if the prevailing interest rate were 5 per cent but prices were expected to rise by 10 per cent, lenders would demand (and borrowers would cheerfully pay) a price premium of 10 per cent, bringing the market rate up to 15 per cent.[6] The price premium completely offsets the effect of rises or falls in the purchasing power of money.

Possible miscalculation. Outside this hypothetical world, however, the price premium found in loan transactions is far from being a secure and rigid arithmetical relationship between prices and interest rates. And this, argues Mises, is a potential source of major miscalculations by lenders, borrowers, investors, indeed by all economic agents.

In the first place, mankind is not blessed with perfect foresight about future prices, and so the price premium at any moment may be too large or too small to compensate for the eventual change in prices. Furthermore, different lenders and borrowers will form different judgements about the future movement of prices, and it is only within the context of the interplay of those personal decisions that the price premium will emerge. Moreover, prices do not move up or down uniformly, but are always changing relative to one another, so that the price premium in the loan market will overcompensate or undercompensate in particular sectors.[7] The price premium might *tend* to compensate for changes in the purchasing power of money, therefore, but because of the unavoidable imperfections in human knowledge and foresight, they will never leave interest rates completely unaffected. That implies that changes in the quantity of money are not neutral: they do not simply push prices up generally while leaving the underlying structure of the economy unchanged. They set changes in train that have a real and perverse effect on business calculations and investment.

The miscalculations are likely to be all the more profound due to the fact that the price premium on loan interest will tend to lag behind the movement of prices. It takes time to collect the data to construct a price index, or for lenders and borrowers to recognize fully how prices are moving. Then, when they have agreed on a compensating price premium, yet further price changes might occur which again will take time to be recognized and then to become incorporated in loan agreements. If the price movements persist, observes Mises, the lag persists, giving a systematic inaccuracy to one of the data that indicate to entrepreneurs whether they should invest in new production or not.

Some monetary theorists, such as Friedman, would be a little more precise on this last point. For the distortion caused in the investment markets might not be so systematic. Those dealing in credit may be fooled by events for a certain time, but eventually, lenders will recognize that they are losing out because of the lag in collecting and acting upon price data. Their tendency then might be to *over*compensate somewhat: and the final track of interest rates may well be a series of oscillations, about the new rate that would be required to offset price increases, gradually diminishing until the compensating level is reached.[8]

Attractive prices. Mises is particularly concerned with interest rates in his analysis. Like the medium of exchange, interest rates have a bearing on every transaction that occurs in the market economy.

However, for the sake of completeness, it must be reiterated that the changes in relative prices, caused by the fact that monetary changes do not occur globally but affect one part of the economy initially and then spread out, also have a profound distorting effect, because high relative prices in the markets first affected by the inflationary boom are a source of false signals that beckon entrepreneurs towards them. When the boom in those markets first affected begins to subside and prices start rising in other markets, then the surge of entrepreneurial effort and capital into them can be seen to have been a mistake. The loans that entrepreneurs took out to finance new factories and production lines are revealed as a poor investment. The higher prices did not indicate a larger consumer demand, but a fleeting wave of credit. Once again we see that money is not neutral but has a profound effect on the structure of production.

More immediate effects

The first effects following monetary changes, then, unleash unpredictable and conflicting forces upon interest rates. In consequence, they frustrate entrepreneurial calculation, for which interest rates are important data, promoting malinvestment and lowering productivity. Nevertheless, it is not clear that they drag the economic system into a cycle of boom and slump.

A second set of effects, Mises surmises, is a much more direct culprit, and systematic in the damage it causes. This is the set of effects on the volume of credit available on the loan market.

The point here is that changes in the supply of money and fiduciary media can have an immediate impact on the amount of lending given to customers by the banks. Banks might expand their fiduciary issue, for example, in order to extend the credit granted to their borrowers (and thus to boost their income in the form of repayments). The resulting surge of new funds onto the loan market, and the banks' attempts to attract new customers by making loans cheaper, leads to a bidding down and reduction of market interest rates.

Meanwhile, the inflationary surge is pushing up the prices of goods and services. The effect of these divergent pressures is to destroy the congruity of net market rates (that is, excluding the price premium and entrepreneurial components) and the rate of originary interest that prevails in the stable situation. And such dislocation prompts entrepreneurs into a new (and, as it turns out, inappropriate) pattern of investment decisions that, ultimately, are manifested in the trade cycle.

THE PROGRESS OF THE CYCLE

Interest and production processes

The rate of originary interest is an important factor in this theory of the trade cycle as outlined by Mises because it defines the length of production process that is just profitable. It represents the willingness of individuals in the marketplace to forgo present consumption for greater consumption later on, and as such is a crucial guide to the entrepreneur who is committing resources today on productive processes that will generate consumable goods at some point in the future.

Thus, a process with a higher rate of return than the originary rate of interest is justifiable; but one with a lower rate of return is not, since people would prefer to have their resources now than the feeble increment promised later. Because economic goods are scarce and the available subsistence fund diverted from present consumption is limited, it is the shorter processes, with the most immediate reward, that will be preferred first. As more capital goods are accumulated, it then becomes possible to embark on longer processes with a lower rate of return.

In consequence, the prevailing production processes at any moment will be (in theory) just long enough to exhaust the fund put aside as a result of the phenomenon of originary interest. If they were shorter, there would be unused capital that could in principle be used on longer, more marginal projects; if they were longer, the fund would be used up before production was completed.

The upswing

When the outpouring of new funds onto the loan market depresses net market rates below the originary rate, this neat balance is disrupted. Although the entrepreneur's wage and materials bill has not changed, an important element in business calculations, the cost of borrowing the funds needed to sustain the production process, has fallen. This reduction in costs makes profitable a range of processes that were previously dismissed as too long to be justified. Heartened by this, entrepreneurs embark on new projects, buying in materials and manpower, and ordering new capital equipment. The boom has begun.

Entrepreneurs may have more to spend, but competition between them for the labour and capital goods currently available will drive up wage rates and the prices of producers' goods. The bigger wage packets of the labour force will raise the demand, and therefore the prices, of consumer goods too. This again gives heart to the entrepreneurs, who now anticipate a healthy price for their final product. They are reassured that increased production will pay, even though their costs are higher, and they resolve to go on. The boom spreads and continues.

The downswing

Greater costs, however, mean that entrepreneurs old and new must each borrow more to sustain their production processes. If the credit expansion that precipitated the boom does not continue, market interest rates will be bid up because this greater demand for loans is not balanced by an increase in the supply of loanable funds. Entrepreneurs will find their budgets squeezed, and will start to cut back; commodity prices will be bid down again, and wage rates, prices, and individuals' cash holdings will all have to adjust back to the new money relation. If wage rates are sticky downwards, entrepreneurs will reduce their labour as a total by laying off workers. If commodity prices do not fall, a smaller volume of them will be bought. Whatever the details, depression spreads. The downswing of the cycle has begun.

A swing back to consumption. It is possible to explain the phenomenon in another way, according to Mises. The credit expansion has prompted entrepreneurs to embark upon new production processes, investing additional factors of production. The decision to commit resources in these ways was taken in the erroneous belief that people were more willing than before to forgo consumption for additional future benefits: interest rates, after all, were falling.

If anything, however, the boost to wages in the upswing of the cycle produces an overall *increase* in consumption, rather than diminution, and the lower rates of interest available on the market discourages new saving and capital accumulation, rather than boosting it. But even if consumption and saving continued at their former rate, the seeds of the crisis would have been sown. For now, the entrepreneur is like a builder who has oversized a set of foundations and discovers that there are insufficient bricks to complete the house only when most of the structure has been raised. Similarly, the new production processes embarked upon by entrepreneurs require a longer waiting time, but the subsistence fund is insufficient to last until they are concluded. That puts an upward pressure on consumption goods prices, which in turn has the unfortunate effect of urging entrepreneurs to expand and borrow even more in an effort to capture the gains of what appears to be a booming market. Regrettably, it requires an *accelerating* expansion of credit if the boom is to be maintained. Even a continuing expansion of undiminished size will be unable to feed it.

The end and consequences of the cycle

The breakdown of the boom, according to Mises's analysis, comes when the banks (and perhaps today we would add the government) become worried by the accelerating pace of credit and begin to exercise more prudence and to curb it. But this reveals the illusory nature of the business boom. Plans that were suggested by the cheapness of loan rates can be continued only if new funds can continue to be borrowed at artificially low rates. It is this margin that gave them the false appearance of being profitable. When the credit expansion comes to an end, it

297

does not *cause* a disaster; it merely *reveals* a disaster that has already occurred:

> the return to monetary stability does not *generate* a crisis. It only brings to light the malinvestments and other mistakes that were made under the hallucination of the illusory prosperity created by the easy money.[9]

Nor could the boom continue if the credit expansion were ruthlessly accelerated. Banks, for their part, would come up against the institutional barriers designed to prevent large expansions of credit: or, in the case of free and competitive banking, traders would begin to doubt the security of their paper issues, and begin to accept their paper only at a discount or demand that it should be immediately redeemed in commodity money. The government would similarly have to end an ever-accelerating issue of its own fiduciary media as prices spiralled higher and higher and the circulating medium became unacceptable to the point where the monetary system broke down completely. In short,

> Any attempt to substitute additional fiduciary media for nonexisting capital goods . . . is doomed to failure.[10]

Real waste. The real losses in all this can be considerable indeed. As previous chapters have revealed, capital goods are more or less convertible. In the upswing, entrepreneurs were ordering new equipment to use in the production processes that began to appear profitable, causing a great rush to acquire capital goods. But it takes time to build productive machinery, and faced with the shortage of capital goods, entrepreneurs may have shut down some production processes and transferred equipment to others that seemed more profitable.

As economic reality reasserts itself, however, it becomes clear that the new processes cannot be sustained. So, much of that effort and equipment will be lost. The refurbishment and retooling of plants and production lines will have been a waste of time and money. Firms in need of urgent cash will dispose of their inventories cheaply; factories will be closed, construction projects abandoned, and workers fired. Lenders will suffer the increasing risk that their debtors might fail, and the entre-preneurial component of loans will rise, making it even more difficult for firms to get the funds they need to stay afloat. Even prudent firms will be hit by the squeeze. The downswing turns into a panic.

No painless escape. Faced with such a recession, some politicians might argue that panic itself and panic alone is the cause, and that because people see things getting worse, they are more inclined to abandon their investments and less willing to begin new enterprises – all of which continues the spiral. Nevertheless, insists Mises, no mere restoration of confidence can return things to their original state. Consumers are generally worse off than before because capital has been destroyed and must be accumulated once again if the standard of living is to be restored. The credit expansion has not enriched them, but taxed them. At the same time, the balance of wealth and income has changed, so that the old price structure can never be restored. New patterns of spending power have arisen and new price relationships will have to be learnt. It will take time before production can be adjusted to serve the new pattern of consumer demands. And as prices fluctuate, first rising in the upswing and then plummeting in the panic, people will fail to anticipate them precisely, generating further sources of loss. In the attempt to maintain confidence, firms and governments might conceal the extent of business losses,[11] but they nonetheless exist.

There is no way out of the process, says Mises, except the dismal route of falling prices and wages. Any attempt to delay such falls (by trade unions, for example) simply prolongs the stagnation and delays the eventual collapse. The sad truth of the matter is that the artificial boom was not in fact a period of 'good business' but an enormous waste of resources on bad invest-ments. No subsequent efforts can rewrite that historical fact.

CONCLUSION

The origin of the business cycle, then, is ultimately the govern-ment's policy on fiduciary issues. True, even an expansion in commodity money (say, due to the discovery of new gold reserves) would have rather similar effect, but Mises insists that money in the narrow sense never in practice demonstrates the unbridled tendency to expansion that is a common feature of fiduciary media – indeed, a commodity would become useless as a currency if it were overly prone to such fluctuations.

Once one has understood their source in credit expansion, one can see that it is quite wrong to think of trade cycles as regular and unavoidable natural phenomena, like the phases of the moon or sunspots (to which some people have linked them). In the economic record, we do not find any regular and episodic 'long waves' of economic prosperity and decline, just a patchwork of booms and busts brought on by credit expansion. In many cases, it is the deliberate attempt of the government to lower interest rates and create a boom which is to blame:

True, governments can reduce the rate of interest in the short run . . . issue additional paper currency . . . open the way to credit expansion by the banks. They can thus create an artificial boom and the appearance of prosperity. But such a boom is bound to collapse soon or late and to bring about a depression.[12]

The moral shortcomings of politicians, who might be quite prepared to accept the immediate applause for the boom and leave others to worry about the depression, are well known. The trouble is that the careful investors who lose all or part of their fortunes in the cycle are more inclined to blame the obvious target of the capitalists rather than the less obvious but more guilty culprits in the political world.[13]

PART FOUR: MISES'S THEORETICAL CONTRIBUTION

CHAPTER FIFTEEN

The Scientific Foundation of Economics

> ... economics ... is a deductive system. It draws its strength from the starting point of its deductions, from the category of action. No economic theorem can be considered sound that is not solidly fastened upon this foundation by an irrefutable chain of reasoning.[1]

THE CHALLENGE OF MISES'S METHOD

For Mises, the character of economics is quite unlike that of the natural sciences. The natural sciences, such as physics or chemistry, deal with *things* and the regular relationships that we can discover operating between those things. They are concerned with objective events that can be measured, repeated, tested in experiments, and predicted.

The events with which the economist wants to deal, on the other hand, are not mechanical; not the regular and predictable consequences of observable, objective, prior events. They depend instead upon *subjective* factors – on the particular *meaning* of events and things for those individuals who happen to be in the marketplace at that moment, and the particular personal *judgements* they form about the world and their needs. Economic events are the outcome of acts of *valuation* – the emotional reaction of men and women to the external world and their physiological condition at that moment[2], and as such, are immune to measurement and defy precise prediction.

Nor are the natural scientist's tools of repetition and experiment open to the economist. The economic process is an unremittingly complex web of interrelationships between large numbers of individuals, each with their own unique aims and values, those subjective factors upon which the result turns. As time marches on, things and people change, and the precise complex of conditions that exists at any one time can never be exactly repeated, making experimentation impossible.

Insurmountable dualism

On the basis of his analysis of such important differences, Mises concludes that we face 'an insurmountable *methodological dualism*'.[3] The approach we use to gain scientific knowledge about the natural world is simply inappropriate to the 'internal world' of human thought, feeling, valuation, and purposeful action, and thus to the social studies in which they inevitably feature. A special method is needed for these 'sciences of human action' – one branch of which is formed by the historical sciences, the other comprising what Mises calls *praxeology*, the human sciences of more universal application such as economics.[4]

Because the natural scientist's methodological toolkit contains nothing with which to grip values, no instrument to measure human purposes or to predict individuals' judgements,[5] and no workbench on which the complexity of human society can be reproduced and subjected to experimental test, it is no wonder that we make an appalling mess of things when we try to engineer our societies in a fashion that is more suited to designing a bridge.

A deductive system

However, once we have rejected the general strategy used in the natural sciences, with its reliance on the testing of theories and models, on observation, on experiment, and on prediction, there are precious few other routes left by which we might derive any useful knowledge about social phenomena. To Mises, the choice was plain enough: the principles of economics and of the sciences of human action generally, he maintained, are not discovered by the methods of observation and experiment used in the natural sciences, but through a process of deduction. They can be derived quite logically from basic axioms that are self-evident, much as the complex proofs of geometry or mathematics could be derived from the self-evident qualities of points, lines, and numbers. Our observation of the world might tell us which particular parts of this deductive system it is most interesting to concentrate on; but the principles of human action are in fact implied in the idea of action itself, and the proper method of the social studies is to draw out those implications.[6]

If this seems odd to mainstream students of economics, or sociology, or history, that is because it is indeed an 'extreme position methodologically'[7] which has never been congenial to the orthodox practitioners of those subjects. Their support could never be won by what they see as Mises's misrepresentation and abuse of their approach. And students, expecting economics to be more a practical enquiry rather than an exercise in pure reason, have unfortunately been inclined to treat the works of Mises and others in his tradition as inaccessible or sterile.

Modern reconstructions

The philosophy of science was young when Mises was developing his own approach, and its leading theorists then undoubtedly misrepresented how natural scientists actually proceed. Mises was perhaps correct to reject that representation, particularly to reject any attempt to apply it to the science of society. Today, however, we have a clearer and more sensitive picture of scientific method, one which can be more plausibly applied to social studies, and some Austrians have begun to reconstruct Mises's approach in the terms of this new view,[8] and to show how the general strategy of scientific discovery is also relevant to the study of society – if applied with due sensitivity to the nature of the material and with the understanding that what science can teach us about so complex a phenomenon as society is inherently rather limited.[9] It may be, therefore, that Austrian economics is gradually emerging from something of a methodological cul-de-sac – entered to escape what we now see was a grotesque apparition, the early philosophical misrepresentation of the methods of the natural sciences.

The problem in describing and evaluating Mises's contributions on this score, then, is that many of his warnings against the insensitive application of scientific techniques to the study of society still ring loud and true. But those alarm bells no longer make us jump so swiftly into a deductive methodology that gives little credit to observation and experiment. Today, we can agree that much of economic theory 'consists merely in working out the logical implications of certain initial facts'[10] without wholly abandoning the empirical approach. The problem left by Mises is to heed his alarm bells but not to run away without salvaging what still works.

Before deciding how that can be done, however, it would be right to examine in more detail some important aspects of Mises's own viewpoint.

THE RIFT BETWEEN SCIENCE AND SOCIETY

There are three main problems in applying the approach of the natural sciences to the study of society, according to Mises: that the subject-matter of science is human values and not directly observable events, that social phenomena do not display the regularity we normally expect of scientific observations, and that no experimentation is possible in the social sciences. The first of these has been discussed briefly above and at more length in Chapter 7; so it is time to move on to the other two.

The lack of regularity in economics

There is certainly no denying the fact: economic forecasts are notoriously imprecise. According to the quantity theory of money, for example, changes in the quantity of money or money substitutes lead to changes in national income or prices; in the stricter versions of the theory, the relationship is held to be exact and proportional. Even the most ardent exponent of the theory, however, has to admit that the actual pattern of changes in prices or incomes fits very imprecisely on the pattern of monetary movements. Optimistic monetarists suggest other events which may have caused the link to be loose. Their critics deny that the evidence suggests any link at all. And many other economic events, from stock market prices to the demand for potatoes, show a similarly vague relationship to the observable phenomena which are supposed to cause them.

Fickle origins. For Mises, this is entirely unsurprising. For economic events such as these depend not on objective facts, but on the subjective *meaning* of facts and events for the particular individuals in the marketplace at the time. Their *purposes* and their *values*, upon which the outcome turns, are emotional reactions that, like the emotion of love or the feeling of beauty, can never be measurable, precise, or predictable, and scientific predictions cannot be made on such foundations.

Furthermore, the exact result observed by the economist will depend not on the subjective state of a single individual, but on the concatenation of the actions of a multitude of individuals, each one of whose actions is likely to affect the decisions of the others. It is too much to expect regularity in the outcome of this complex business.

Textbook economists, argues Mises, are very fond of searching for 'constants' and 'functions' that link different economic magnitudes. But because of the inherently subjective and non-mechanical nature of valuation and exchange, no such precision exists. In economics,

the alleged 'correlations' and 'functions' do not describe anything else than what happened at a definite instant of time in a definite geographical area as the outcome of the actions of a definite number of people.[11]

Even if some statistical correlation does appear, say between the money supply and prices, it may not be enough on which to suppose the existence of a firm link that will continue into the future.[12] Statistics can deal only with historical events: people tomorrow will have different purposes, and will face a particular pattern of events that might prompt them to make quite different choices, completely shattering the 'constants' we had imagined to exist.

The impossibility of experiment

The other difference which Mises detects between the natural and social sciences is the impossibility of performing controlled experiments in the latter. The physical scientist seeks out regularities by controlling the various events which might confuse the issue. Thus, a relationship between the volume of a gas and the pressure applied to it can be found, but only because the scientist can control the temperature, which also has a bearing on the result. In economics, however, background events and conditions are always changing, and no such experimentation is possible.

One reason is that ethical factors prevent us from interfering in the economy just to test our theories. We cannot rob people of half their incomes to see what effect it would have on the price structure, for example. And even so, says Mises, the exact circumstances in the market, or in any segment of history for that matter, are never repeated. The same people will not be alive, or if they are, they will be older and wiser and will not make the same decisions. Their emotional state, their environment, and their physiological condition will all be different. Consequently, we cannot replay economic events to test the relative weight of any particular factor. All we can do is try to *interpret* past events; we can never perform *experiments* to check our analysis of them.

This critique, however, might be overdrawn. Astronomy is still regarded as a science, even though the astronomer cannot turn the universe into reverse to check his theories. Human society, of course, is more complex and less mechanical, but the essential point is the same: genuine sciences do not cease to be genuine sciences just because experimentation within them is hard or even impossible.

The engineering analogy

Mises understood the problems posed by the complexity of human societies. The purposes and values which large numbers of individuals hold at any moment, the exact pattern by which their actions are adjusted each to the other, and even the incidence of lucky or unlucky accidents all affect the result. He recognized the harm that could be done in treating human society as if it were a machine that could be engineered or even rebuilt in order to make it operate as we would choose.

Living under the shadow of Marx and Sombart, this was a

very real and frightening prospect to Mises. For as the nineteenth-century physical sciences had produced a dramatic expansion in our ability to control the natural world, political philosophers looked on enviously and concluded that they, too, could achieve the same degree of control over the human world. There persisted well into the twentieth century

some confused ideas about a 'unified science' that would have to study the behaviour of human beings according to the methods Newtonian physics resorts to in the study of mass and motion.[13]

The analogy went further: on the basis of this 'positive' approach, it was imagined that 'social engineering' could fashion a new society of living people just like the mechanical engineer would fashion a motor or a bridge.

So seductive is this misleading analogy that it has persisted in some degree even to this day; and in 1962, Mises felt its presence so strongly that he was driven to intemperate language against all versions of it:

Their authors are driven by the dictatorial complex. They want to deal with their fellow men in the way an engineer deals with the materials out of which he builds houses, bridges, and machines. They want to substitute 'social engineering' for the actions of their fellow citizens and their own unique all-comprehensive plan for the plans of other people. They see themselves in the role of the dictator – the *duce*, the *Führer*, the production tsar . . .[14]

Protecting the social sciences

Mises recognized very clearly that human societies could not be so easily manipulated. Their unfathomable complexity throws up institutions that are of the greatest benefit but which were never planned in advance; and that same complexity can throw up the most vicious of unintended consequences when we do start trying to plan and manipulate human actions. The analogy of the natural sciences suggests to some people that in the social world too, anything can be achieved if enough force is applied; but it is not so. Unfortunately, our utopias run aground against the firm tendency of human societies not to conform to them.[15]

The reason, concludes Mises, is that the sciences of human action are of a completely different character to the natural sciences. Just as their subject-matter is different, so are the methods by which we can understand and interpret that material. The two are *logically* different.

Is economics a science?

This radical departure might save us from the grim side-effects of social engineering by denying that society throws up any simple laws and constants which can be used by an engineer. But it leaves us with the bitter question whether what we have left can really be called a science at all. After all, the traditional techniques of physical sciences – observation, experiment, testing, making predictions, and so on – have all be abandoned in the process.

Are there no patterns or lessons in history, or is it all just gossip about past events, interesting but uninstructive? Are there no principles which distinguish good from bad economics, or is it just like good and bad art, a matter of personal taste?

Timeless principles. Mises, of course, wanted to argue that even though he believed that economics and history were of a different logical character to the natural sciences, they were still, in an important sense, scientific: that they were more than mere gossip about past events that would never be repeated, and that we *could* discern a set of universal principles about human action from their study.

First, he says, we can and do find principles that apply in every society and in every period of history. It is wrong to suggest that because historical events are never exactly repeated that they are a meaningless jumble of unique things which defy any comprehension. In fact, the principles by which we interpret economic events today are just as relevant in any historical era. The analysis we use to investigate the effects of price controls today is precisely applicable to price controls in the middle ages.[16] The prices and the nature of the controls

310

may have changed, but the principles that must operate have not:

Goals change, ideas of technology are transformed, but action always remains action.[17]

Second, Mises insists that the study of human action *does* give us useful scientific information because it *is* possible to make predictions on the strength of it, although they are rather different from the predictions of the natural sciences. For the latter are expected to be precise quantifiable and originate (says Mises) in our observation of the regular association of different events. In the realm of human action, predictions must be less accurate, and come from a different source, having their origins in pure theory rather than applied science:

This is not to say that future human actions are totally unpredictable. They can, in a certain way, be anticipated to some extent. But the methods applied ... are logically and epistemologically different from those applied in anticipating natural events ...[18]

There is, it seems, some semblance of order in the buzzing confusion of human society. But the way we grasp that limited regularity, says Mises, is not by trying to observe and measure repeated conjunctions of events and then supposing that they will necessarily continue in the future, but by understanding 'from within' how people think, value, and choose. To make progress in the science of economics, as Wieser explained, we need to begin with a clear understanding of human nature and the human mind.

A deductive system

The science of praxeology, of which economics is a component, is therefore not an empirical science but a deductive one, Mises concludes. Like mathematics or geometry, it is a case of drawing out the logical implications of a few initial axioms. Although it is different in character from physics or chemistry in that it relies on logical deduction rather than empirical testing, it has just as much scientific status as mathematics and geometry.

However, Mises attributed to praxeology a status much firmer than that of mathematics or geometry, because in his view, the axioms from which it starts can not be chosen arbitrarily, but are a necessary part of the way in which we see the world.[19] The principles of human action, he argues, follow logically from our very concept of action itself.

Logical character of the mind. A short explanation is in order to show how Mises believes that an understanding of our own minds can reveal truths about the external world. When we start to think about how the human mind addresses the world, says Mises, we realize that it is inevitably constrained to understand events in a particular way. For example, we cannot defy the rules of logic: it is impossible to conceive of a world in which logical contradictions exist, in which an event happens and does not happen, in which an object exists and does not exist at the same time.

The fundamental relationships of logic, then, permeate every experience we have of the world. Drawing on the thinking of the eighteenth-century German philosopher, Immanuel Kant, Mises explains that this is simply because the human mind orders its experiences in certain ways. What comes in through our eyes and ears has to be compartmentalized so that we can make sense of it. Experience provides the raw material to work on, and then the mind breaks it into intelligible 'categories'. They are prior to experience – what philosophers call *a priori* – because they are the mental system we use to process experience.[20]

As we have evolved over the millennia, Mises goes on, we have developed mental categories that have become better and better adjusted to the conditions of reality. So they are not to be dismissed as arbitrary prejudices: they have helped us to construct theories and strategies which have been of very great benefit to our survival when they have been applied. They *do* provide some information about the reality of the universe.

Economics and the mind

In terms of the methodology of the sciences concerned with human action, this is an important result. For the concept of *action*, states Mises, is itself one of these mental categories. It comes not from experience, but from within our own minds. The idea that there is such a thing as action, that we can consciously aim to achieve some particular state of affairs, is a fundamental part of how our minds categorize and deal with the world.

A basic category. The logical category of action, this idea of action by which the mind brings order to a certain part of our world, is the self-evident axiom from which a very considerable body of knowledge can be deduced. Once we have the concept of action, which is automatically built into our mental structure, we must have concepts of time (for action takes time), value (for action aims at substituting one state for a preferred one), ends and means (for we may be prepared to sacrifice one thing in order to gain something we value more), success and failure (for the desired end may not be achieved), profit and loss (for what is gained may or may not be valued more than what is given up), regularity (we must have an idea that a certain action will be likely to achieve the desired end), of costs and marginal costs, and much more.[21]

Without too much strain, we can see that the basic principles of human action – of preferring, choosing, economizing and so on – can be drawn quite logically out of the basic concept of action itself. Economics is not a science whose principles are inferred from observation, but a process of deduction from knowledge that is already contained in the human mind, knowledge that is valid through all time and in all circumstances because it is derived logically and not through observation. It is, in a sense, a pure theory of choice, the logic of action.[22]

Practical application. This is all very well as far as pure theory is concerned, but Mises concurs that the end of a science is to know reality, not mental gymnastics. In deriving the implications contained in the concept of action, we confine ourselves to how they apply to the real world. We do not think abstractly about disutility, the costs of giving up one thing for another, for example, but apply our findings to the disutility of labour – and so on with the other principles we can discover.[23] We bring observation into our science of economics, true enough, but only to help us apply productively an understanding that we have already without any observation and experience. Economics remains a science with a methodological character quite different from that of the natural sciences.

ISSUES IN MISES'S FORMULATION

At this point, the yawning depth of the division between Mises's viewpoint and that of the mainstream economists becomes apparent. One prominent author on economic method concluded that 'his later writings on the foundations of economic science are so cranky and idiosyncratic that we can only wonder that they have been taken seriously by anyone',[24] while even (the generally sympathetic) James Buchanan has confessed that he has 'never been able to appreciate fully the Misesian emphasis on praxeology or "the science of human action"'.[25]

It would be a pity if the radical nature of Mises's conclusions caused mainstream economists to ignore many of the insights he had along the way, insights which should remind them how limited the claims of applied economics should be. For example, there can be little objection to Mises's observation of the importance of the acts and judgements of individuals in determining economic events, nor that the observer can never hope to get into the mind of the individual and so predict with certainty what action he or she will take in any given circumstance. It should be plain to all that empirical predictions rest on a very shaky foundation in the social sciences.

But many scholars who accept this conclusion still resist Mises's radical nonempirical alternative. Buchanan, for example, voices the same criticism that must be voiced by all those schooled in traditional scientific method. That is, Mises has developed a theory of choice which can 'explain' *any* course of action an individual might be observed to take; but a theory which admits everything in fact explains nothing.[26]

Some of the Austrians who have followed Mises have been constructive in their criticism – most notably F.A. Hayek, who in his later writings has argued that the empirical scientific method *is* appropriate to the social sciences, although what it can achieve is more limited than what it can achieve in the realm of the nature.[27] Others, such as Rizzo, have thought it necessary to reformulate Mises's method within the framework of the mainstream view, while still trying to preserve the deductive methodology.[28]

Evidently, Mises's stark methodology causes problems, even for his sympathizers. Is it really wrong, overblown, or an unnecessary departure from established methods?

The understanding of scientific method

It would leave no mark of shame on Mises if we discovered it to be a misunderstanding of what the methodology of the natural sciences actually was that drove him to seek out such a radical alternative for the social sciences. For at the time when he was developing his own approach, the methodology of the natural sciences was much misunderstood.

This was, after all – and particularly in Vienna – the age of logical positivism, which distinguished science from non-science on the principle that it must be possible to *verify* the statements of the former. That treatment actually corresponds very much to most ordinary people's view of science: that scientists discover laws, and experimental evidence confirms or verifies them. But Mises, and many others, correctly argued that such 'laws' could not be proven: no amount of experience can *verify* the law of gravity, for example, because tomorrow, or today in some corner of the universe we have not yet examined, apples might fall *up*.

The Popperian sea-change. It took Sir Karl Popper to shatter this deeply ingrained idea of science as a process of verification.[29] To him, science was a matter of putting forward theories that could be *falsified*: we continue to accept our working theories of how things function until experimental observation shows them false – then we know that we need a better theory, and our knowledge has expanded to the extent that we now have a better of idea of what *is not* the case.

Popper's analysis certainly convinced Hayek, and became the point of departure for the next half century's discussion of scientific method; but by the time it was published, Mises had already worked out his own stance.[30] Thus, we find him demanding a new method for the social sciences because he is worried that there is 'no proof' of scientific laws and 'no certainty' in empirical knowledge[31] – while contemporary philosophers sleep quite calmly with their belief that science cannot discover universal truths, but advances our knowledge by systematically unmasking the theories that *do not* work.

Mises's view of empiricism

Mises was scornful of the 'empiricism' that he saw as a method inappropriate to social studies – and perhaps rightly so, given what its advocates were claiming before the Popperian sea-change. But today, the term has a different meaning: no longer is it about 'deriving . . . laws from historical data'.[32] Experiment and observation today is seen more as *testing hypotheses* rather than confirming alleged 'laws'.

Modern empiricism, then, is less arrogant than its earlier manifestation. It does not claim to discover certain truth, only to reveal when a theory is unacceptable – though that in itself is a powerful tool which can be wielded with self-confidence. Mises, for his part, remained unable to take seriously the suggestion that scientific 'knowledge' amounted to a web of yet-unrejected guesses rather than a wall of certain fact.[33] But the distinction may be of the greatest moment for the social sciences, since it could well take the edge off 'the viciousness of positivism . . . that it does not acknowledge any other ways of proving a proposition than those practised by the experimental natural sciences'.[34] Mises is right that to claim a sure knowledge of how people *will* act denies them any scope for free choice; but merely to accept the working hypothesis that certain sorts of action normally *are not* found recognizes human individuality and admits a wide scope for choice while still conveying useful information about the world.

Observation and reality. The widely held belief that science was a search for irrefragable 'laws' and certain knowledge led Mises to suppose that 'radical empiricism and positivism' claimed observation could give us a direct and incontrovertible access, indeed our only access, to an objective reality.[35]

Empiricists today, however, are more inclined to believe that the concept of 'objective' reality is an empty one. To take an exaggerated example, it is clear that different creatures with different sense organs would probably see things in completely different ways. At a more down to earth level, we would have to admit that, similarly, different human beings, whether scientists or those with different cultural, ideological, or religious viewpoints can and do come to different conclusions about the way the world works. What then counts as 'objective'?[36]

Modern empiricists have therefore come to argue that there can be many different ways of seeing, producing many different 'systems of knowledge' that can exist in competition. The aim of science is to decide whether any particular way of seeing, any specific system, is better than the others – for example, if it is more consistent.[37] For example, if research shows up findings that are inconsistent with our accepted ideas, we might want to reconsider whether our orthodox way of seeing things is really the best. So experimentation remains important, even though it is not believed to disclose any 'certain' truths, only to decide between alternative systems. We do not test scientific theories against an unknowable 'objective reality' but to see how they fit against the other theories that we generally accept. Often, experimental results do require us not to reject the new findings, but to reshape our deeply entrenched views of reality, as when scientific orthodoxies are revolutionized by the new views of Copernicus, Newton, Einstein, and thousands of lesser innovators. It might cause us to doubt whether anything in science is unimpeachable, but the empiricist accepts this happily enough.

Mises's epistemology. This analysis is obviously at odds with Mises's notion that the human mind, and the way of seeing determined by its structure, has evolved closer and closer to 'reality', that

Only those groups could survive whose members acted in accordance with the right categories, i.e., with those that were in conformity with reality and therefore . . . worked.[38]

For it suggests that there is no point in talking about, or claiming inside knowledge of, an 'objective' world at all. The particular viewpoint, the particular system of knowledge imposed by the structure of our minds is only one possibility among many. Others may exist, and we might develop better ones.

Even Mises's assertion that praxeological knowledge is prior to experience 'like logic and mathematics',[39] has been challenged. To Mises, the logical structure of the mind is how we think: it is no good trying to prove or disprove the rules of logic, because every such argument would automatically assume their validity, and we could not discuss the question without them.[39]

By the 1920s, however, Alfred Tarski had already broken the circle by developing a 'metalogic', a calculus which uses different rules to discuss entire systems of logic.[40] Furthermore, our minds are notoriously drawn to accept illusions and superstitions. Are we to accept these as a priori knowledge, or to submit them to the rigorous tests that will reveal them as mere mistakes?

Can it really be said, then, that the structure of our minds gives us objective knowledge – or has evolution simply left us with one way of seeing, one system of 'knowledge' that we have the ability to discuss critically and replace with better ones?

The aim of science

Interestingly, although Mises did not share this view of the process of scientific enquiry, it is redolent of the subjective view of economics that he adopted. Thus, in science there can be many competing theories, many possible systems of knowledge, just as in economics there are different individual value systems. In science, what people see as a 'fact' depends upon their viewpoint or scientific 'paradigm':[41] economic affairs turn on the equally subjective *meaning* of events for the individuals concerned.

However, science does not allow us to cling to any theory we happen to like. Lysenko might have gained wealth and power because his views were agreeable to Stalin, but he is not now recorded as a good scientist, because his views are judged today by the conventional standards of science.[42] The generally agreed purpose of scientific activity is to acquire an increasing ability to predict the operation of external objects and forces.[43] That is why science has no interest in theories that do not yield any testable conclusions.

SCIENTIFIC METHOD IN ECONOMICS

Mises's view

Mises suggested that history and economics were not empirical sciences like physics or chemistry because they began not from observed facts but from theories. Our understanding in history, for example, comes not by observing what people do and then trying to fashion 'laws' out of that raw data, but from our own knowledge of how people think, value, and choose. We do not need to observe numerous cases of revolution to know that oppressed people are likely to turn to violence: we know enough about human nature from within to state that fact from the outset.

Alternatives. Popper, however, seems to have eroded that distinction by his suggestion that all empirical science too starts with a theory. We cannot 'observe' before we know what we want to observe – in other words, we have to have an initial theory, an idea that some correlation might exist and is worth seeking out, before we can make observations and experiments at all.

If this view is accepted, it seems that natural science starts from the propagation of theories just as much as history or economics. In both cases, then, we must be aware that our initial theories are not a priori knowledge, but conjectures that can be improved and modified according to how well they help us to interpret and predict events. In science, our theories may be very complex, because it is possible to perform controlled experiments and to whittle away quickly the theories that do not fulfil our purposes so well. In history and economics, however, they may really be rather trite because of the difficulties of eliminating inadequate ones. Even some natural sciences, geology and astronomy for example, make only slow progress because of the problems of re-creating past conditions in a controlled test.

This kind of reasoning led Hayek to depart from Mises's view, and to conclude that the general strategy used in other sciences was also appropriate in history and economics, although there were special problems in its application. He agreed with Mises that the complexity of human society and our lack of practical access to the inner psychology of the individuals involved, makes all predictions vague and imprecise. Yet he thought it possible to predict *patterns* of events, just as the natural scientist may be able to predict accurately the half-life of a particular element without knowing in detail *which* atoms will decay.[44]

Mises does seem to have accepted that the general nature of limited economic events might be predicted in a qualitative way, but he assumed that such predictions could not be the result of general scientific method because:

What characterizes the natural sciences as such is the fact that they approach the material of experience with the category of a strict regularity in the succession of events. History . . . i.e., the totality of experience concerning human action, must not and does not refer to this category.[45]

Even while admitting that their theories are necessarily less precise than those of physicists, however, such 'historians' may yet insist that their methodological strategy of testing new theories by searching the available evidence is completely similar.

The restoration of science

Mises had a marked tendency to presume, on the basis of how fickle he knew human beings to be, that no prediction is possible in economics.[46] But the idea that patterns of activity can be predicted, even when the actions of the particular individuals who generate that pattern cannot be, must disallow that presumption.

Certainly, such predictions must be vague. We may be unable to predict what *will* happen – inventions and acts of creativity are bound to surprise the forecasters – only to close off a few possibilities that we predict *will not*. Nevertheless, such predictions remain truly scientific in character. And it remains clearly true that our 'inside' knowledge of human psychology helps us to form new theories and predictions about how people will behave in the future.

Uncharacteristic approach. Mises was correctly worried that the assumption of scientific precision in applied economics would induce those in power to start treating people like data, and lead us into the horrors of social engineering. Some commentators have found it odd that he should therefore develop a system which itself immodestly claims to deduce the principles of action with 'apodictic certainty'.[47] By contrast, Hayek argues that economics proceeds through the same general method used by other sciences, that of constructing simplified models and subjecting them to tests which systematically narrow down the possibilities – with the important rider that a truly scientific approach in economics involves 'a frank admission of how limited our powers of prediction really are'.[48]

Once we abandon the discipline of that method, or pretend to have a degree of knowledge about the complex workings of society that in fact we do not possess, then we surely do leave ourselves defenceless against the unintended evils brought about by the social engineers.[49] The irony is that the rationalistic claim to a priori knowledge made by scores of prominent social theorists over many centuries, has often resulted in those same evils.

CHAPTER SIXTEEN

Economic Theory Before and After Mises

> I have come to realize that my theories explain the degeneration of a great civilization; they do not prevent it. I set out to be a reformer, but only became the historian of decline.[1]

It is a grave misfortune that the ideas of the Austrian School, although spreading much more widely today than many a few years ago would have dared hope, are still seen as something of a bolt-on attachment to mainstream economics. Thus, Austrian marginal utility analysis has been absorbed into the orthodox textbooks; the trade cycle and balance of payments problems are once again being appreciated as monetary phenomena; and with even less acknowledgement, the importance of subjective decision making on economic events has become a sizeable part of practical and textbook economics under the description of 'expectations theory'. In other respects, too, Austrian ideas are generally reckoned to be a good source from which to pilfer when gaps appear in conventional economic theory.

At least that pilfering is positive. The problem is that most Austrian theory since Menger has concentrated so much on a critique of conventional wisdom that it is often relegated to the status of devil's advocate. Students learn the mainstream approach first, and only then are they subjected to Austrian and other criticisms, lumped together, in order to sharpen their minds a little. Because it is seen as negative, Austrian economics remains very much a subject that is considered appropriate only for graduate students. It is no wonder that one leading Austrian scholar has concluded that 'we ought to scale down very sharply the extent to which our future efforts ... are devoted to the refutation of any and every fallacy which others choose to propose'.[2]

Mises's influence

There is no doubt that Mises must be credited with making an enormous contribution to Austrian economics. The colleagues whose views he influenced, the students he taught over a long career, and their students in turn all testify to that fact. The leading Austrian thinkers today – Israel Kirzner, Ludwig Lachmann, F.A. Hayek, Murray Rothbard, and many more – have all been pulled onto new courses by the profound influence of the ideas which he built into a comprehensive system. Barry Smith may not be exaggerating when he says that 'it was above all . . . the circle of thinkers around Ludwig von Mises who did most to establish the characteristic methods of the Austrian school . . . and to spread the Austrian ideas beyond the borders of Austria'.[3]

Nevertheless, the adherents to Austrian ideas remained very much a minority cult during Mises's lifetime, despite their crossing of national boundaries. Only now has the approach (in forms of varying rigour) begun to spread outside a narrow circle of thinkers who were all known to each other.

The charitable explanation of this is that the conclusions of Mises and his colleagues could never have expected much popularity during a period entranced by the charms of a fashionable socialism; perhaps the disappointing practical experience of that flirtation has left more people willing to try a radical alternative. A less complimentary view, from James Buchanan, is that 'Mises and his followers have been too prone to accept the splendid isolation of arrogant eccentrics to divorce their teaching too sharply from mainstream interests, and too eager to launch into polemic'.[4] If that is so, the growth of Austrian ideas today would then have to be put down to Hayek and others who have been less divergent from mainstream methodology, more restrained in their criticism of opposing views, better in tune with the mentality of the English-speaking world.

Linguistic overkill. Mises's *Socialism* is a good example of his 'eager polemic' for those who seek one. To some extent, Mises always seems happiest when he is mincing his opponents with a few sharp phrases of contempt, and it can be effective; but it is hardly calculated to make enemies admit their mistakes, and even friends can be embarrassed. T.W. Hutchison makes this point when he notes that 'the precise and lucid use of language as a means of communication, which might be regarded as specially incumbent on academics disporting themselves in this particular intellectual area, cannot be counted among Mises's more obvious intellectual virtues. For example, his supporters have had to explain that when Mises wrote that socialism is 'impossible', he "obviously meant that the proposed methods of socialism could not achieve what they were supposed to do" '.[5]

Even Mises's most constructive works, such as *Human Action*, are peppered with passages devoted to putting down opponents (the description 'positivist' furnishes Mises and many other Austrians with an all-purpose malediction of which they make full use),[6] and with digressions on tangential points, on issues in the history of ideas, and on specifically German-language problems, all of which can seriously undermine the flow and persuasiveness of the argument. It is a matter of debate how much this, rather than any unpopularity of the ideas themselves, has reduced Mises's influence in the English-speaking world.

This again makes it hard to estimate Mises's importance – and perhaps easy to underestimate it, because many of his ideas have come into currency through third parties,[7] often in the shape of his colleagues and students, instead of directly from his own writings. One could argue, for example, that Mises's observation of the subjective nature of costs, which comes out of his discussion of the socialist calculation problem, was the sole origin of the opportunity-cost tradition developed in the London School of Economics during the 1930s.[8] Today, everyone knows the principle, but few would associated the name of Mises with it.

The attack on formalism

The development of a thoroughgoing subjectivism, whether it is seen as intellectually isolated by mainstream economists or not, must be one of Mises's most significant contributions to Austrian theory. Resolutely he rejected any suggestion still lurking in the works of Menger that values inhered in things or 'essences',[9] or that values and utility can be measured,[10] insisting on them being purely personal judgements. With Mises, subjectivism became a confident, consistent, comprehensive approach.

Lachmann, and Buchanan, have therefore thought it surprising that Mises did not extend it still further to cover the problem of expectations that grew in economic debate in the 1930s.[11] Was it that he thought expectations were a merely empirical matter and not a fit subject for analytical inquiry? Or was it that his theory considered aims, values, and expectations alike as simply 'given'? In any event, modern Austrians have been keener to apply subjectivist principles in the renewed debate about expectations that followed the inflations of the 1970s and the demise of the Phillips Curve; and the influence of the subjectivist approach is seen even in the contributions of non-Austrians such as Milton Friedman.[12]

Modern Austrians have continued to extend the application of subjectivism. Professor G.L.S. Shackle, for example, argues that values are not just individual judgements about *things*, as Menger and Mises suggest, but that an individual's economic decisions depend also upon his or her reaction to the purely hypothetical results that are *imagined* to occur as a result of different actions being taken. Any theory that seeks to explain economic phenomena in terms of mechanical relationships between things, and ignores subjective reactions to real events and imagined possibilities, is therefore doubly mistaken.[13]

The importance of time. Another of Mises's achievements was to make clear exactly why *time* is of central importance in any study of human action, an importance well beyond even the concept of time *preference* that features in the work of Böhm-Bawerk as a key determinant of the capital structure.[14] While that analysis is confined to a limited aspect of human nature,[15] and is largely macroeconomic in its approach,[16] Menger and Mises recognized that time had a much more general, subjective significance. The value of time pervades every action.

Mises, therefore, could never treat time as a mere continuum in which economic events smoothly unfold, a homogeneous factor to be placed on one axis of an unintermitting graph in the manner of the orthodox economists. Economic events are not the result of immutable forces but of human action; and as time elapses, the perspective from which individuals see the world, and hence their action within it, changes. Over time, people acquire new knowledge about present conditions and past events, and they must abandon old ideas that are now redundant. Such changes will undoubtedly affect the pattern of choices they make, altering the data upon which others in turn base yet further choices – and so it continues. Economics is not a clockwork mechanism: time is creative, generating unpredictable novelties as the competing and often incompatible plans of different individuals develop, mature, and interact within it.

As time progresses, then, knowledge itself changes, making the future inevitably uncertain. In this insight, kept alive by Mises, modern Austrians have found a valuable tool that they have put to good use in recent years – exploring the importance of subjective factors in the capital structure,[17] emphasizing the frailty of our knowledge and expectations when we make economic plans of whatever size,[18] breathing life into the dead textbook concept of competition by reinterpreting it as a discovery procedure,[19] and undermining the general equilibrium orthodoxy in which the change and uncertainty wrought by time are ignored.[20] G.L.S. Shackle,[21] and Gerald O'Driscoll and Mario Rizzo,[22] have in particular made the study of time and its associated uncertainty a major theme of modern Austrian theory.

Mathematics and macroeconomics. Mises's subjectivist critique of orthodox equilibrium analysis enjoined him into a long and lonely vigil during the 1950s and 1960s,[23] but the attractiveness of the modern Austrians has grown as they have more and more confidently pieced together their view that a recognition of the incomplete, inconstant, and dispersed nature of human knowledge is essential if the economic process is to be understood.

Thus, Shackle has noted that the data upon which general equilibrium concepts are founded can never be constant: as time moves on, human knowledge develops and human actions consequently change, making the equilibrium of one moment obsolete the next.[24] Hayek has observed that knowledge is necessarily dispersed between many different minds, so that *communication* becomes the key problem,[25] although orthodox theory makes no mention of it. And then there is the difficulty even of measuring macroeconomic variables, founded as they are on subjective valuations.[26]

The Austrian approach, however, remains rather negative in this sector. Certainly, Lachmann has proposed that Austrians should focus on *dis*equilibrating forces rather than equilibrium,[27] and Shackle has suggested a 'kaleidic' method which seeks to identify the range of short-run possible outcomes rather than to state with supposed certainty what *will* happen.[28] Otherwise, all the Austrian eulogies of market *process* seem to leave us still lacking a 'coherent, precise account of how a complex of interacting markets works' – although that objection might be gladly accepted by the Austrians as the necessary price of subjectivism.[29]

Specific applications

Economists building on the work of Mises have made a number of interesting developments on more specific issues such as entrepreneurship, competition theory, the idea of monopoly, money and inflation, and interventionism.

Entrepreneurship. For most early economists (and even today in the patois of many mainstream textbooks), the role of the entrepreneur was indistinguishable from that of a manager. Even the older Austrian school had little to say on the subject; and so it was with Mises that the entrepreneur began to be represented for the first time as no mere organizer, but the mainspring of economic action, innovation, and discovery, the prime mover of progress.

In so doing, Mises uncovered a rich vein that has yielded many valuable insights resulting from the further and systematic exploration by Israel Kirzner in particular. And in recent years there has been a lively debate among the Austrians about what *are* the salient features of entrepreneurship. Both sides are agreed that the entrepreneur's function is more than to allocate known resources optimally between competing ends, for such knowledge is inevitably dispersed and incomplete; the question is whether the key element of entrepreneurship is an *alertness* to new market niches and previously overlooked production possibilities, or (as Mises stressed) the ability to make a good *judgement* about the market conditions that will prevail in an inevitably uncertain future.[30]

Other debates have also arisen. Murray Rothbard, for example, takes to its extreme Mises's notion that a 'pure' entrepreneur is never found, and talks of 'capitalist-entrepreneurs';[31] Kirzner and Lachmann, on the other hand, although recognizing that the two functions are typically integrated in every 'businessman', want to preserve the distinction for analytical purposes;[32] while Schumpeter went to the other extreme by arguing that the pure entrepreneur bears no risks, and that only the capitalist has something to lose.[33]

Profit and competition. The modern Austrian views of entrepreneurial profit and of competition also illustrate how this aspect of the theory has departed radically from orthodox textbook analysis. To Mises and those who have followed him, profit is not the entrepreneur's 'wage', nor a 'residue' after other costs have been met, nor even objective at all: profit is a cryptic message about what is entrepreneurially successful, and it needs *judgement* to be interpreted. Competition, another of the dead textbook forms resuscitated by Mises, has also been nursed back to health by Hayek in particular, who has stressed its creative nature as a *process* of discovery about how we can best co-ordinate our actions with those of others in the marketplace, and who repeats that the traditional view of competition simply would not work.[34]

Monopoly. For orthodox textbooks, monopoly is assumed to be a common market imperfection, and the only questions to be addressed are how to define it and what its effects will be on supply and price. Mises does not altogether escape this formal approach, although he consigns much of the textbook theorizing to unimportance by defining monopoly rather narrowly. Modern Austrians, however, are even more interested than he in whether monopoly *can* exist at all, and where it comes from. Most have been pleased to accept Mises's conclusion that outside resource monopoly, government intervention is the principal source.

An exception appears to be Israel Kirzner, who scarcely mentions it, but who has nevertheless taken Austrian monopoly theory into a new round by stressing the effect of monopolies in *blocking* the dynamic and creative process of competition, an approach again in marked contrast to the mainstream models.[35] Rothbard too rejects the orthodox view – and its echoes in Mises: how can we say that a monopolist raises prices above the competitive level when competition, and so the competitive price, does not even exist?[36] And still the debate remains lively, with some calling for a reinstatement of Menger's position, that monopoly is quite common (in early stages of economic development, or when a new product is introduced, for example) but that the market invariably erodes it, so that the only question is where we are in the process.[37]

Intervention. The broader problem of government intervention raised by Mises is being given more attention today, perhaps as a result of growing and bitter practical experience. Rothbard has identified many different types of intervention, and classified them according to who is affected and the mechanism used.[38] This typology embraces government actions that Mises excluded from his definition of 'intervention', and the modern consensus is that this wider remit is sound.[39]

Mises's underlying assumption was that the objectives of interventionism might be laudable, but that each intervention unfortunately led to side-effects that needed further measures to correct. Rothbard, for his part, is less charitable, and argues that the objectives of interventionists may be purely selfish. And this ties in with the public choice school, of which James Buchanan is the leading exponent, where political measures are seen more as the result of agitation by vested interest groups than as the product of selfless public servants.[40]

This is an important development, and perhaps potentially

more so is the 'micropolitics' approach, which asks how such political interests can be assembled to reduce intervention rather than install it.[41] Mises has argued strongly *against* interventionism: but what we really need today is a second-best solution, or a cure, once it has occurred.

Money and inflation. Inflation was a pressing problem during Mises's lifetime, although his analysis and recommendations were largely unheeded: and the problem arose again after the Second World War in the wake of the Keynesian suggestion that money did not matter, or at least, did not matter very much.[42] The fierce inflations that occurred when this restraint was removed have prompted a revival in the quantity theory, led in particular by Milton Friedman.[43]

The practical experience of inflation, however, has shown the weaknesses in the macroeconomic 'monetarist' approach, such as the occurrence of pronounced distributive effects elucidated by Mises. Hayek[44] and others have sought to remind policy-makers of the dislocation caused by inflation but left unexplained by the monetarist approach, and have argued against the monetarists that inflation cannot be gradually reduced nor suffered in a small amount, but must be stopped dead.[45] It is yet unclear how deeply this message has penetrated, and whether the end result will be simply the abandonment of all forms of quantity theory. Nevertheless, many of Mises's points, such as the view that balance-of-payments problems are *monetary* problems, and that inflation is inextricably linked with government interventionism, have indeed hit home.

Mises recognized that what is normally regarded a uniform stock of money actually contains many heterogeneous elements, and so can have diverse results; and much modern Austrian effort has been devoted to building up a working description of the money supply. Recognizing that it is the subjective *meaning* of each element that is important, Rothbard,[46] for example, would include many items not normally put down as 'money', such as insurance policy surrender values, and would redraw the traditional distinctions between different kinds of deposits on the basis of how people regard them, not on how they happen to be classified by the bankers.

On the purpose of economics

Mises's methodological approach remains his most enigmatic facet. While many of his disciples, such as Rothbard, defend it tenaciously, many others, such as Hayek,[47] accept many of his conclusions but cannot themselves take the same methodological route.

Indeed, this polarization of opinion is almost as old as Austrian economics itself. Although Menger apparently rejected a priori axioms,[48] he did distinguish what he called 'empirical laws' from 'exact laws'. The former were like any observation of the real world – conforming to a general rule or pattern, but full of exceptions and slight irregularities, the sort of 'error' that every practising scientist knows only too well. The latter are best regarded as a sort of 'ideal' rules, in principle neither falsifiable nor proveable, since they did not describe real things, only how we conceive 'ideal' things to behave.

To Böhm-Bawerk, who had little interest in methodological theory,[49] most of this could be accepted, and it showed the close parallel between the methods of economics and of natural science. For the scientist, he thought, starts with observations that may be rough and full of error, but uses them 'to build general laws' that are the pure theory, the 'exact laws' describing 'ideal' relationships mooted by Menger.[50] This is not so far from the modern notion that the 'ideal' relationships in pure scientific theory are simply hypotheses made in the light of our observational findings and the testing of other hypotheses in the past.

Although Mises wrote disparagingly of Wieser,[51] he did absorb Wieser's 'psychological method', the point that the economist has a 'huge advantage' over the natural scientist because he or she can draw on 'inner observation' to understand directly the values and purposes that motivate individuals.[52] And Mises seems to have fused this notion with Menger's 'exact laws', concluding that the pure theory of economics came from 'inside' or a priori knowledge, rather than being built up from observations (as Böhm-Bawerk supposed).

Unfortunately for us today, this conclusion also rules out the possibility that the pure theory is no more than conjectural, a hypothetical framework that we have devised on the basis of our empirical testing of other hypotheses in the past. Mises held fast to his central conclusion, but the world was already changing about him. In the post-Popperian world, we face new options that he did not recognize: and it will be interesting to see how Austrian economics ultimately responds.

Co-ordination and knowledge. Nevertheless, we must still explain why the method of hypothesis and testing that works so well in the physical sciences seems unable to produce accurate and quantitative predictions in economics.

Mises's main answer was that we cannot get inside the minds of those whose decisions will ultimately determine the outcome; but he also recognized that human societies were extremely complex, and that the results of any action depend upon what other people are doing at the same time, what they know about the action, how their own plans are affected, how they respond, and so on. In the midst of such pressures, not all action is successful, but as Mises's critique of interventionism shows, action can have completely unintended consequences. The more people involved, the harder it is to predict the outcome. The entrepreneur may speculate with fair success in a limited section of the market, on the basis of his understanding of the minds of customers and competitors; but when we try to control the entire economy or make quantitative predictions, the sheer complexity of human interactions must overwhelm us.

If the world of human action is so complex, how do people make their way within it? How do they co-ordinate their actions with those of others and produce a result which is, quite evidently, not one of bewildering chaos? Menger gave the Austrians an explanation by observing that the unintended consequences of action do in fact include *beneficial* and orderly social institutions, such as language, the law, and the market order. These, he says, were never consciously designed, but were thrown up and developed in the process of human beings dealing with one another.[53]

Mises certainly shared this understanding that the market order helped us to co-ordinate our actions, and developed the notion of the market as a spontaneous process which promotes the mutual adjustment of individual actions with a speed and accuracy that deliberate economic planning cannot match. The theory underlying this approach has been advanced most spectacularly by Hayek, who has stressed the *knowledge content* of such institutions. To him, institutions such as language, morality, religion, the law, and the market order flourish and develop in so far as they help the groups which practise them: they contain, as it were, knowledge about how to act that benefits their practitioners. Thus, following the rules of grammar or of morality helps us co-ordinate our actions efficiently and peacefully with others, and those rules persist and grow as a result.[54] Or again, although the price mechanism was never consciously designed by human beings, it perists because it is a remarkable way of transmitting information about abundance and scarcity. It allows millions of individuals to adjust their actions to one another without needing any central planning authority to decide the (impossible) questions of what should be done, what resources exist to do it, and how they would be best used.[55]

CONCLUSION

This kind of analysis is helping more and more students today to understand that good economics does not attempt to describe the conditions that produce a world of general equilibrium – for such a world of perfect balance must be necessarily imaginary, unchanging, and dead. The really important and interesting questions in economics are the very live issues of how people adjust their actions to one another in a world of complexity and change, of how information about supply and demand conditions diffuses through the market, and how people perceive and respond to new data and new opportunities.

For the Austrian economist, then, there can be no such thing as 'perfect' markets and 'perfect' competition, because the textbook assumptions – that all buyers and sellers are identical, that the traded products are identical in price and quality, and that knowledge is already spread perfectly – can never hold. Indeed, the market process, a process of discovery and adjustment, would be unnecessary if they did, so to assume them simply assumes away the main question, how markets work.

Paradoxically perhaps, Mises's rejection of interventionism is shared most strongly by those who have the most straightforward faith in the ability of perfect competition to make free markets adjust perfectly and instantly back to equilibrium following any disturbance. Unfortunately, that conclusion is undermined easily by the observation that real-world markets are never perfect, and then the naive faith in the benefits of textbook perfection is used to justify all kinds of interventions on the ground that they will make markets 'more' perfect and correct 'market failure'. The anti-interventionism of Mises and the Austrians, on the other hand, is built on a much stronger foundation. It rests on our inability to control a very complex process, on the folly of crediting ourselves with the ability to make accurate forecasts of economic events, on the impossibility of perfection, and on the understanding that the market process is a continuing attempt to deal with changing *dis*equilibria.

Such understanding is spreading, and with it is spreading a recognition of the importance of many issues explored by Mises: the subjectivist foundation of economics; the role of the entrepreneur in setting off and navigating through the process; the unpredictable lags, imbalances, and transition effects caused by the fact that all adjustment takes time; the inevitability of error in a world where knowledge is not perfect; expectations about the future; and the complexity of human interactions. In developing such parts of economic theory yet further, present and future economists will be drawing on an approach kept alive, and on the many insights collected and developed, by Ludwig von Mises.

Notes

Mises's main works have been through several editions. Some of the early printings are now difficult to obtain, others have been revised by the author, and many have been put into new English translations from the original German. Rather than give page references to first editions, therefore, it seems sensible to refer to the editions most easily available today. These notes consequently match editions cited at the start of each entry in the select bibliography.

Chapter 1: Mises's life and work

1. *Notes and Recollections*, p.109.

2. Henry Hazlitt, 'Salute to Von Mises', in *Barron's National Business and Financial Weekly*, 1 October, 1973, reprinted in *Planning for Freedom*, pp.271–5 (p.271).

3. Alvin H. Hansen, *A Guide to Keynes* (New York: McGraw-Hill, 1953). A possible exception is Murray N. Rothbard, 'The Essential Von Mises', in *Planning For Freedom*, pp.234–70, although this is a rather rapid summary of Mises's main work.

4. The most notable discussions are probably Laurence S. Moss (ed.), *The Economics of Ludwig von Mises* (Menlo Park, California: Institute for Humane Studies, 1976); Israel M. Kirzner (ed.), *Method, Process, and Austrian Economics* (Lexington: D.C. Heath & Company, 1982); and, exclusively on Mises's monetary economics, James Rolph Edwards, *The Economist of the Country* (New York: Carlton Press, 1985).

5. Carl Menger, *Principles of Economics*, translated by James Dingwall and Bert F. Hoselitz (New York: New York University Press, 1981), first published as *Grundsätze der Volkswirtschaftslehre* (Vienna: 1871). This volume is also available in Carl Menger, *Collected Works*, edited by F.A. Hayek (London: London School of Economics, 1933–6).

6. For a brief overview of the main elements of the subjectivist approach, see Alexander H. Shand, *Subjectivist Economics* (London: The Pica Press, 1981).

7. *The Ultimate Foundation of Economic Science*, p.138.

8. *Die Entwicklung des Gutsherrlich-Bäuerlichen Verhaltnisses in Galizien: 1772–1848* (Leipzig: Franz Deuticke, 1902).

9. *A Contribution to Austrian Factory Legislation* (1905).

10. *Notes and Recollections*, p.16.

11. *Ibid.*, p.33.

12. Of Wieser, Mises writes: 'He enriched the thought in some respects, although he was no creative thinker and in general was more harmful than useful. He never really understood the gist of the idea of subjectivism in the Austrian School of thought, which limitation caused him to make many unfortunate mistakes.' *Notes and Recollections*, pp.35–6.

13. *Notes and Recollections*, p.79.

14. Recounted by Hayek in 'Coping With Ignorance', in his *Knowledge, Evolution, and Society* (London: Adam Smith Institute, 1983), pp.17–27 (p.17).

15. James Rolph Edwards, *The Economist of the Country* (New York: Carlton Press, 1985), p.19.

16. *Notes and Recollections*, pp.91–2.

17. Margit von Mises, *My Years With Ludwig von Mises* (New Rochelle, New York: Arlington House, 1976).

18. Margit von Mises, 'Ludwig von Mises, The Man', in John K. Andrews Jr (ed.), *Homage to Mises* (Hillsdale, Michigan: Hillsdale College, 1981), pp.10–13 (p.12).

19. Many examples of Mises's difficulty with English could be produced. Among the most evident is Mises's repeated but odd description of the division of labour as 'one of the great basic principles of cosmic becoming . . .' Perhaps worse is his frequent use of 'the masses' to signify the general population, which to an English reader suggests an authoritarian and aristocratic attitudes which is in fact the precise opposite of Mises's true philosophy. He was mindful that clear language was essential for clear thinking, and (according to his wife in her foreword to Percy Greaves's *Mises Made Easier*), even with *Human Action*, a massive work in a language not native to him, he carefully 'chose every single word and fought with the editor about the slightest editorial change'. But he did make slips (for someone so hostile to mechanical analogies in economics, his observation on p.309 of that work that 'the entrepreneurial activities are automatically, as it were, directed by the consumers' wishes' could be seen as one such), and from the point of view of style, the success of his fights with the editor might well be judged a misfortune.

20. Murray N. Rothbard, 'The Essential Von Mises', in *Planning for Freedom*, pp.234–70 (p.245).

21. *Notes and Recollections*, p.55.

22. For a brief survey, see Eamonn Butler, *Milton Friedman: A Guide to his Economic Thought* (New York: Universe Books, and London: Gower, 1985), Chapter 2.

23. F.A. Hayek, *Monetary Theory and the Trade Cycle* (London: Routledge, 1933) was the first to appear in English, followed soon by *Profits, Interest, and Investment* (London: Routledge, 1939) and *The Pure Theory of Capital* (Chicago: University of Chicago Press, 1941).

24. For example, Milton Friedman, in his book written with Anna J. Schwartz, *Monetary Trends in the United States and the United Kingdom* (Chicago and London: University of Chicago Press, 1982), pp.29–31.

25. Rolph James Edwards, *The Economist of the Country* (New York: Carlton Press, 1985).

26. *Notes and Recollections*, p.66.

27. *Ibid.*, p.18.

28. Murray N. Rothbard, 'The Essential Von Mises', in *Planning for Freedom*, pp.234–70 (pp.255–6).

29. Margit von Mises, *My Years with Ludwig von Mises* (New York: Arlington House, 1976), pp.57–62, gives a graphic and moving account of Mises's immigration to the United States and the events that led up to it.

30. F.A. Hayek, *The Road to Serfdom* (London: Routledge, 1944).

31. *Notes and Recollections*, p.115

32. For a survey of these economic and social changes, see David Howell MP, *Blind Victory: A Study of Income, Wealth, and Power* (London: Hamish Hamilton, 1986), and James Robertson, *Future Work* (Aldershot, Hampshire: Gower/Temple Smith, 1985), and Charles Handy, *The Future of Work* (Oxford, Basil Blackwell, 1984).

Chapter 2: The logical problems of socialism

1. 'Economic Calculation in the Socialist Commonwealth', p.110.

2. *Liberalism*, p.60, and pp.60–63.

3. *Socialism*, p.20.

4. *Omnipotent Government*, pp.242–3.

5. For a review of war socialism, see *Nation, State, and Economy*, pp.141–7.

6. *Socialism*, pp.240–9. The term 'state socialism' is seen by Mises as a misnomer, since socialism *always* requires the apparatus of the state to give directions and ensure compliance, no matter how much Marx and Engels might have looked forward to 'the withering away of the state'.

7. *Socialism*, pp.256–8. The instability of economic planning is well explained in S.C. Littlechild, *The Fallacy of the Mixed Economy* (London: Institute of Economic Affairs, 1978).

8. *Socialism*, p.269.

9. For these points, see *Human Action*, pp.812–16, and *Socialism*, pp.270–5.

10. *Human Action*, p.813.

11. *Socialism*, p.269.

12. *Ibid.*, p.13.

14. 'Economic Calculation in the Socialist Commonwealth', p.103.

15. On this point, T.W. Hutchison writes: 'German historical economists, and others . . . had discered the main critical point decades before – and this had even been briefly but clearly glimpsed by Friedrich Engels . . .' See T.W. Hutchison, *The Politics and Philosophy of Economics* (Oxford: Basil Blackwell, 1981), p.208. Another good review of the course of the debate and its prehistory is found in Karen Vaughan's 'Introduction' to her translation of Trygve J.B. Hoff, *Economic Calculation in the Socialist Society* (Indianapolis: Liberty Press, 1981).

16. Trygve J.B. Hoff, *Economic Calculation in the Socialist Society* (Indianapolis: Liberty Press, 1981), pp.1–2.

17. David Ramsay Steele, 'Posing the Problem: The Impossibility of Economic Calculation Under Socialism', *Journal of Libertarian Studies*, Vol.5, No.1 (Winter 1981), pp.7–22 (p.10).

18. *Ibid.*, pp.11–12.

19. *Socialism*, p.115.

20. *Ibid.*, p.122. Interestingly, Max Weber, writing independently a year after Mises, agreed that socialism was not rational when economic decisions became highly complex.

21. *Economic Policy*, p.34

22. 'Economic Calculation in the Socialist Commonwealth', p.102.

23. *Human Action*, p.207.

24. 'Economic Calculation in the Socialist Commonwealth', p.103.

25. *Ibid.*, p.116.

26. *Human Action*, pp.710–15. The point, in fact, goes back to Wieser, and G.L.S. Shackle has explored it fully in his concept of the 'kaleidic' nature of human action. See G.L.S. Shackle, *Decision, Order, and Time in Human Affairs* (Cambridge: Cambridge University Press, 1961) and his *Epistemics and Economics* (Cambridge: Cambridge University Press, 1972).

27. See F.A. Hayek, 'The Use of Knowledge in Society', in his *Individualism and Economic Order* (Chicago University Press, 1948), pp.77–91.

28. Boris Brutzkus puts the problem succinctly in his *Economic Planning in Socialist Russia* (London: George Routledge & Sons, 1935). For Hayek's comments, see 'The use of Knowledge in Society' in his *Individualism and Economic Order* (Chicago: Chicago University Press, 1948), pp.77–91 (p.79), and Eamonn Butler, *Hayek: His Contribution to the Political and Economic Thought of Our Time* (London: Maurice Temple Smith, 1983).

29. H.D. Dickinson, *The Economics of Socialism* (Oxford: Oxford University Press, 1939). See Karen Vaughan, 'Introduction' to Trygve J.B. Hoff, *Economic Calculation in the Socialist Society* (Indianapolis: Liberty Press, 1981), p.xiii.

30. For a description, see Robert Bradley Jr, 'Market Socialism: A Subjectivist Evaluation', *Journal of Libertarian Studies*, Vol.5, No.1 (Winter 1981), pp.23–39 (pp.24–6).

31. *Socialism*, p.255.

32. *Ibid.*, p.136.

33. *Nation, State, and Economy*, p.172.

34. *Omnipotent Government*, p.243.

35. *Socialism*, pp.129–30.

36. *Ibid.*, p.161.

37. *Ibid.*, p.199.

38. *Omnipotent Government*, pp.51–2.

39. *Socialism*, p.562. Despite Trotsky's long political dispute with Stalin, says Mises, the only thing which really divided them was the fact that one rose to supreme power and the other desired it. F.A. Hayek has summed up this

view of socialist planning pithily in his *The Road to Serfdom* (London: Routledge, 1944) quoting as the motto for Chapter 9 a 1937 remark by Trotsky: 'In a country where the sole employer is the state, opposition means death by slow starvation. The old principle: who does not work shall not eat, has been replaced by a new one: who does not obey shall not eat.'

40. *Socialism*, p.185.

41. Donald C. Lavoie, 'A Critique of the Standard Account of the Socialist Calculation Debate', *Journal of Libertarian Studies* Vol.5, No.1 (Winter 1981), pp.41–87.

Chapter 3: The theoretical basis of Marxism

1. *Human Action*, p.83.
2. *Socialism*, pp.15–17.
3. *Ibid.*, p.31. H.B. Acton, in *What Marx Really Said* (London: Macdonald & Co, 1967), pp.131–41, likens Marxism to a religion because of this.
4. *Theory and History*, p.105.
5. *Ibid.*, pp.109–112.
6. *Human Action*, pp.79–80.
7. *The Ultimate Foundations of Economic Science*, pp.31–2.
8. *Theory and History*, pp.110–20.
9. *Human Action*, pp.75–6.
10. *Ibid.*, pp.77–8 and *Epistemological Problems in Economics*, pp.191–5.
11. *Human Action*, pp.78–9.
12. *Theory and History*, pp.138–9.
13. *Ibid.*, pp.139–40.
14. *Human Action*, p.81.
15. *Theory and History*, p.113.
16. *The Epistemological Problems of Economics*, p.188.
17. *Theory and History*, pp.121–2.
18. *The Historical Setting of the Austrian School*, p.21.
19. *The Ultimate Foundations of Economic Science*, p.31.
20. *Theory and History*, pp.188–197.
21. *The Ultimate Foundation of Economic Science*, p.59.

Chapter 4: Anti-capitalism, interventionism, and bureaucracy

1. *Economic Policy*, p.51.
2. *Human Action*, pp.851–3.
3. *Ibid.*, pp.872–6.
4. *Planning for Freedom*, pp.161–72.
5. *Epistemological Problems of Economics*, pp.183–4.
6. *Socialism*, pp.463–8; *The Anticapitalist Mentality*, pp.66–72.
7. *Economic Policy*, pp.96–100.
8. *Liberalism*, p.160.

9. For an outline of this development, see Henri Lepage, *Tomorrow, Capitalism*, translated by Sheilagh C. Ogilvie (La Salle, Illinois: Open Court, 1978), pp.81–106; and James M. Buchanan, *Public Finance in Democratic Process* (Chapel Hill, North Carolina: University of North Carolina Press, 1967).

10. *Socialism*, p.23.

11. For Mises's critique of Myrdal, see *Epistemological Problems of Economics*, pp.58–62.

12. *Human Action*, pp.835–40. An excellent short work that corrects many of the modern myths about the early factory system and its social consequences is F.A. Hayek (ed.) *Capitalism and the Historians* (Chicago: University of Chicago Press, 1954).

13. *Liberalism*, pp.85–7. The point is expanded greatly by Hayek in *Knowledge, Evolution, and Society* (London: Adam Smith Institute, 1983) and *The Fatal Conceit* (forthcoming).

14. *Socialism*, 'Epilogue' p.531 (this also appears as *Planned Chaos*, p.21).

15. See *Socialism*, pp.442–50.

16. *Socialism*, pp.442–50.

17. *Nation, State, and Economy*, p.171.

18. *Socialism*, p.43.

19. *Liberalism*, pp.67–70.

20. *A Critique of Interventionism*, p.54.

21. *Planning for Freedom*, p.9.

22. *Ibid.*, pp.32–3.

23. *Interventionism*, p.20.

24. *Ibid.*, pp.19–20.

25. *Ibid.*, p.19.

26. *Ibid.*, p.20.

27. Robert L. Schuettinger and Eamonn F. Butler, *Forty Centuries of Wage and Price Controls: How Not to Fight Inflation* (Washington, DC: Heritage, 1979).

28. This example occurs in *Socialism*, pp.533–4, and variants are repeated in a number of places, such as *Economic Policy*, pp.41–6, *A Critique of Interventionism*, pp.24–9 and 144–50, and *Liberalism*, pp.76–85.

29. *Economic Policy*, p.46.

30. On rent control, see *Economic Policy*, pp.50–1 and *Human Action*, pp. 765–6.

31. *Liberalism*, pp.79–85 and *Human Action*, pp.775–6.

32. *Liberalism*, pp.79–85.

33. A consequence of all intervention (*Human Action*, pp.743–4).

34. *A Critique of Interventionism*, pp.27–9.

35. *Socialism*, 'Epilogue', p.533 (*Planned Chaos*, p.23).

36. *A Critique of Interventionism*, p.30.

37. *Planning for Freedom*, p.229.

38. Such as *Human Action*, pp.743–57.

39. *Human Action*, p.756.

40. *Ibid.*, pp.737–42. On this point, see, for example, Donald C. Lavoie, 'The Development of the Misesian Theory of Interventionism', in Israel M.

Kirzner, *Method, Process, and Austrian Economics* (Lexington: D.C. Heath & Company, 1982), pp.169–83 (especially pp.174–7).

41. For example, see Murray N. Rothbard, 'Interventionism: Comment on Lavoie', in Israel M. Kirzner, *Method, Process, and Austrian Economics* (Lexington: D.C. Heath & Company, 1982), pp.185–8.

42. See *Bureaucracy*, pp.59–63.

43. *A Critique of Interventionism*, pp.161–2.

44. *Bureaucracy*, pp.65–9. This government extinction of the benefits of the profit motive may well explain why so many large firms seem to become self-perpetuating empires rather than profit-making concerns, a point made forcefully over the years by J.K. Galbraith.

45. *Liberalism*, p.104.

46. *A Critique of Interventionism*, p.154.

47. *Ibid.*, p.159.

48. 'Economic Calculation in the Socialist Commonwealth', p.120.

49. Peter Young and Madsen Pirie, *Privatization Worldwide* (London: Adam Smith Institute, 1986).

Chapter 5: Nationalism versus liberalism

1. *Epistemological Problems of Economics*, p.196.

2. *Nation, State, and Economy*, p.13.

3. *Ibid.*, p.50.

4. *Omnipotent Government*, p.5–6. Mises's views on nationalism and and the economic foundations of war are found particularly in *Nation, State, and Economy*, in *Omnipotent Government*, and in Chapter 34 of *Human Action*, 'The Economics of War'.

5. *Economic Policy*, p.88.

6. *Liberalism*, p.122.

7. *Omnipotent Government*, pp.99–100. In support of Mises, it might be pointed out that the rate of return from investments in India and other parts of the British Empire was lower than that available at home. Economic necessity and 'exploitation' were clearly not the motivating forces of the imperial drive.

8. *Omnipotent Government*, p.44. The word 'etatism', derived from French, is used by Mises to signify that the idea has only recently taken root in the Anglo-Saxon mind (*Omnipotent Government*, p.5n. But today, he thinks, it is a principle that leads to complete war (*Omnipotent Government*, p.93). See *Socialism*, pp.245–6.

9. *Liberalism*, p.107. While this may be true, recent events have shown that a much stronger deterrent to military action is the presence of a country's own nationals working abroad. This is, however, a barrier to warfare that exists in a world of strong national identies. Perhaps the elimination of national identities desired by Mises is not the only route to avoiding war.

10. *Omnipotent Government*, p.3.

341

11. In *Human Action*, Mises came to recognize that the free movement of capital, rather than of people, was a more realistic target which would have many of the same economic benefits, whatever the restrictions on personal freedom.

12. *Human Action*, p.825.

13. *Economic Policy*, p.2.

14. *Ibid.*, p.23.

15. *Socialism*, pp.289–99.

16. This analysis is developed in detail by Hayek. For a synopsis of his view, see Eamonn Butler, *Hayek: His Contribution to the Political and Economic Thought of our Time* (London: Maurice Temple Smith, and New York: Universe Books, 1983), pp.15-40.

17. *Liberalism*, p.19.

18. *Ibid.*, p.21.

19. *Omnipotent Government*, pp.46–7.

20. *Liberalism*, p.37.

21. For insights on this, see Murray N. Rothbard, *Power and Market: Government and the Economy* (Menlo Park, California: Institute for Humane Studies, 1970), especially pages 151–88.

22. *Socialism*, p.57.

23. *Nation, State, and Economy*, p.184.

24. *Liberalism*, p.88.

25. *Economic Policy*, p.9, a point reiterated by Arthur Shenfield, 'Morality and Capitalism', in his *Myth and Reality in Economic Systems* (London: Adam Smith Institute, 1981), pp.44–60 (p.47).

26. *Ibid.*, p.6. On the factory system, see F.A. Hayek (ed.) *Capitalism and the Historians* (Chicago: University of Chicago Press, 1954).

27. *Economic Policy*, pp.81–4.

28. *Human Action*, pp.730–2, and *Socialism*, pp.534ff. The point has been elaborated by F.A. Hayek, 'The New Confusion about "Planning"', in his *New Studies in Philosophy, Politics, Economics, and the History of Ideas*, pp.232–46.

29. For Hayek's views on the 'marvel' of the price system, see F.A.Hayek, 'The Use of Knowledge in Society', *American Economic Review*, Vol.35, No.4 (September 1945), pp.519–30. Reprinted in F.A. Hayek, *Individualism and Economic Order* (Chicago: University of Chicago Press, 1948), pp.77–91.

30. *Human Action*, pp.287–8.

31. See *Nation, State, and Economy*, pp.188ff., and *Human Action*, p.320.

32. *Nation, State, and Economy*, p.214–5.

Chapter 6: Welfare, taxation, and the market

1. *Socialism*, p.469.

2. *Human Action*, Chapter 35.

3. *Ibid.*, p.836.

4. Chapter 4 above.

5. *Human Action*, pp.837–9.

6. *Ibid.*, p.841.

7. *Ibid.*, pp.845–6.

8. *A Critique of Interventionism*, pp.157–8. Hayek reiterates the point in *The Constitution of Liberty* (Chicago: Chicago University Press, 1960), pp.44–6. For a discussion, see Eamonn Butler, *Hayek: His Contribution to the Political and Economic Thought of Our Time* (London: Temple Smith/Gower, and New York: Universe Books, 1983), pp.98–100.

9. *Human Action*, p.852.

10. *A Critique of Interventionism*, pp.49–50.

11. *Bureaucracy*, p.24.

12. *Socialism*, p.491.

13. Not, of course, in the rigid socialist model, where incomes are controlled, since no tax would be necessary (*Socialism*, p.492).

14. *Planning for Freedom*, p.32.

15. *Economic Policy*, p.84.

16. *Human Action*, p.806.

17. *Liberalism*, p.74.

18. *Nation, State, and Economy*, p.186.

19. *Human Action*, p.659.

20. *Bureaucracy*, p.81.

21. *The Theory of Money and Credit*, p.83.

22. *Human Action*, pp.740–1. The point might be reinforced by a reading of the American supply-side economists, who reveal that tax rates above a certain level actually produce *less* revenue for the authorities, such is their depressive effect on incentives and their other destructive tendencies. See Andrew Neil *et al.*, *It Pays to Cut Taxes* (London: Adam Smith Institute, 1986).

23. *Planning for Freedom*, p.138.

Chapter 7: Individual values in economics

1. *Human Action*, p.96. For Mises's work on this point, perhaps the principal foundation of Austrian Economics, see especially *Human Action*, pp.92–8; *Epistemological Problems of Economics*, pp.146–82; *The Ultimate Foundation of Economic Science*, pp.37–8; and *Theory and History* pp.19–34.

2. *The Ultimate Foundations of Economic Science*, p.37.

3. *Human Action*, p.92.

4. *Theory and History*, p.6.

5. *Epistemological Problems in Economics*, p.208.

6. *Human Action*, p.21.

7. *Epistemological Problems in Economics*, p.208. This is a very narrow definition of 'subjective', as pointed out in Ludwig Lachman's essay 'Ludwig von Mises and the Extension of Subjectivism' in Israel M. Kirzner (ed.), *Method, Process, and Austrian Economics* (Lexington: D.C. Heath & Company, 1982), pp.31–40, and modern usage has changed. In fact, the term 'subjective' has several different meanings today, even as it is used by economists of the

Austrian School (see Stephan Boehm, 'The Ambiguous Notion of Subjectivism: Comment on Lachmann', in Israel M. Kirzner (*Ibid.*), pp.41–52.

8. *Human Action*, p.95.

9. See *Human Action* pp.119ff.

10. *Human Action*, pp.119–27.

11. *The Theory of Money and Credit*, p.52.

12. *Human Action*, p.122.

13. For example, Paul Samuelson, *Economics: An Introductory Analysis* (New York: McGraw-Hill, Seventh Edition, 1967) p.418.

14. *Human Action*, p.95.

15. *Human Action*, p.93.

16. F.A. Hayek, 'Scientism and the Study of Society', in his *The Counter-Revolution of Science* (Indianapolis: Liberty Press, 1979), pp.17–182 (pp.44–5).

17. *Human Action*, p.97.

18. *Socialism*, pp.113–4.

19. *The Theory of Money and Credit*, p.52.

20. *Ibid.*, p.121.

21. *Human Action*, p.210.

22. *Ibid.*, p.392.

23. *Ibid.*, p.217.

Chapter 8: The crucial importance of change

1. *Human Action*, p.223.

2. On this, see *Socialism*, Chapter 6.

3. See, for example, G.K. Shaw, *Rational Expectations: An Elementary Exposition* (Brighton, Sussex: Wheatsheaf, 1984). Friedman's analysis of the role of expectations in making inflations more pronounced is another example. See Eamonn Butler, *Milton Friedman: A Guide to His Economic Thought* (London: Temple Smith/Gower and New York: Universe Books, 1985), Chapter 7, and Friedman's own Nobel lecture, reprinted as *Inflation and Unemployment* (London: Institute of Economic Affairs, 1977). Although regarded as very much a free-market economist, Friedman also shows how traditional Marshallian market analysis is being overwhelmed more and more by subjectivist elements. Even proponents of the market do not say that markets are always perfect; interventionists' caricatures are simply wrong.

4. See, for example, Israel M. Kirzner, *Competition and Entrepreneurship* (Chicago: University of Chicago Press, 1973), and Gerald P. O'Driscoll Jr and Mario J. Rizzo, *The Economics of Time and Ignorance* (Oxford: Basil Blackwell, 1985).

5. This, and the ping-pong ball analogy, are not Mises's own examples.

6. *Human Action*, p.250.

7. *Planning for Freedom*, p.148.

8. *Human Action*, pp.55–6.

9. F.A. Hayek, 'The Theory of Complex Phenomena', in *Studies in Philoso-*

phy, Politics, and Economics (Chicago: Chicago University Press, 1967), pp.22–42. For a discussion of Hayek's view on this, see Eamonn Butler, *Hayek: His Contribution to the Political and Economic Thought of Our Time* (London: Maurice Temple Smith and New York: Universe Books, 1983), pp.132–150.

10. *Human Action*, p.222
11. *Ibid.*, p.329.
12. *Ibid.*, p.257.
13. *Economic Policy*, p.17.
14. *Epistemological Problems of Economics*, pp.161–2.
15. *The Ultimate Foundations of Economic Science*, p.51.

Chapter 9: Entrepreneurship, profit, and loss

1. *Socialism*, p.538.
2. See, for example, Israel M. Kirzner, *Competition and Entrepreneurship* (Chicago: University of Chicago Press, 1973) his essay 'Uncertainty, Discovery, and Human Action: A Study of the Entrepreneurial Profile in the Misesian System', in Israel M. Kirzner (ed.), *Method, Process, and Austrian Economics: Essays in Honor of Ludwig von Mises* (Lexington and Toronto: D.C. Heath & Company, 1982), pp.139–60; and his paper 'The Primacy of Entrepreneurial Discovery', in Arthur Seldon (ed.) *The Prime Mover of Progress* (London: Institute of Economic Affairs, 1980), pp.3–30.
3. *Human Action*, p.297.
4. *Ibid.*, pp.254–5. On this point, it is interesting to note that Mises's follower, Murray N. Rothbard, has no difficulty in merging the roles of entrepreneurs and capitalists, when he speaks of 'capitalist-entrepreneurs' in *Man, Economy, and State* (Los Angeles: Nash, 1962).
5. *Human Action*, p.234.
6. *Economic Policy*, p.36.
7. *Human Action*, pp.297–8.
8. For this and the following analysis, see *Human Action*, pp.327–331.
9. *Human Action*, p.338.
10. See Chapter 7, above, 'Individual Values in Economics'.
11. *Bureaucracy*, p.29.
12. *Economic Policy*, p.5.
13. See Alexander H. Shand, *The Capitalist Alternative: An Introduction to Neo-Austrian Economics* (Brighton, Sussex: Wheatsheaf, 1984), pp.92–5

Chapter 10: Competition, co-operation, and the consumer

1. *Planning for Freedom*, pp.72–3.
2. See F.A. Hayek, 'Competition as a Discovery Procedure' in his *New Studies in Philosophy, Politics, Economics, and the History of Ideas* (London: Routledge, 1978), pp.179–190, and 'The Meaning of Competition' in F.A. Hayek, *Individualism and Economic Order* (Chicago: University of Chicago

Press, 1948), pp.92–105 for this argument. Although it forms the under-current in Mises's work, Hayek's exposition of the phenomenon is probably clearer.

3. F.A. Hayek, *Ibid.*

4. *Human Action*, p.270. More generally, see *Human Action* pp.269–75.

5. *Human Action*, p.271, and *Socialism*, 'Appendix', p.535.

6. *Socialism*, p.535.

7. *Economic Policy*, p.9; see also *Human Action*, p.271.

8. *Economic Policy*, p.3.

9. *Ibid.*, p.4.

10. *A Critique of Interventionism*, p.84.

11. *Liberalism*, p.88.

12. *Socialism*, p.299.

13. *Economic Policy*, p.5. Hayek puts the figure much higher, noting that the capitalist system today supports two hundred times as many people as existed before civilization began. See F.A. Hayek, 'Our Moral Heritage', in his *Knowledge, Evolution, and Society* (London: Adam Smith Institute, 1983), pp.45–57 (p.47).

14. *Human Action*, p.673.

15. *Socialism*, p.397.

16. *Socialism*, p.397.

17. *Ibid.*, pp.40–41. On the identification of ownership and control, see *Socialism*, p.37: 'Ownership appears as the power to use economic goods. An owner is he who disposes of an economic good'.

18. *Ibid.*, p.41.

19. *Ibid.*,pp.372–3.

20. *Ibid.*, p.380.

21. *Human Action*, p.277.

22. *Liberalism*, p.93ff.

23. *A Critique of Interventionism*, p.48.

24. *Liberalism*, p.93.

25. *Human Action*, p.369.

26. *Socialism*, pp.390–1.

27. *Omnipotent Goverment*, p.68ff.

28. *Omnipotent Government*, p.72.

29. W. Baumol, 'Contestable Markets: An Uprising in the Theory of Industrial Structure', *American Economic Review*, March 1983.

Chapter 11: Capital and interest

1. *Economic Policy*, p.87.

2. For Mises's views on capital, see especially *Human Action*, pp.480–522 and *Epistemological Problems of Economics*, pp.215ff.

3. *Human Action*, p.493.

4. For this, see *Epistemological Problems of Economics*, pp.215ff.

5. *Human Action*, p.506.

6. See Chapter 13 below, 'Inflation and Its Effects'.

7. *Human Action*, p.515.

8. Not Mises's example.

9. *Human Action*, p.515. For a discussion of the error of conceptual realism (and many others), see Madsen Pirie, *The Book of the Fallacy* (London: Routledge, 1986).

10. *Ibid.*, p.263.

11. *Ibid.*, p.263.

12. *Socialism*, p.202.

13. *Ibid.*, p.494.

14. *Planning for Freedom*, pp.5–6.

15. *Economic Policy*, p.81.

16. *Human Action*, p.532.

Chapter 12: The nature and value of money

1. *The Theory of Money and Credit*, p.144.

2. For example, the 'mutual determination' method of Don Patinkin, J.R. Hicks, and Oskar Lange.

3. Milton Friedman and Anna J. Schwartz, *Monetary Trends in the United States and the United Kingdom* (Chicago: University of Chicago Press, National Bureau of Economic Research Monograph, 1982), pp.26–36 See also Eamonn Butler, *Milton Friedman: A Guide to His Economic Thought* (London: Temple Smith/Gower, and New York: Universe Books, 1985), pp.242–5.

4. The example here is not one from Mises.

5. *Human Action*, p.401.

6. *Ibid.*, p.401.

7. *The Theory of Money and Credit*, p.88.

8. *Human Action*, p.401.

9. *The Theory of Money and Credit*, p.125.

10. *The Theory of Money and Credit*, pp.76–81.

11. *Human Action*, p.432.

12. *The Theory of Money and Credit*, p.85.

13. Actually, in *The Theory of Money and Credit* (pp.95–102), Mises does talk about increase in the nominal quantity of money resulting in changes in prices which tend to restore the real quantity of money – suggesting equiproportionality. But this is in the context of demonstrating that money is not a production or a consumption good (in which case increases or decreases in its quantity obviously *would* affect welfare), and is obviously intended to be just a general result of long-run comparative statics rather than a precise and necessary principle of economics.

14. *The Theory of Money and Credit*, p.309.

15. *Ibid.*, p.135.

16. *Ibid.*, p.132.

17. Indeed, modern expectations theory and even Friedman's 'permanent

income' hypothesis put great reliance on past experience, suitably weighted, as a guide to individuals' appraisal of the future. See Milton Friedman, *A Theory of the Consumption Function* (Princeton, New Jersey: Princeton University Press, 1957); and G.K. Shaw, *Rational Expectations: An Elementary Exposition* (Brighton, Sussex: Wheatsheaf, 1984).

18. Don Patinkin, *Money, Interest, and Prices* (Evanston, Illinois: Row, Peterson, & Co, 1956), especially pp.115–6.

19. See, for instance, Laurence S. Moss, 'The Monetary Economics of Ludwig von Mises', in Laurence S. Moss (ed.), *The Economics of Ludwig von Mises* (Kansas: Sheed and Ward, 1976), pp.13–49, (especially pp.21–3), and James Rolph Edwards, *The Economist of the Country: Ludwig von Mises in the History of Monetary Thought* (New York: Carlton Press,1985), pp.58–61.

Chapter 13: Inflation and its effects

1. *The Theory of Money and Credit*, pp.163–4.

2. *Ibid.*, p.411.

3. *Ibid.*, p.159.

4. *Ibid.*, p.164.

5. *Economic Policy*, p.59.

6. *Human Action*, p.412.

7. F.A. Hayek, 'Three Elucidations of the Ricardo Effect', in *New Studies in Philosophy, Politics, Economics, and the History of Ideas* (London: Routledge, 1978), pp.165–78 (p.173).

8. *The Theory of Money and Credit*, p.168.

9. See, for example, Friedman's defence against Mises's views in Milton Friedman and Anna J. Schwartz, *Monetary Trends in the United States and the United Kingdom* (Chicago: University of Chicago Press, National Bureau of Economic Research Monograph 1982), pp.29–31. For a discussion, see Eamonn Butler, *Milton Friedman: A Guide to his Economic Thought* (Aldershot, Hampshire: Gower/Temple Smith, and New York: Universe Books, 1985), pp.242-5.

10. *The Theory of Money and Credit*, pp.220–21.

11. *Ibid.*, pp.218–9.

12. *Ibid.*, p.26.

13. *Ibid.*, p.455.

14. *Ibid.*, pp.434–5.

15. *On the Manipulation of Money and Credit*, p.189.

16. For a survey of Friedman's view, see Eamonn Butler, *Milton Friedman: A Guide to his Economic Thought* (Aldershot, Hampshire: Gower/Temple Smith, and New York: Universe Books, 1985).

17. *The Theory of Money and Credit*, p.257.

18. Actually, this principle might provide an argument to the effect that a commodity standard would *not* produce the falling prices we so commonly fear. Technological progress in the production or extraction of a commodity

currency is likely to improve over the years, just as much as progress in the production of other goods. This will tend to keep prices on a more even path than if the supply of the commodity currency was unalterably fixed in volume.

19. *Economic Policy*, p.65.
20. *The Theory of Money and Credit*, p.270.

Chapter 14: The tragedy of the trade cycle

1. *Human Action*, p.561. A thorough explanation of Mises's views on on the trade cycle is found in *Human Action*, pp.538–86.

2. For this analysis, see Chapter 13 above, 'Inflation and Its Effects', and *Human Action*, pp.416–86; on the observed movement of interest rates, see *The Theory of Money and Credit*, pp.384–8, and *Human Action*, pp.548–71.

3. *The Theory of Money and Credit*, p.386.

4. *Ibid.*, pp.387–8.

5. *Ibid.*, pp.388–9.

6. Or possibly a little more, to compensate lenders for interest lost over the year of the price escalation.

7. *Human Action*, pp.541–8.

8. See Milton Friedman and Anna J. Schwartz, *Monetary Trends in the United States and the United Kingdom* (Chicago: University of Chicago Press, National Bureau of Economic Research Monograph, 1982), p.493. For a review, see Eamonn Butler, *Milton Friedman: A Guide to his Economic Thought* (Aldershot, Hampshire: Gower/Temple Smith, and New York: Universe Books, 1985), pp.166-8.

9. *Planning for Freedom*, p.156.

10. *Human Action*, p.562.

11. *Epistemological Problems of Economics*, p.226.

12. *Omnipotent Government*, p.251.

13. *Human Action*, pp.576–7.

Chapter 15: The scientific basis of economics

1. *Human Action*, p.68.

2. *The Ultimate Foundations of Economic Science*, p.37.

3. *Human Action*, p.18.

4. *Ibid.*, pp.30–32.

5. *The Ultimate Foundations of Economic Science*, pp.37–8.

6. For an overview of Mises' concept of praxeology, see the Introduction and Part 1 of *Human Action*; Chapter 1 and Chapter 2 of *Epistemological Problems of Economics*; and the 'Preliminary Observations', Chapter 1, and Chapter 2 of *The Ultimate Foundation of Economic Science*.

7. James M. Buchanan, 'The Domain of Subjective Economics: Between Predictive Science and Moral Philosophy', in Israel Kirzner (ed.), *Method*,

Process, and Austrian Economics: Essays in Honor of Ludwig von Mises (Lexington and Toronto: D.C. Heath and Company, 1982), pp.7–20 (pp.13–14).

8. See Mario J. Rizzo, 'Mises and Lakatos: A Reformulation of Austrian Methodology', in Israel M. Kirzner (ed.), *Method, Process, and Austrian Economics: Essays in Honor of Ludwig von Mises* (Lexington and Toronto: D.C. Heath and Company, 1982), pp.53–73.

9. See F.A. Hayek, 'Coping with Ignorance', in *Knowledge, Evolution, and Society* (London: Adam Smith Institute, 1983), pp.17–27.

10. *Ibid.*, p.22.

11. *The Ultimate Foundation of Economic Science*, p.63.

12. *Epistemological Problems of Economics*, pp.117–8.

13. *Ibid.*, p.xiii.

14. *The Ultimate Foundation of Economic Science*, pp.40–1.

15. *Epistemological Problems of Economics*, p.200.

16. *Theory and History*, p.215.

17. *Epistemological Problems in Economics*, p.56.

18. *Theory and History*, p.5.

19. *The Ultimate Foundation of Economic Science*, pp.4–5.

20. See, for example, *The Ultimate Foundations of Economic Science*, pp.11–33 and *Human Action*, pp.32–6.

21. *The Ultimate Foundations of Economic Science*, pp.35–6.

22. *Epistemological Problems in Economics*, pp.12–13.

23. *Human Action*, pp.65–6.

24. Mark Blaug, *The Methodology of Economics* (Cambridge: Cambridge University Press, 1980), p.93.

25. James M. Buchanan, 'The Domain of Subjective Economics: Between Predictive Science and Moral Philosophy', in Israel Kirzner (ed.), *Method, Process, and Austrian Economics: Essays in Honor of Ludwig von Mises* (Lexington and Toronto: D.C. Heath and Company, 1982), pp.7–20 (p.14).

26. *Ibid.*, p.14.

27. See F.A. Hayek, 'The Theory of Complex Phenomena' in M. Bunge (ed.) *The Critical Approach to Science and Philosophy* (New York: The Free Press, 1964), reprinted as Chapter 2 of F.A. Hayek, *Studies in Philosophy, Politics, and Economics* (London: Routledge and Chicago: University of Chicago Press, 1967), pp.22–42. It is interesting to compare this with his earlier 'Scientism and the Study of Society' and 'The Counter-Revolution of Science', published together as *The Counter-Revolution of Science: Studies in the Abuse of Reason* (Glencoe, Illinois: The Free Press, 1952), and the later 'Coping With Ignorance' in F.A. Hayek, *Knowledge, Evolution, and Society* (London: Adam Smith Institute, 1983), pp.17–27. For a brief discussion of the subject, see Eamonn Butler, *Hayek: His Contribution to the Political and Economic Thought of Our Time* (London: Maurice Temple Smith, and New York: Universe Books, 1983), pp.132–50: 'Epilogue: Sense and Sorcery in the Social Sciences'.

28. See Mario J. Rizzo, 'Mises and Lakatos: A Reformulation of Austrian Methodology', in Israel M. Kirzner (ed.), *Method, Process, and Austrian Economics: Essays in Honour of Ludwig von Mises* (Lexington and Toronto: D.C. Heath and Company, 1982), pp.53–73.

29. Karl R. Popper, *The Logic of Scientific Discovery* (London: Hutchinson & Co, 1959), originally published as *Logik der Forschung* (Vienna: 1934).

30. *Epistemological Problems in Economics*, containing the first discussion of the concept of a science of human action, was published in 1933, a year before Karl Popper's *Logic of Scientific Discovery*, in the same city of Vienna. Had the dates been transposed, the history of Austrian Economics might have been entirely different.

31. *Human Action*, p.31.

32. *Epistemological Problems of Economics*, p.8.

33. See his brief dismissal of Popper in *The Ultimate Foundations of Economic Science*, pp.69–70.

34. *The Ultimate Foundation of Economic Science*, p.xii.

35. *Ibid.*, p.18.

36. Imre Lakatos, and others, objected on this ground even to Popper's formulation. Popper argues that, while we have no criterion of truth, we do have a limited criterion of falsity, and talks about 'testing in the light of our objective knowledge', saying the process reveals 'falsity'. But Lakatos objects that we have no way of establishing any scientific proposition as definitely false, any more than we have of establishing it to be definitely true: for in either case, where does the 'objective' standard of truth or falsity come from? See Imre Lakatos, 'Falsification in the Methodology of Scientific Research Programmes', in Imre Lakatos & Alan Musgrave (eds) *Criticism and the Growth of Knowledge* (Cambridge: Cambridge University Press, 1970), pp.91–196.

37. Madsen Pirie, *Trial and Error and the Idea of Progress* (La Salle, Illinois and London: Open Court, 1978), especially pp.24-45.

38. *The Ultimate Foundation of Economic Science*, p.15.

39. *Human Action*, pp.25, 34, and 64.

40. For a survey of this, see Alfred Tarski, *Logic, Semantics, Metamathematics* (Oxford: Oxford University Press, 1956).

41. A point made by Rizzo in 'Mises and Lakatos: A Reformulation of Austrian Methodology', in Israel M. Kirzner (ed.), *Method, Process, and Austrian Economics: Essays in Honour of Ludwig von Mises* (Lexington and Toronto: D.C. Heath and Company, 1982), pp.53–73, his attempt to bring Mises's methodology more into line with the more recent approaches of Imre Lakatos and Thomas Kuhn. For the views of the latter, see Thomas S. Kuhn, *The Structure of Scientific Revolutions* (Chicago: Chicago University Press, 1962). Kuhn's book was published in the same year as Mises's radically different *The Ultimate Foundation of Economic Science*.

42. Madsen Pirie, *Trial and Error and the Idea of Progress*, (La Salle, Illinois: Open Court, 1978), p.38.

43. *Ibid.*, p.25.

44. *Ibid.*, p.90.

45. *The Ultimate Foundation of Economic Science*, p.45.

46. In fact, the ethologists and sociobiologists are now exploring the view that human action might be rather more predictable than our elevated opinion of ourselves causes us to admit. See, for example, Hilary Callan,

Ethology and Society (Oxford: Oxford University Press, 1970), Irenäus Eibl-Eibesfeldt, *Ethology: The Biology of Behaviour* (New York: Holt, Reinhart and Winston, 1970), and Edward O. Wilson, *Sociobiology: The New Synthesis* (Cambridge, Massachussetts: Harvard University Press, 1975).

47. See, for example, T.W. Hutchison, *The Politics and Philosophy of Economics* (Oxford: Basil Blackwell, 1981), p224.

48. F.A. Hayek, 'Coping With Ignorance', in *Knowledge, Evolution, and Society* (London: Adam Smith Institute, 1983), pp.17–27 (p.21).

49. F.A. Hayek, 'The Pretence of Knowledge', in *New Studies in Philosophy, Politics, Economics, and the History of Ideas* (London: Routledge and Kegan Paul, 1978), pp.23–34.

Chapter 16: Economic theory before and after Mises

1. *Notes and Recollections*, p.115

2. Louis M. Spadaro, 'Toward a Program of Research and Development for Austrian Economics', in Louis M. Spadaro (ed.) *New Directions in Austrian Economics* (Kansas City: Sheed Andrews and McMeel, 1978), pp.205–227 (pp.208–9).

3. Wolfgang Grassl and Barry Smith (eds) *Austrian Economics* (London and Sydney: Croom Helm, 1986), p.viii.

4. James M. Buchanan 'Introduction: LSE Cost Theory in Retrospect', in James M. Buchanan and G.F. Thirlby (eds) *LSE Essays on Cost* (New York: New York University Press, Institute for Humane Studies Series in Economic Theory, 1981; originally published in London by the London School of Economics, 1973) pp.1–16 (p.11).

5. T.W. Hutchison *The Politics and Philosophy of Economics* (Oxford: Basil Blackwell, 1981), p.209, quoting F.A. Hayek, *New Studies in Philosophy, Politics, Economics, and the History of Ideas* (Chicago: Chicago University Press, 1978), p.297.

6. T.W. Hutchison, *Ibid.*, p.204

7. It is interesting, for example, how most of the leading English-language critics of Marxism, though plainly influenced directly or indirectly by Mises's arguments, acknowledge no debt to him. See for Example, John Plamenatz, *Man and Society* (London: Longman, 1963) and H.B. Acton, *What Marx Really Said* (London: Macdonald, 1967, and *The Illusion of the Epoch* (London: Routledge and Kegan Paul, 1955).

8. For views in this tradition, see James M. Buchanan and G.F. Thirlby, *LSE Essays on Cost* (New York: New York University Press, Institute for Humane Studies Series in Economic Theory, 1981; originally published in London by the London School of Economics, 1973).

9. Wolfgang Grassl and Barry Smith, *Austrian Economics* (London and Sydney: Croom Helm, 1986), p.81, quoting Carl Menger's *Principles of Economics* (Vienna: 1871), in his *Works* edited by F.A. Hayek (London: London School of Economics, 1933–6), p.87; and p.3, quoting a letter of 1884 written to Walras.

10. Menger, for example, used a table of figures to illustrate his argument about marginal utility. See Carl Menger, *Principles of Economics*, translated by James Dingwall and Bert F. Hoselitz from the German edition of 1871 (New York: New York University Press, Institute for Humane Studies Series in Economic Theory, 1981), p.204. Although he certainly did not want to suggest that utility was measurable, that conclusion has unfortunately permeated into much of the neoclassical theory.

11. Ludwig M. Lachmann, 'Ludwig von Mises and the Extension of Subjectivism', in Israel M. Kirzner (ed.), *Method, Process, and Austrian Economics: Essays in Honor of Ludwig von Mises* (Lexington and Toronto: D.C. Heath and Company, 1982), pp.31–40 (p.36), and James M. Buchanan, *Cost and Choice* (Chicago: Markham, 1969), p.8.

12. See, for example, Milton Friedman, *Inflation and Unemployment* (London: Institute of Economic Affairs, 1977) and *Unemployment Versus Inflation?* (London, Institute of Economic Affairs, 1975). For a discussion, see Eamonn Butler: *Milton Friedman: A Guide to His Economic Thought* (Aldershot, Hampshire: Gower, and New York: Universe Books, 1985), pp.133–148. Expectations theory should have been seen as a crucial contribution of the subjectivist scholars, and is claimed as such by Ludwig M. Lachmann. But Mises's reluctance to explore it may have critically reduced that link; expectations theory has now gone into mainstream teaching with hardly any acknowledgement of Mises and the subjectivist writers.

13. See G.L.S. Shackle, *Epistemics and Economics* (Cambridge: Cambridge University Press, 1972), and also his *Imagination and the Nature of Choice* (Edinburgh: Edinburgh University Press, 1979).

14. A point made by Ludwig M. Lachmann, 'An Austrian Stocktaking: Unsettled Questions and Tentative Answers', in Louis M. Spadaro (ed.) *New Directions in Austrian Economics* (Kansas City: Sheed Andrews and McMeel, 1978), pp.1–18 (pp.1–2).

15. Murray N. Rothbard, 'The Essential Von Mises', in *Planning for Freedom*, pp.234–270 (p.241).

16. Ludwig M. Lachmann, 'On Austrian Capital Theory', in Edwin G. Dolan, *The Foundations of Austrian Economics* (Kansas City: Sheed and Ward, 1976), pp.145–159 (p.145–6).

17. This is a part of the theory in which Ludwig M. Lachmann has set the pace. See, for example, his *Capital, Expectations, and the Market Process* (Kansas City: Sheed Andrews and McMeel, 1977). See also Gerald P. O'Driscoll and Mario J. Rizzo, *The Economics of Time and Ignorance* (Oxford: Basil Blackwell, 1985) pp.160–187; and F.A. Hayek, *The Pure Theory of Capital* (Chicago: University of Chicago Press, 1941), which started the Austrian retreat from Böhm-Bawerk's classical objectivism, according to Ludwig M. Lachmann, *The Market as an Economic Process* (Oxford: Basil Blackwell, 1986), p.x.

18. See, for example, Gerald P. O'Driscoll and Mario J. Rizzo, *The Economics of Time and Ignorance* (Oxford: Basil Blackwell, 1985) pp.62–9.

19. See, for example, F.A. Hayek, 'Competition as a Discovery Procedure', in his *New Studies in Philosophy, Politics, Economics, and the History of Ideas*

(London: Routledge & Kegan Paul, 1978), pp.179–190; and Gerald P. O'Driscoll and Mario J. Rizzo, *The Economics of Time and Ignorance* (Oxford: Basil Blackwell, 1985), pp.95–129.

20. See, for example, Gerald P. O'Driscoll and Mario J. Rizzo, *The Economics of Time and Ignorance* (Oxford: Basil Blackwell, 1985), pp.71–91; and Mario J. Rizzo, 'Disequilibrium and All That: An Introductory Essay', in Mario J. Rizzo (ed.) *Time, Uncertainty, and Disequilibrium*, pp.1–49. For a summary of Shackle and Lachmann on equilibrium theory, see Alexander H. Shand, *The Capitalist Alternative: An Introduction to Neo-Austrian Economics* (Brighton, Sussex: Wheatsheaf, 1984), pp.39-40.

21. See, for example, G.L.S. Shackle, *Time in Economics* (Amsterdam: North Holland, 1958), and *Decision, Order, and Time in Human Affairs* (Cambridge: Cambridge University Press, second edition, 1962).

22. Gerald P. O'Driscoll and Mario J. Rizzo, *The Economics of Time and Ignorance* (Oxford: Basil Blackwell, 1985).

23. Israel M. Kirzner, 'Mises and the Renaissance of Austrian Economics', in John K. Andrews, *Homage to Mises* (Hillsdale, Michigan: Hillsdale College, 1981), pp.14–18 (p.16).

24. G.L.S. Shackle, *Epistemics and Economics* (Cambridge: Cambridge University Press, 1972).

25. See, for example, F.A. Hayek, 'Coping With Ignorance' in his *Knowledge, Evolution, and Society* (London: Adam Smith Institute, 1983), pp.17–27. For a summary of Hayek's points, see Eamonn Butler, *Hayek: His Contribution to the Political and Economic Thought of Our Time* (London: Maurice Temple Smith, and New York: Universe Books, 1983), pp.15–65.

26. Ludwig M. Lachmann, *Macroeconomic Thinking and the Market Economy* (London: Institute of Economic Affairs, 1973), and 'Toward a Critique of Macroeconomics', in Edwin G. Dolan, *The Foundations of Modern Austrian Economics* (Kansas City: Sheed and Ward, 1976), pp.152–159.

27. Ludwig M. Lachmann, *Capital, Expectations, and Market Process* (Kansas City: Sheed, Andrews and McMeel, 1977), p.39.

28. G.L.S. Shackle, *Epistemics and Economics* (Cambridge: Cambridge University Press, 1972).

29. Alexander H. Shand, *The Capitalist Alternative: An Introduction to Neo-Austrian Economics* (Brighton, Sussex: Wheatsheaf, 1984), p.41.

30. For a discussion of the entrepreneurial function, see Israel M. Kirzner, 'Uncertainty, Discovery, and Human Action: A Study of the Entrepreneurial Profile in the Misesian System', in Israel M. Kirzner (ed.), *Method, Process, and Austrian Economics: Essays in Honor of Ludwig von Mises* (Lexington and Toronto: D.C. Heath and Company, 1982), pp.139–160; and the reply by Jack High, 'Alertness and Judgment: Comment on Kirzner' in the same volume, pp.161–168.

31. Murray N. Rothbard, *Man, Economy, and State* (Los Angeles: Nash, 1962), p.463.

32. See Ludwig M. Lachmann, *Capital, Expectations, and Market Process* (Kansas City: Sheed, Andrews, and McMeel, 1977), p.316; and Israel M.

Kirzner, 'The Primacy of Entrepreneurial Discovery' in Arthur Seldon (ed.) *The Prime Mover of Progress: The Entrepreneur in Capitalism and Socialism* (London: Institute of Economic Affairs, 1980), pp.3–30 (p.29).

33. Joseph A. Schumpeter, *History of Economic Analysis* (London: Oxford University Press, 1954).

34. See, for example, F.A. Hayek, 'Competition as a Discovery Procedure', in his *New Studies in Philosophy, Politics, Economics, and the History of Ideas* (London: Routledge & Kegan Paul, 1978), pp.179–190.

35. Israel M. Kirzner, *Competition and Entrepreneurship* (Chicago: Chicago University Press, 1973).

36. Murray N. Rothbard, *Man, Economy, and State* (Los Angeles: Nash, 1962), p.608.

37. For a review of this, see Gerald P. O'Driscoll, 'Monopoly in Theory and Practice', in Israel M. Kirzner (ed.), *Method, Process, and Austrian Economics: Essays in Honor of Ludwig von Mises* (Lexington and Toronto: D.C. Heath and Company, 1982), pp.189–213.

38. Murray N. Rothbard, *Man, Economy and State* (Los Angeles: Nash, 1962). For a review see Donald C. Lavoie, 'The Development of the Misesian Theory of Interventionism', in Israel M. Kirzner (ed.), *Method, Process, and Austrian Economics: Essays in Honor of Ludwig von Mises* (Lexington and Toronto: D.C. Heath and Company, 1982), pp.169–186 (pp.177–180).

39. Donald C. Lavoie, 'The Development of the Misesian Theory of Interventionism', in Israel M. Kirzner (ed.), *Method, Process, and Austrian Economics: Essays in Honor of Ludwig von Mises* (Lexington and Toronto: D.C. Heath and Company, 1982), pp.169–186 (pp.177–180).

40. See, for example, James M. Buchanan, *Public Finance in Democratic Process* (Chapel Hill, North Carolina: University of North Carolina, 1967).

41. For an example of this approach, see Madsen Pirie, *The Logic of Economics* (London: Adam Smith Institute, 1981).

42. The importance of money was downgraded more and more in Keynes's writings, culminating in its virtual omission (despite the title) from his *General Theory of Employment, Interest, and Money* (London: Macmillan, 1936).

43. For an overview of Friedman's work, see Eamonn Butler, *Milton Friedman: A Guide to His Economic Thought* (Aldershot, Hampshire: Gower, and New York: Universe Books, 1985).

44. For example, Hayek's essays in inflation in Sudha R. Shenoy (ed.) *A Tiger by the Tail* (London: Institute of Economic Affairs, 1978).

45. F.A. Hayek, *1980s Unemployment and the Unions* (London: Institute of Economic Affairs, 1980), p.23.

46. Murray N. Rothbard, 'The Austrian Theory of Money', in Edwin G. Dolan (ed.), *The Foundations of Austrian Economics* (Kansas City: Sheed & Ward, 1976), pp.160–184.

47. See, for example, 'Coping With Ignorance', in F.A. Hayek, *Knowledge, Evolution, and Morality* (London: Adam Smith Institute, 1983), pp.17–27 (especially p.18 and pp.21–2).

48. For a discussion, see T.W. Hutchison, *The Politics and Philosophy of Economics* (Oxford: Basil Blackwell, 1981), pp.166ff.

49. Ludwig M. Lachmann, 'Ludwig von Mises and the Extension of Subjectivism', in Israel M. Kirzner (ed.) *Method, Process, and Austrian Economics: Essays in Honor of Ludwig von Mises* (Lexington and Toronto: D.C. Heath and Company, 1982), pp.31–40 (p.32).

50. See T.W. Hutchison, *The Politics and Philosophy of Economics* (Oxford: Basil Blackwell, 1981), pp.203–4.

51. See especially *Notes and Recollections*, pp.35–6.

52. For a review see T.W. Hutchison, *The Politics and Philosophy of Economics* (Oxford: Basil Blackwell, 1981), pp.204-7.

53. Carl Menger, *Problems of Economics and Sociology*, edited by L. Schneider and translated by F.J. Nock from the original German edition of 1883 (Urbana, Illinois: University of Illinois, 1963).

54. The most forthright expression of this is to be found in Hayek's *The Fatal Conceit* (forthcoming). His evolutionary view is also to be found in *Knowledge, Evolution, and Society* (London: Adam Smith Institute, 1983), and is reviewed in Eamonn Butler and Madsen Pirie (eds) *Hayek on the Fabric of Human Society* (London: Adam Smith Institute, 1987).

55. For Hayek's views on the 'miracle' of the price system as a communicator of market information, see especially F.A. Hayek, 'The Use of Knowledge in Society', in his *Individualism and Economic Order* (Chicago: University of Chicago Press, 1948), pp.77–91.

Select Bibliography

Below are listed Mises's main works which are mentioned in the text. For a more comprehensive list, perhaps the best is still that of Bettina Bien Greaves, *The Works of Ludwig von Mises* (Irvington-on-Hudson, New York: Foundation for Economic Education, 1969), although several new editions and reprints have emerged since then – in particular, the Institute for Humane Studies has made possible a number of new editions and reprints.

The first reference given in each item below represents what is probably the most widely available editions in English at the time of writing – and these are the editions to which page numbers in the footnotes refer. However, the order of the list itself follows the order of the first editions, many of them originally in German. In each case, the original titles and publication dates are given.

BOOKS AND ARTICLES BY MISES

The Theory of Money and Credit, translated by H.E. Batson (Indianapolis: Liberty Fund, 1980). The 1980 edition follows closely the translations by H.E. Batson published in London by Jonathan Cape Limited (1934) and in New Haven, Connecticut by Yale University Press (1953). The first German edition appeared in 1912 as *Theorie des Geldes und der Umlaufsmittel*.

Nation, State, and Economy, translated by Leland B. Yeager (New York and London: New York University Press, Institute for Humane Studies Series in Economic Theory, 1983). Originally published in 1919 as *Nation, Staat, und Wirtschaft*.

'Economic Calculation in the Socialist Commonwealth', translated by S. Adler, in *Collectivist Economic Planning: Critical Studies on the Possibilities of Socialism*, edited by F.A. Hayek (London: Routledge, 1963). The book was first published by Routledge in 1935, and the article by Mises originally appeared as 'Die Wirtschaftsrechnung im socialistischen Gemeinwesen', *Archiv für Socialwissenschaften*, Vol.47 (1920), pp.86–121.

Socialism: An Economic and Sociological Analysis, translated by J. Kahane (New Haven, Connecticut: Yale University Press, 1951). This includes an epilogue, *Planned Chaos* but is otherwise similar to the translation from the second German edition of 1932 that was published in London in 1936 by Jonathan Cape. The first edition appeared as *Die Gemeinwirtschaft: Untersuchungen über den Socialismus* (Jena: Gustav Fischer, 1922). A new printing of the English edition appeared from Jonathan Cape in 1969, and a version with a Foreword by F.A.Hayek was published in 1981 by the Liberty Press, Indianapolis.

Liberalism: A Socio-Economic Exposition, translated by Ralph Raico and edited by Arthur Goddard (Kansas City: Sheed Andrews and McMeel, Institute for Humane Studies Series in Economic Theory, 1978). The earlier English-language edition by the same translator was published under the title *The Free and Prosperous Commonwealth: An Exposition of the Ideas of Classical Liberalism* (Princeton, New Jersey: D. Van Nostrand, 1962). It has now been released as *Liberalism in the Classical Tradition* by the Foundation for Education in Economics (Irvington on Hudson, New York: Foundation for Education in Economics, 1985). The original German edition was *Liberalismus* (Jena: Gustav Fischer, 1927).

A Critique of Interventionism, translated by Hans F. Sennholz (New Rochelle, New York: Arlington House, 1977). Originally published in 1929 as *Kritik des Interventionismus* (Jena: Gustav Fischer Verlag, 1929) and again in German by the same publisher in 1976, with the inclusion of the essay 'Die Verstaatlichung des Kredits: Mutualisierung des Kredits' which Mises had intended to include originally.

On the Manipulation of Money and Credit, translated by Bettina Bien Greaves and edited by Percy L. Greaves Jr (Dobbs Ferry, New York: Free Market Books, 1978). Based primarily on Mises's essays 'Die geldtheoretische Seite des Stabilisierungsproblems', in *Schriften des Vereins für Socialpolitik*, Vol.164, Part 2 (Munich and Leipzig: Duncker & Humblot, 1923); *Geldwertstabilisierung und Konjunkturpolitik* (Jena: Gustav Fischer, 1928); and *Die Ursachen der Wirtschaftskrise: Ein Vortrag* (Tübingen: J.C.B. Mohr, Paul Siebeck, 1931).

Epistemological Problems of Economics, translated by George Reisman (New York and London: New York University Press, Institute for Humane Studies Series in Economic Theory, 1981). An edition based on the Reisman translation published in Princeton, New Jersey by D. Van Nostrand, 1960. Originally published as *Grundprobleme der Nationalökonomie: Untersuchungen über Verfahren, Aufgaben, und Inhalt der Wirtschafts und Gesellshaftslehre* (Jena: Gustav Fischer, 1933).

Nationalökonomie: Theorie des Handelns und Wirtschaftens (Geneva: Editions Union, 1940).

Notes and Recollections (South Holland, Illinois: Libertarian Press, 1978). An intellectual autobiography written by Mises in 1940 but not published until after his death.

Omnipotent Government: The Rise of the Total State and Total War (New Rochelle, New York: Arlington House, 1969). Reprinted from the original edition under the same title (New Haven, Connecticut: Yale University Press, 1944)

Bureaucracy (Cedar Falls, Iowa: Center for Futures Education, 1983). Also available in the 1969 edition published by Arlington House of New Rochelle, New York, which was reprinted without change from the original 1944 edition published by Yale University Press.

Planned Chaos (Irvington-on-Hudson, New York: Foundation for Economic Education, 1961). Originally written as an epilogue to the Spanish edition of *Socialism* that appeared in 1947, and included in the Yale edition of 1951.

Human Action: A Treatise on Economics (Chicago: Henry Regnery Company, 1966). A revised edition from an original under the same title published by Yale University Press in 1949, now also available in the Liberty Press, Illinois, *Liberty Classics* series. The book has its roots in the earlier *Nationalökonomie*.

Planning for Freedom, and Sixteen Other Essays and Addresses (South Holland, Illinois: Libertarian Press, 1980). This is the fourth edition, enlarged from the 1952 original from the same publisher.

The Anti-Capitalistic Mentality (South Holland, Illinois: Libertarian Press, 1978). Reprint of the 1956 edition published in Princeton New Jersey by D. Van Nostrand.

Theory and History: An Interpretation of Social and Economic Evolution (New Rochelle, New York: Arlington House, 1969). A reprint of the original edition published in 1957 by Yale University Press of New Haven, Connecticut.

Economic Policy: Thoughts for Today and Tomorrow (Chicago: Regnery Gateway, 1979). A collection of lectures given by Mises in South America in 1958.

The Ultimate Foundation of Economic Science: An Essay on Method (Kansas City: Sheed Andrews and McMeel, 1977). Originally published by D. Van Nostrand of Princeton, New Jersey, in 1962.

The Historical Setting of the Austrian School of Economics (Auburn, Alabama: The Ludwig von Mises Institute of Auburn University, 1984). Original edition published in 1969 by Arlington House of New Rochelle, New York.

Money, Method, Intervention, and Trade: Essays by Ludwig von Mises, edited with an introduction by Richard M. Ebeling (Fairfax, Virginia: Institute for Humane Studies, in preparation).

BOOKS ABOUT MISES

Mary Sennholz (ed.) *On Freedom and Free Enterprise: Essays in Honor of Ludwig von Mises* (Princeton, New Jersey: D. Van Nostrand, 1956).

Bettina Bien Greaves, *The Works of Ludwig von Mises* (Irvingon-on-Hudson, New York: Foundation for Economic Education, 1969).

F.A. Hayek (ed.) *Toward Liberty: Essays in Honour of Ludwig von Mises on the Occasion of his 90th Birthday* (Menlo Park, California: Institute for Humane Studies, 1971).

Laurence S. Moss (ed.), *The Economics of Ludwig von Mises: Toward a Critical Reappraisal* (Kansas City: Sheed and Ward, Institute for Humane Studies Series in Economic Theory, 1974).

Index